Utilitarianism, Institutions, and Justice

UTILITARIANISM,

INSTITUTIONS,

and

JUSTICE

James Wood Bailey

New York • Oxford
Oxford University Press
1997

Oxford University Press

Oxford   New York
Athens   Auckland   Bangkok   Bogota   Bombay   Buenos Aires
Calcutta   Cape Town   Dar es Salaam   Delhi   Florence   Hong Kong
Istanbul   Karachi   Kuala Lumpur   Madras   Madrid   Melbourne
Mexico City   Nairobi   Paris   Singapore   Taipei   Tokyo   Toronto   Warsaw

and associated companies in
Berlin   Ibadan

Published by Oxford University Press, Inc.
198 Madison Avenue, New York, New York 10016

Oxford is a registered trademark of Oxford University Press

Library of Congress Cataloging-in-Publication Data
Bailey, James Wood, 1967–
    Utilitarianism, institutions, and justice / James Wood Bailey.
        p.   cm.
    Includes bibliographical references.
    ISBN 0-19-510510-9
    1. Utilitarianism.   2. Institutions (Philosophy)
3. Justice (Philosophy)   I. Title.
B843.B35   1997
171'.5—dc20   96-41290

9 8 7 6 5 4 3 2 1

Printed in the United States of America
on acid-free paper

Dedicated to
my mother and father

PREFACE

I did not know it at the time, but I was well on my way to becoming a utilitarian when, as a wet-behind-the-ears graduate student, I first heard an intemperate debate between a group of free-speech advocates and a group of feminists over the legal regulation of pornography. What was remarkable about this debate was not just the wide gulf between factual premises that separated the two groups but also the relative insensitivity each expressed toward the moral concerns of the other. The free-speech advocates were willing to concede, at least *arguendo*, that pornography might have negative consequences for the behavior of at least some people but that a supposed right of free expression required us to live with these consequences. The feminists were willing to concede, in considering questions of public policy, that any strong program for regulating pornography would be expensive and intrusive, but they were unwilling to concede that these costs ought to be a barrier to such a legal regime. Surely, I thought, all costs should matter. The end of moral rights should be to secure a decent existence for human beings, not to allow some to run roughshod over others.

If I had to summarize the doctrine of utilitarianism in one sentence, it would be as follows: the imposition of a cost can only be justified by the avoidance of a greater cost, and all costs matter equally. It does not matter whether the cost is immediately observable or it exists only in the form of an opportunity foregone. And what is more, it does not matter on whom the cost may fall. Man or woman, rich or poor, fellow countryman or foreigner, quick or yet unborn, the burdens of life on each count the same. Utilitarianism tells us to do the best we can, with utter impartiality. As such, it is a powerful engine both for justifying and for criticizing the way we live. Small wonder that it should hold such an attraction for a young political theorist.

But striving for the best leads to both a problem and a paradox. The problem has two branches. A system of ethics that tells us to achieve the best at once permits too much and demands too much. Achieving the best overall outcome can mean imposing very large costs on some people, and this is something many of us find intuitively to be horrible. We do not want to sacrifice an innocent person to achieve some other end, perhaps any other end. If we are told that we can save the lives of five dying persons by murdering some unsuspecting fellow, we would not do so even if the magnitude of the cost works out in favor of doing it. Most of us accept that there are moral constraints on what use we can make of other people; but utilitarianism, it is alleged, tells us to override this constraint in some instances, and so permits too much. At the same time, it also appears to demand too much because, given the amount of suffering and unhappiness in the world, the amount of time and energy any one agent could devote to bringing about the best outcome overall would be formidable. I do not give away almost all of my income to feed starving children, even though some have argued that a good utilitarian would do just that.

The paradox follows quickly on the second branch of the problem. In principle, it would appear that utilitarianism tells us to make each and every choice such that it leads to the best consequences overall. But an insight made clearer by the development of game theory is that no choice has consequences in isolation, only in conjunction with many other choices of many other agents. So while utilitarianism gives us the duty to make things go as well as possible, it does not give to any individual agent at any particular juncture any definite responsibility because causally the outcome of his or her choice lies in the hands of so many other agents. My individual contribution to the overall good may be consequential if and only if others also contribute in the right way. In the absence of some knowledge about how others are likely to act, the principle of utility alone can tell me nothing useful about what I should do.

I have written this book to show that both the problem and the paradox can be resolved simultaneously. The resolution of the paradox of individual responsibilities is achieved by elaborating an account of institutions as equilibria in complex games. Within institutions, individuals have specific responsibilities they cannot get from the principle of utility alone. But the principle of utility still has work to do even in an institutional account because it can help us identify some institutions as more morally desirable than others. When we have identified those institutions, we find that utilitarianism is not the doctrine that makes the horrible recommendations it is accused of making. Utilitarianism can thus be the basis for a viable public philosophy, the kind of doctrine capable of resolving precisely those problems of difficult trade-offs that first led me to its study.

ACKNOWLEDGMENTS

Many people have provided help and encouragement over the years without which this book would not have been possible. I am grateful most of all to Alan Ryan, who supervised this project as a doctoral dissertation at Princeton University, and to Amy Gutmann, Russell Hardin, and Elizabeth Kiss, who served on my dissertation committee and were tireless in providing useful comments, criticism, and support. I owe special thanks also to Tim Scanlon, who made me feel welcome during my academic year (1991–92) at Harvard, learning as best I could how to think like a philosopher. I was helped in this endeavor by the excellent teaching and occasional encouragement of Robert Nozick, Derek Parfit, and Amartya Sen. I received the financial support of the Woodrow Wilson Fellowship Foundation in the form of a dissertation-year award.

As I was turning the dissertation into a book, Jon Elster, David Johnston, Andrew Koppelman, Dan Sabia, and two anonymous reviewers for Oxford University Press read the manuscript either in whole or in part while it was in preparation and contributed helpful comments. Other helpful comments were made at lectures I gave on my version of utilitarianism by my colleagues David Austen-Smith, Steven Brams, Joshua Cohen, Andrew W. Dick, Jim Johnson, and Ken Oye.

Finally, I feel a gratitude hard to express in words to those friends whose conversation and companionship were able to sustain me in both heart and mind through the long process of thinking and writing: Jonathan Allen, Astrid Arraras, Tomas Chuaqui, George W. Downs, Roxanne Euben, Kyle Hudson, George Kateb, Cliff Landesman, Chris Marrison, Jamie Mayerfeld, Pratap Mehta, Jason Scorza, Jeannie Sowers, and Stuart White.

CONTENTS

Utilitarianism, Institutions, and Justice

ONE

Introduction to Utilitarianism

What Is Utilitarianism?

In this book, I propose to make a contribution to the doctrine of utilitarianism. Readers familiar with the history of ethics will know that ever since Jeremy Bentham coined the term in 1781 (or at least since he introduced it to the public in 1802), the doctrine has been subject to any number of understandings or, more typically, misunderstandings.

If one were to sample definitions of utilitarianism even from the literate and well-educated part of the public, one would be likely at best to get only some half correct half-definitions. Some think that utilitarianism has something to do with recommending material acquisition over spiritual accomplishments. Others might recall the names of Bentham and Mill. A few might remember the none-too-helpful formula about bringing about the greatest good for the greatest number.

So before setting about the task of defending any doctrine, I had better try to explain just what is to be defended. Much of the confusion about utilitarianism stems from the fact that it really is not a single doctrine but a family of doctrines defined by the following four characteristics: (1) evaluative consequentialism, (2) a theory of the personal good, (3) interpersonal comparability, and (4) distributive indifference about the good.

Evaluative consequentialism is the doctrine that acts are right only to the extent that they in some way contribute to the bringing about of a state of affairs that is optimal, and wrong only to the extent that they contribute to bringing about a state of affairs that is less than optimal. Consequentialism holds that the end of ethics is to maximize the amount of good in the world.

"Contribute to" can have a number of meanings for consequentialists. In act-consequentialism, the way for an agent to do right is to calculate the actual amount of good that each action one could perform would bring about in the world and to select from that entire set of acts that particular act that would do the greatest amount of good. It is not necessary, however, to be an act-consequentialist to contribute to

3

bringing about the greatest amount of good in the world. One's contributive obligations might be fulfilled in other ways. For instance, a moral agent may choose his or her acts based on their conformity to rules that, if acts are generally chosen thereby, will bring about the greatest amount of good in the world.[1] Or an agent may choose the act that contributes to bringing about the greatest amount of good by acting on those motives, that, if generally cultivated, would lead agents to act in such a way as to bring about the greatest amount of good in the world.[2]

Consequentialism alone does not determine what the good is. It is possible to have a consequentialist moral theory in which the intrinsic character of acts and not just their physical consequences can be said to contribute to the amount of goodness or badness in the world. There is a kind of consequentialism that holds that the fact that an innocent person's death is brought about by an intentional act makes that death worse than one that occurs simply by a preventable accident. In such an account, murdering someone contributes more badness to the world than simply letting that person die. What makes consequentialist moral views distinctive is that even when they recognize that acts may have intrinsic badness, they permit agents to balance or aggregate goodness and badness.

This license to aggregate distinguishes consequentialists from *deontologists*, who hold that there are certain actions that an agent must never do, no matter what the consequences.[3] Thus even a consequentialist who holds that murder is such a bad thing that the murder of one innocent person can never be justified by the bringing about of any amount of any other good—such as preventing the accidental deaths of many other innocent people—would have to maintain that the murder of one innocent person might be justified in order to prevent more than one other innocent person from being murdered.[4] A deontological view would hold that an agent must not commit murder, even if by committing murder an agent could prevent other persons from being murdered.

The *theory of the personal good*[5] holds that in order for us to claim that one state of the world contains more good than another, at least one person must be better off in that state. Likewise, for one state of the world to be worse than another, at least one person must be worse off in it. Under the principle of the personal good, an act cannot contribute to the good of the world without being good for someone, nor can it contribute to the badness of the world without being bad for someone.

The principle of the personal good seems intuitively well supported, although it is not universally accepted. G. E. Moore maintained that between two uninhabited and self-contained universes that would never be experienced by any conscious being, one of which contained a beautiful planet and one of which did not, the former would be in some deontic sense better or preferable.[6] Some moral perfectionists may also reject the principle of the personal good. The perfectionist who believes that individuals should show heroism may think that Achilles has an obligation to act heroically even though his heroic acts are not good for him or for anyone else. The holder of this view believes that a universe that contains heroism that leads to suffering and defeat for all persons connected with it might at least in one way be a better universe than a universe with more cowardice and more prosperity.

Interpersonal comparability extends the reach of the principle of personal good. It holds that we can make comparative judgments about worlds in which some persons are made better off and others worse off. So, for example, the principle of interpersonal comparability would hold that if we are given two worlds—one in which the rich do well because of wealth and the poor do badly because of poverty, and another in which some wealth is redistributed from rich to poor and levels of personal good are adjusted accordingly—we can make a judgment about which of these is the better world.

The principle of interpersonal comparability plays a role in many theories of justice other than utilitarianism. Egalitarian theories hold that worlds in which redistribution from rich to poor has taken place are ceteris paribus better than those in which there is no redistribution, even though the gains to the poor may be outweighed by the losses to the rich. The situations of the rich and the poor must be comparable in order to make judgments about whether they are more or less alike. Many versions of the so-called "difference principle" implicitly accept interpersonal comparability by much the same reasoning. The difference principle requires that any inequalities generated by a set of social institutions make the position of the worst-off person as well off as possible. But to identify that worst-off person as worst off, there must be some means of comparing his or her lot with that of others.

Not all theories of justice accept this principle, however. Traditional welfare economics uses a Pareto criterion of evaluation similar but not identical to the principle of the personal good. Under this criterion, states of affairs in which at least one person is made better off without making anyone worse off are adjudged superior. But any states in which some persons are made better off and others worse off are thought to be either simply incomparable or equally good.[7]

The principle of *distributive indifference* holds that increases in personal good make worlds superior to the same degree without regard for the person in which those increases take place. This concept is somewhat abstract. Perhaps it can best be grasped through an example. Imagine a world in which there are two persons: Lucky, whose life is quite good, and Unlucky, whose life is quite poor. There are two possible states into which the world could proceed, World-1 and World-2. In World-1, a large gain in personal good goes to Lucky. In World-2, a small gain in personal good goes to Unlucky. The principle of distributive indifference maintains that it is the size and not the location of the gain that matters. Thus, in this principle, which is part of utilitarianism, World-1 is better than World-2.

It is precisely here that utilitarianism parts company from other potentially consequentialist and welfarist doctrines. An egalitarian or a Rawlsian might claim that World-2 is better than World-1, either because in World-2 Lucky and Unlucky have more equal lives or because in World-2 the position of Unlucky is the best it can be. As we shall see, it is on precisely this parting of company that utilitarianism gets in the most trouble.

Some Historic Forms of Utilitarianism

It is common knowledge that for Bentham the personal good that is to be maximized is pleasure. This common knowledge probably oversimplifies a bit. We must remember that Bentham begins his treatise on laws and morals with the sentence "Nature has placed mankind under the governance of *two* sovereign masters, *pain* and *plea-*

sure."[8] For Bentham, the personal good—utility—seems not to have been just a matter of counting up psychological units of pleasure but rather a function of pleasure and pain.

J. S. Mill's utilitarianism is rather more complicated. While supposedly maintaining a link between pleasure and utility, Mill sees personal good as being more complex than the apparently simple psychological phenomenon that Bentham had envisioned. For Mill the pleasures are plural and rather more problematical in comparison to one another: the pleasures of a Socrates are different and apparently superior phenomena to those of a fool.[9]

In the twentieth century, the concept of a personal good achieved a sophisticated mathematical articulation.[10] Both the ordinal utility of economists and the axiomatic utility theory of von Neumann and Morgenstern broke the connection between utility and virtually any psychological concept.[11] In the former, utility was simply defined by concave sets that describe the indifference of consumers among different possible bundles of consumer goods; in the latter, by expressed orderings of preferences over varying degrees of risk. Whether individual economic agents got any more pleasure or satisfaction or anything else when they did better at maximizing utility was and largely is a question about which contemporary economists remain serenely agnostic.

The most plausible concept of personal good for purposes of a moral theory would be one that recognizes multiple dimensions of possible human satisfaction. Bentham thought that there was either a single dimension of aggregate hedonic satisfaction or (arguably) two dimensions of pleasure and pain. Mill thought that there were several different psychological dimensions and, further, that these dimensions might vary across persons. We may generalize beyond Mill's thesis and say that a person's good has many dimensions, not all of which are psychological. What could this generalization mean?

The idea that one's personal good may have many dimensions simply means that what makes one's life go well may be the experience of a wide variety of different phenomena that cannot be lumped together under generic categories of pleasure and pain. There is the pleasure of listening to music and the pleasure of having sex and the pleasure of finishing one's first book; all these things are personal goods, but they are not simply fungible. Likewise, there is the pain of having a tooth drilled and the pain of losing a lover and the pain of editing one's manuscript; these things are all personal bads, but they, too, are not simply fungible.

The notion that personal goods may be individuated suggests that for different persons different possible dimensions will have different weights. Indeed, different persons may have different dimensions altogether. The pleasure of listening to Verdi is a dimension of my personal good that is of great importance, but it is of little or no personal importance to many other people. Some may have personal goods that are dominated by a single dimension. The lives of some persons will go best when they are fanatically devoted to music or sexual pleasure or whatever. Others will have personal goods with many dimensions. It may even be the case that there are no goods that are identifiably goods for all actually existing persons, and there may be goods that are goods for only one person.

A person's good may not be transparently obvious even to a person whose good it is. Though many neoclassical economists write as if they believe so, it is not axiomatic that a person is automatically better off when his or her preferences are better satisfied.[12] Such disjunctions between preferences and personal good are possible; and since, no doubt, many of us have had the experience of getting something we once wanted and finding it disappointing, we might even say that such disjunctions are likely. If it is the case, however, that we can learn about our personal goods through our own lives, then the preferences that we have and express in our choices will be reasonably accurate reflections of our own personal goods.

Thus for a utilitarian, personal good might consist in any number of things. There is, however, one limit on this concept when it is used in utilitarianism. John Broome has suggested that one's personal good may include moral goods, so that one's life may be said to go worse if one is treated unequally or suffers injustice.[13] In Broome's conception, what may matter is not necessarily the suffering or lack of opportunity one faces from being at the bottom of an unequal distribution, nor is it necessarily the envy one feels of those who are better off or the resentment generated by unjust treatment. It can be just the bare fact of being treated unequally or unjustly, even if one does not perceive one's treatment as wrong. If one conceives the personal good in this way, one could pack many moral theories, conceivably any moral theory, into utilitarianism.

This manipulation of the personal good threatens to rob utilitarianism of any distinctive content, which would render the whole theoretical enterprise nugatory. Utilitarianism, after all, is supposed to provide an independent theory of justice and not just tell us what we already know. So herein I use the term *personal good* rather more narrowly than Broome does, to specify those states of the world—independent from moral descriptions, states of mind, and relations of states of the world to states of mind—that can be said to make one's life go better or worse.

Why Study Utilitarianism?

In chapter 2 I discuss why utilitarianism may be plausible as a moral doctrine. Indeed, the whole of this book is an attempt to vindicate that plausibility. But even if I were to provide such a vindication, the obvious question that should be asked is this: who cares? What would we learn if we come to believe that the doctrine is true?

Rights Talk and Moral Trade Offs

A number of observers of contemporary moral discourse[14] have noted the existence of an increasingly expansive and intransigent use of the language of rights as a means of advancing political claims. Indeed, it is hard to think of any significant public policy debate today, in the United States especially, in which opposing sides claim not just to have "right" but also "rights" on their side. Proponents of a national health service claim that every American has a right to medical care,[15] while opponents of such policies make much of the right of every economic agent to make one's own decisions about which medical services to purchase. Proponents of gun control advance the right of individual citizens to live in safety, while opponents counterattack with the right to bear arms that is guaranteed in the Second Amendment. Feminists who want to extirpate pornography claim that it interferes with the right of women to be treated as the moral equals of men—a right based in a not-implausible reading of the Fourteenth Amendment—while those who oppose such a ban cite the right to free expression that is enshrined in the First.

Environmentalists worry about the rights of future generations and sometimes even of nonhuman natural entities, while industrialists and their workers claim a right to make a living. Defenders of abortion propound a woman's right to do as she sees fit with her own body, while opponents claim a right of a developing fetus to go on developing unmolested. Fundamentalists attack public education for allegedly inter-fering with the right of parents to bring up their children in a religious environment, while liberals defend the right of society to educate children for democratic citizen-ship. Opponents of the war on drugs insist on a plausible right of adults to make decisions about what chemicals they will expose themselves to, while supporters sug-gest that there exists a right of parents to rear children in an environment free of po-tentially addictive and dangerous substances. This list of debates could be extended indefinitely, but the point should be clear: the moral dimension of contemporary policy discourse is all too often shrill and confused.

Not surprisingly, the claims of rights begin to become rather dizzying after a while. Sometimes it seems as if the language of rights has simply been worn out through overuse: with so many rights claims about we are liable to become weary and cynical about any new ones. We may become suspicious of every claim, thinking it just an attempt at political advantage by some self-interested faction. In other cases, we suf-fer not weariness but perplexity since both claims seem serious but conflicting: in burning issues like pornography and abortion, this is especially true.

Both cynicism and perplexity are problematic: cynicism because at least some moral claims really do demand our attention, and perplexity because it is a require-ment of civilized living that we actually resolve some of our public policy disputes in an equitable manner. Utilitarianism holds out a hope of resolving these disputes in a determinate and equitable way: exactly what the way may be I try to clarify in this book. The principle itself is simple enough. The achievement of determinate solu-tions to vexing moral questions is only a matter of having adequate empirical knowl-edge. To be sure, the amount of empirical knowledge that is "adequate" for resolving any given question about rights may be very large indeed. This book does not attempt to address particular questions of policy in detail; the most I can hope to achieve is a broad outline of a theory of what utilitarianism would recommend and some prom-ising starting places for further investigation.

Of course, utilitarianism is not the only theory that could help us with vexing rights questions; there are an indefinite number of other theories, both consequentialist and deontological, that could also do so. What possible advantages could a utilitarian theory have over its many rivals in this respect?

The first advantage is *sensitivity to empirical conditions*. Often the question about which right should prevail in a conflict of plausible rights has to do not so much with the actual weight of the rights themselves—which is usually quite vague in any event—

as with the empirical presuppositions under which the claim has been advanced. Thus, in the claim that pornography should be banned to serve the plausible right of women to be treated as the moral equals of men, there are a number of tacit empirical claims. It is often either tacitly or explicitly claimed that pornography has a positive causal effect on sexual violence and sexual discrimination against women. But this positive causal effect is not a given: both the size and sign (if any) of the effect and our cognizance of it are likely to vary with historical circumstance. We might assume, *arguendo*, that in a society with robust and exogenously-supported gender-egalitarian norms, the effects of even the worst pornography are likely to be minimal, while in a highly sexist society its inegalitarian effects could be quite severe. The degree to which our society is gender-egalitarian varies over time.

A consequentialist moral theory can take account of this variance and direct us in our decision about whether a plausible right to equality ought to outweigh a plausible right to freedom of expression.[16] In some circumstances the effects of pornography would surely be malign enough to justify our banning it, but in others they may be not malign enough to justify any interference in freedom.[17]

A deontological theory, in contrast, would be required either to rank the side constraints, which forbid agents from interfering in the free expression of others and from impairing the moral equality of others, or to admit defeat and claim that no adjudication between the two rights is possible. The latter admission is a grave failure since it would leave us no principled resolution of a serious policy question. But the former conclusion is hardly attractive either. Would we really wish to establish as true for all times and circumstances a lexical ordering between two side constraints on our actions without careful attention to consequences? Would we, for instance, really wish to establish that the slightest malign inegalitarian effect traceable to a form of expression is adequate grounds for an intrusive and costly censorship? Or would we, alternatively, really wish to establish that we should be prepared to tolerate a society horrible for women and children to live in, for the sake of not allowing any infringement on the sacred right of free expression?[18]

Consequentialist accounts can avoid such a deontological dilemma. In so doing, they show a certain healthy sense of realism about what life in society is like. In the world outside the theorist's study, we meet trade-offs at every turn. Every policy we make with some worthy end in sight imposes costs in terms of diminished achievement of some other plausibly worthy end. Consequentialism demands that we grapple with these costs as directly as we can and justify their incurrence. It forbids us to dismiss them with moral sophistries or to ignore them as if we lived in an ideal world.

But as has already been noted, utilitarianism is only a family within the order of consequentialism. What might be particularly attractive about utilitarianism in particular? Here I would argue that the doctrine has the advantage of proximity to real human interests. Within the consequentialist family there are perfectionist doctrines that deny the principle of the personal good: versions of such theories might maintain that it is better if there are fewer rights violations or more heroism or more artistic beauty or whatever, whether or not the coming about of these states is good for anyone. Certainly we can generate theories like these—G. E. Moore did—but it is far from clear why anyone should pay them any heed. Not only does it seem counterintuitive to most people that we should bring about states from which no person could be in the position to benefit, but also it seems irrational for each and every possible agent to do so.

The consequentialist who believes that Achilles should act courageously would have a rather hard time convincing him to be courageous if he did not share the courage-consequentialist's moral theory *ex ante*. Were Achilles to ask of an act of courage that does no one any good, "Why should I do it?" it is hard to imagine what answer the courage-consequentialist would give. Of course, perhaps Achilles would think badly of himself if he were to act like a coward, but in that case acting courageously, or at least being able to think of himself as courageous, is in fact a part of Achilles's personal good.

Likewise, it is far from clear what rational motivation any agent could have to minimize the number of rights violations he or she commits if the rights violations themselves do not affect anyone's personal good. Suppose I care impartially about the welfare of six persons, and I have the choice of intentionally killing one or letting the five others die. Suppose further that (1) I have a special psychology in which I never feel guilt or any other bad emotion for doing what would be recommended by act-utilitarianism and (2) I can make the death of the one look infallibly like a natural event, so that no other agent can feel resentment or anguish over that person's death. Consequently, the killing of the one would be no worse in the principle of personal good than the letting die of any other one. Suppose further that act-utilitarianism recommends killing the one, while rights-violation-minimizing consequentialism condemns it. Does not the former recommend the thing that is rational to do, whereas the latter recommends something that would be irrational?

That utilitarianism seems like a multiagent version of individual rationality is one of its strengths. For this rationality connects utilitarianism with the real preferences of real persons—a theme I explore further in the next chapter.

Classical welfare economics and distribution-sensitive versions of consequentialism share in utilitarianism's congruence with individual rationality while rejecting some of its other assumptions. Classical welfare economics rejects interpersonal comparability (which I defend in the next chapter). Distributive indifference, however, creates a number of its own problems. Most of this book is an attempt to deal with them, but I should at first say why it is that distributive indifference is at least a somewhat plausible principle.

The plausibility of distributive indifference comes from two sources: its connection to a fundamental moral principle of impartiality and potential problems suffered by other interpretations of the same norm. The fundamental principle of impartiality requires that we have the same degree of concern and respect for all persons without regard for their ascriptive characteristics: the fact that they may be remote from us in time, in space, in character, or in our affections should not affect the degree of our concern with their fates. Under this norm we should be prepared to tolerate the less good lives of other persons only for relevant reasons.

Utilitarianism claims that a relevant reason for tolerating inequalities is a gain in efficiency; that is, we should be prepared to tolerate the fact that some persons' lives go less well than others if some aggregate of personal good is greater. Most contemporary theorists of justice hold this claim to be incorrect; they maintain that impartiality makes equality itself a kind of good or that it requires us to give priority to the personal good of those who are worst off under any possible set of social institutions and practices.

Let us distinguish between those who think that equality is an intrinsic social good—egalitarians—and those who want to give priority to the worst off, whom we can call *prioritarians*. An extreme egalitarianism would hold that the actual level of personal good is irrelevant to any ranking of states of the world, that is, that only the amount of equality between the goods of different persons is relevant in determining what makes a better or a worse world. A moderate egalitarian would hold that the actual level of personal goods does matter but that the ranking of different states of the world must also include the degree of equality in personal goods between different persons. Thus a moderate egalitarian might be willing to rank a world with more inequality as a better world than one with less if the former has a much higher level of personal good than the latter.

A lexical prioritarian would hold that in ranking the states of the world, the personal good of the worst-off person is the only one that is to be counted. Thus, in a lexical view, the personal good of better-off persons counts not at all. The holders of this view would maintain that if we could make the worst-off person only slightly better off by making better-off persons much worse off, we should do so. A weighted prioritarian holds that while the worst-off person is not to be give absolute priority over those who are better off, his or her personal good is to be given greater weight in determining the rankings of states of the world than those who are better off.

Prioritarian and egalitarian views are not the same, although they are often conflated.[19] One way of making the distinction clear is the following: a prioritarian is willing to tolerate any amount of inequality for the sake of making the worst off better off. Thus, if a prioritarian were faced with a choice of a world in which there were almost no inequalities, but the worst-off person is badly off, and a world in which there are vast inequalities (the best-off person being perhaps millions of times better off than the worst-off person), but the worst-off person is not so badly off, the prioritarian would opt for the latter. The extreme egalitarian would opt for the former. Exactly which world the moderate egalitarian would choose is more in doubt since it would depend on one's weighings of the relative virtues of equality and efficiency.

The extreme egalitarian and the lexical prioritarian are alike, however, in being vulnerable to an intuitive objection, which I call the "objection to leveling." In the extreme egalitarian's principles, a world with a very low level of personal good and much equality would be ranked higher than one in which there is more inequality but a higher level of personal good. A world in which everyone had nothing but Muzak and potatoes[20] would be preferable to a world in which some had fine music and fine food and others did not—indeed, preferable to a world in which some had fine things and others had slightly less fine things. Equality of poverty would be preferred to inequality of riches. A lexical prioritarian, while willing to tolerate an inequality of riches if the worst-off person would be better off under this arrangement than under an equality of poverty, would still be vulnerable to a version of this objection. This prioritarian would require that all kinds of personal good—all the best imaginable things one could have in life—be sacrificed or taken from the better off in order to produce even a tiny gain for the worst off. If shutting down the Opera House is the only way to free enough resources so that the most miserable member of our society can have an extra pat of butter on a slice of bread, then *è sia*: shut the Opera House we must.

The extreme egalitarian and lexical prioritarian principles seem at once counter-intuitive and irrational: counterintuitive because it seems morally insensitive to treat the personal goods of so many persons—even the better off—in so cavalier a fashion, irrational because it seems hard to understand how anyone would want a society in which we have nothing but Muzak and potatoes for the sake of pursuing an alleged condition of justice. Such harsh conclusions could not possibly be correct. We do not live our own lives in accordance with anything like such principles. We would not live a life of utter poverty and dullness for the sake of not having too much in-equality between our good moments and our bad. Neither do we give priority to our own expected worst moments, turning down every good opportunity for the sake of not risking really bad moments.[21] It would be disingenuous to recommend to an entire society principles we would be unwilling to apply to ourselves. I thus take the objection to leveling to be fatal to extreme egalitarianism and lexical prioritarianism.

The moderate egalitarian and weighted prioritarian views can avoid the objection to leveling by giving appropriately light weights to their respective desiderata: lighter weight to equality in a calculus of overall goods in the egalitarian case or to the priority of the personal good of the worst off in the prioritarian case. But for these doctrines I would formulate a second—admittedly weaker—objection, which I call the "objection to arbitrariness."

I can put this objection in the form of a series of rhetorical questions: in the egalitarian case just how much are we to weigh equality versus efficiency? If we assume that we have a cardinal metric of personal good, just what numerical measure of inequality are we prepared to tolerate for what level of general personal good? What should the trade-off curve look like? In the prioritarian case, again by assuming a cardinal metric of personal good, just how much are we to weigh the personal good of the worst-off person against that of the best-off? Five times? Ten times? One hundred? One thousand? Every opinion is bound to be different: some people are just more egalitarian than others. Some care about the worst-off person a great deal, others very little. Moreover, opinions are likely to vary from context to context. Intuitions about how much priority to give to the personal good of persons in generally poor societies may be different from intuitions about how much priority to give to it in rich societies.

I would not want to venture the opinion that there is no principled answer to the rhetorical questions I have just posed. Perhaps a clever enough thinker can elucidate the right answer in reflective equilibrium through enough intuition pumping and theorizing. Thus, the objection to arbitrariness need not be as fatal as the objection to leveling. The considered opinion of many moral philosophers is that it is better to struggle with potential arbitrariness than to go for a simple principle of aggregation as that offered by utilitarianism: what is recommended by utilitarianism, it is often claimed, is sufficiently horrible that we have no choice but to grapple with egalitarian or prioritarian arbitrariness. A central aim of this book is to take issue with that last contention. Before I begin to do so, however, I must deal with some potentially distracting side issues.

What Is Not Wrong with Utilitarianism

Is Consequentialism Impossible?

A naive argument often made against utilitarianism and related consequentialist doc-trines is that they demand something that is virtually impossible. Utilitarianism re-quires us to act in such a way as to contribute to the best outcome. Presumably, this means taking into account all of the relevant causal forces in making some kind of complex calculation about what outcome will in fact result from our actions. And since utilitarianism in particular requires that we be indifferent among those on whom the consequences of our actions fall, we must calculate not just the proximate but the remotest consequences of our actions. The effects on the well-being of those who will be born a thousand generations hence are to be weighed equally with those on the generation now living. But, this line of argument holds, to make these calculations we are required to have simply vast amounts of knowledge about how the world works and vast calculative capacities to apply that knowledge. It is impossible, however, for actual human agents to have all the relevant causal knowledge or to calculate the re-mote causes of their actions with any degree of accuracy. Since it is held as a general rule of ethics that ought implies can, utilitarianism must be false.[22]

The objection might be made clearer by a little story put to me in the first under-graduate course in philosophy I ever took.[23] Dr. Myopic travels through a stormy night to reach a remote Austrian village to help a woman in labor. Hers is a particularly difficult labor, and neither mother nor child is likely to survive. But because of the skillful application of medical knowledge and heroic efforts by the doctor, both pull through, and by morning the woman has delivered a healthy baby boy. Exhausted but pleased with himself, Dr. Myopic turns to the happy new mother and says, "Frau Hitler, here is your baby."

If we assume for the moment that had Hitler never existed the Third Reich and its associated train of horrors would never have existed either, it seems that the utili-tarian thing for good Dr. Myopic to have done would have been to spend the night in a biergarten and let little Adolf perish in utero.[24] But surely Dr. Myopic could not have predicted that helping little Adolf to be born would have the disastrous conse-quences that it in fact had. For him to have done so would have required his posses-sion of more knowledge and calculative capacity than any human being has ever had. But since utilitarians would require him to make such a calculation, utilitarianism must be wrong.

The problem with such an argument is that it proves too much. It undercuts not just utilitarianism but also prudential rationality and perhaps even most plausible deontological theories of morality as well.[25] My prudential rationality, after all, is con-cerned with the effective maximization of good consequences within my own life. But every choice I make in my own life has consequences that I could not remotely esti-mate precisely without an exhaustive causal knowledge and calculative capacities. If I drive across town to save $100 on the purchase of a washing machine and fatally collide with a truck on the way, this is in any plausible account a very bad conse-quence for me. If staying home would have prevented the collision, then I should have done so. But that does not mean that it is rational for me to avoid driving across town, and it does not mean, after my grisly end, that some third party can easily declare that I was irrational for having done so, any more than one could declare that our fictional Dr. Myopic was immoral for helping Adolf Hitler to be born.

With respect to deontological accounts of morality, it must be said that any plausible account of moral side constraints will give agents an obligation not just not to act with the intent of violating other people's rights but also to act in such a way as to not violate other people's rights. One can surely violate the moral space around another person without intending to do so: if I shoot a gun at random in a populated area, even if I do so only for the sheer joy of hearing it go off, I am at risk of violating other people's right to be free from negligent harm. But if we take the anticonsequentialist argument at full force, we cannot actually say that I have no moral obligation not to shoot off the gun since there is no way to know in advance, without an exhaustive knowledge of causal factors, whether one of my bullets will actually harm someone. And on most plausible views of the subject, moral (if not legal) responsibility applies to agents even for certain remote and hard-to-calculate consequences. If I place a mantrap on my property and ten years later it maims a five-year-old child, it is quite reasonable to think I have acted badly.

In ordinary prudential reasoning and in thinking through the requirements of deontological constraints against negligence, we are normally willing to use probabilistic reasoning and rules of thumb. It is rational for me to drive across town based on the savings I could realize and the relative risk associated with driving. Firing a gun at random in a populated area is surely a violation of the rights of my innocent neighbors, whether or not any bullets actually hit them, whereas shooting at cacti in a nearly empty desert probably violates no one's rights, even if by a freak accident someone is hit.

When we wish to evaluate whether an individual acted in accordance with prudential rationality or not, we should actually ask an efficiency question: given the cognitive and other epistemic resources that were available, did the individual make a good decision? We should not and do not ask whether the decision the person in fact made was the same decision he or she would have made had he or she been omniscient. The latter question is virtually meaningless: we ourselves are not omniscient, so we cannot ourselves come to any conclusion about what decision an omniscient being would make. But nonetheless we make judgments about prudential rationality—both our own and others—all the time.

I should also note that in order to be rational we do not even need to gather as much information as possible. Since prudential rationality is an exercise in making one's own life go better, and since time spent in gathering and processing information is costly, it is actually irrational for one to spend too much time and energy actually gathering it. One cannot say of me, after being hit by a truck, that I was irrational for having gone out without first conducting an exhaustive study of the incidence of automobile accidents in my town.

Since utilitarianism is itself only an aggregation of decisions about what would be good for individuals, what holds for prudential rationality holds also for utilitarianism. The correct utilitarian standard by which to judge Dr. Myopic is determined by the cognitive and other resources available to him at the time. As a matter of fact, a fairly large number of infants grow up into moderately happy, noncriminal human beings. Very, very few grow up to become monsters. The cost in information and processing to detect in advance those who will become monsters simply cannot be justified by the low odds of ever finding one. Our good doctor would spend all his time learning historical causation and none learning medicine, and that would be a waste that would produce much worse consequences in the end. Frau Hitler's doctor can be allowed his delivery.

Of course, the question of how much care any individual agent must take in actually calculating the consequences of one's actions becomes very difficult very quickly. Often the best we can do is to follow rules of thumb that replicate the content of deontological theories. Stealing other people's property, for example, usually leads to worse consequences overall, so utilitarianism requires us not to do so, or at least erects a strong barrier of presumption against doing so.

Critics of the theory state that this argument empties the theory of any distinctive content. But even in the most simple-minded ways of thinking about how to predict consequences, utilitarianism will always retain some content of its own. Even if we start just with whatever rules of thumb we happen to have at the time, there is distinct advice in utilitarianism; for even if costs of information and causation do not allow us to make global estimates of what would lead to the best outcomes overall, utilitarianism does enable us to make piecemeal reforms in our practices whenever new information or calculative techniques become available, which they do from time to time. In this way utilitarianism remains a doctrine distinct from a deontological theory, which would hold that the side constraints remain in force even if they are discovered not to be optimizing. Utilitarianism is thus often a doctrine of marginal rather than global analysis.

Critics may repeat that if utilitarianism is concerned largely with local or marginal maximization, it is robbed of distinctive content as a theory, but this is not so. Maximization is a coherent notion even when global maximization is known not to be possible in principle. Engineers, who design machines to be efficient, often face implicit maximization problems with many variables that cannot be solved algorithmicly in finite time. But this does not mean that the activities of these engineers are futile, that some machines are not better designed than others, or that it would be incoherent to describe what the engineers are doing in their design work is designing the most efficient machine they can.

Does Utilitarianism Have an Incoherent Theory of Value?

Another argument made against the prima facie plausibility of utilitarianism is its alleged reliance on an implausible theory of the good life. Because of utilitarianism's historical association with hedonism, it is often assumed that any utilitarian theory must necessarily be concerned with the maximization of the amount of pleasure and happiness in the universe. Certainly the greatest of the nineteenth-century utilitarians wrote as if this were the case. Bentham made a notorious remark to the effect that to the extent that both produce like amounts of pleasure, pushpin is as good as poetry. Mill, while rejecting Bentham's ideas on the relative merits of different kinds of activity, still thought of utilitarianism as a "greatest happiness principle," and Sidgwick thought of the utilitarian method of ethics as being a form of "universal hedonism" (as opposed to egoism, which is particularistic hedonism).[26]

But most people believe that having a good life must surely be more complex than having a life in which there is the greatest possible amount of pleasure or even the greatest amount of happiness. That the best life consists not merely of psychological quanta of pleasure seems easy to demonstrate on simple reflection: few people would choose to become addicted to a drug that gave even very intense and lasting pleasure without painful side effects if in taking it they would become incapable of carrying out other important life projects. Nor would many people voluntarily allow themselves to be permanently attached to a machine that provides any number of pleasurable experiences on demand by feeding them appropriate neural input.[27] The maximum amount of pleasure may not, in fact, be personally good for them.

The idea that the best life is that which contains the most happiness is also open to reasonable suspicion. There are a number of cases in which it seems at least plausible to claim that there are things that can occur that would make my life a worse one even if they do nothing to affect my happiness. If, after my death, it is discovered that because of my carelessness I made mistakes early in my career that rendered my life's work worthless, it may reasonably be said that my life is worse for those mistakes, even though such a postmortum discovery can in no way affect the amount of happiness in my life. It might be good for me to strive to avoid making avoidable mistakes, even if so doing exacts a price in happiness. My life may also go worse if my friends routinely violate confidences behind my back for the sake of laughing at my discomfitures and vices among themselves, even if I never come to know of their untrustworthiness and so happily imagine them to be good friends. It may be worthwhile for my personal good to know the painful truth.[28]

The trouble that afflicts hedonism seems to afflict generally any theory that attempts to reduce a heterogeneous personal good to a single good. Even very general single goods, like success in meeting one's goals or fulfilling one's life plan, seem inadequate for fulfilling the role of final explainers of personal good. One might succeed brilliantly in meeting all one's goals and still have a bad life if one makes oneself miserable; one might have had a better life with less success and more happiness. Furthermore, one-dimensional theories of personal good run afoul of our intuition that some goods may be autonomous. For a true scholar, knowledge is an end with value in and of itself; it need not be justified as something that produces happiness or allows us to meet our other goals, and it may even be worth sacrifices in happiness or success to achieve. For most people the good life seems to consist of many dimensions, which cannot plausibly be reduced to one another. A person's good may consist of some professional accomplishments and some personal cultivation and some true friendships and a number of simple pleasures.

Hedonists may choose to dispute these counterexamples by showing them to be based on an inadequate understanding of hedonism or by showing how they are distracting or misleading. Perhaps the fear people have of pleasure machines is really based on superstition or on holdovers from a Calvinist culture. Perhaps "true scholars" have acquired a subterranean and forgotten internal connection between the acquisition of knowledge and happiness. Perhaps they have been behaviorally conditioned through hedonic stimuli to pursue knowledge and are simply deluded when they claim to be pursuing it for its own sake. But while I have some sympathy for hedonism, I do not myself try to defend it.[29] Rather, I simply sidestep the debate between hedonists and their opponents by arguing that hedonism is not itself a necessary component of utilitarian theories.

While it may not be true that all life's goods can be said to be made good by virtue of their all having a single property, such as providing a certain number of quanta of pleasure or happiness, it does not follow that we cannot rank different states of affairs along a single scale of personal good. As long as we can rank different heterogeneous states by a relation of better and worse, and as long as the ordering of those states is transitive, we can come up with an ordinal scale of personal good. When a few other conditions for making choices are satisfied, we can generate a metric of personal good that has the property of *cardinality*, that is, of having numerical measures of personal good, rather than just ordinality. Such a function is the von Neumann and Morgenstern utility function, to which I have already alluded. To show the power of this concept of utility, it is worth reviewing its logical preconditions.[30]

The first of these requirements is ordering: it must be possible to rank the various alternatives from better to worse on some transitive scale. It is worth noting that such a ranking does not require a single, homogeneous component to human wellbeing. One may simply have brute preferences over states of affairs; or as Brian Barry has pointed out,[31] one may recognize that there are many intrinsic goods, although one has a set of internal indifference functions that tells one how to make trade-offs and rankings among states of affairs in which they may be realized.

The second of these conditions is *monotonicity*. It is satisfied whenever, given equally risky prospects of two states of affairs, we continue to prefer the risky prospect of that state that we would have preferred when both states were certain.

The third condition is a *indifference among probabilistically equivalent prospects*. It is satisfied whenever we are indifferent across sets of risky prospects that are algebraically equivalent. Thus, we should be indifferent between a lottery ticket that gives us a probability of 0.25 of some prize *p* and a lottery ticket that gives us a probability of 0.5 of being allowed to play in a lottery in which there is a probability of 0.5 of winning the same prize *p*.

The fourth condition is *continuity*. This condition is satisfied whenever—given three prospects *A*, *B*, and *C*, such that *A* is better than *B*, which is in turn better than *C*—there is some lottery consisting of *A* and *C* that is equal in goodness to *B*. Such a utility function is consistent with the thesis of a personal good. Hence, whenever I refer to *utility* hereafter in these pages, it is shorthand for "a person's good that may ideally be represented in a von Neumann–Morgenstern utility function."

Must the von Neumann–Morgenstern conditions be satisfied? It is the general opinion of economists that the various conditions are not just any arbitrary collection of axioms but rather conditions that an agent's choices must satisfy for that agent to be rational. An agent who (at least consistently) failed to satisfy them would be wide open to various forms of exploitation. An agent who failed to transitively rank states of affairs would be subject to a form of manipulation called a *money pump*. Suppose an agent consistently finds *A* better than *B*, *B* better than *C*, and *C* better than *A*. Presumably the agent would be willing to trade *C* plus some sum of money for *B*, *B* plus some sum of money for *A*, and *A* plus some sum of money for *C*. The agent would thus have cycled back around to *C* and be nothing but poorer for the process. A clever trader could make the holder of intransitive preferences go round and round indefinitely until either the preference holder changes his or her preferences or runs out of money.[32] Agents who fail in their choices to satisfy the probabilistic axioms would be vulnerable to a probabilistic version of the money pump, called the *Dutch book*.[33] Falling for a money pump or a Dutch book seems pretty clearly to be a paradigmatic case of irrationality, which is why many economists would maintain that the von Neumann–Morgenstern conditions must be normatively acceptable.[34]

It has been objected that if there are different goods, then these goods may be *incommensurable* and cannot be integrated into any single function of personal good.[35] Thus even if we can be compelled to make choices among alternatives, as we are compelled to do in the money pump example, these choices do not reveal anything meaningful about our underlying personal well-being. We simply cannot compare the good of staying alive with, say, the good of self-cultivation. Or if friendship and professional success are both elements of one's personal good, one cannot make any kind of rational judgment in a situation in which one is forced to choose between one or the other. There simply is, for those who believe in incommensurability, no rational choice between these two goods. But if there is no rational choice between these two goods, and thus no rational choice between the different states of affairs containing them, it cannot be possible to rank the two states by a relation of betterness. There would be no possible ordinal value function and, a fortiori, no cardinal value function.

There is a plausible notion underlying arguments from incommensurability, which is that there is no homogeneous and fungible quantity—like wealth or pleasure—that underlies human well-being. The absence of such a quantity would capture many of our intuitions about what makes a life go well or not. Many of us would think that no amount of domestic bliss could make up for the pain of a shattered career, nor that a brilliant career could make up for a miserable and lonely home life, even if both domestic bliss and professional success advance our well-being. Let us call the thesis of the absence of a single homogeneous good the "weak incommensurability thesis." The weak thesis may very well be true. But what is often wrongly inferred from it is a "strong incommensurability thesis," which is a denial that comparisons that trade off different goods are meaningfu , in effect a denial of the ordering axiom or the continuity axiom.[36] This thesis i not really plausible. If we really believed that different goods were incommensurable, we would be forced into one of two doubtful positions: either an untenable form of extreme risk aversion or a Sorites paradox of choices among risky prospects.

A simple question that draws on an example we have already seen should illustrate the problem: should I drive across town to save $100 on a large purchase? Wealth, or at least what wealth can achieve, is undeniably a good, and so is staying whole and alive. In a sense these two goods might be said to be incommensurable: I would not accept any amount of money in compensation for ending my life. As it happens, every time I take a drive of any length there is about a one-in-four-million chance of death in an automobile accident.[37] If the good of staying alive and the good of possessing wealth are really incommensurable, one way of arguing would be to say that there is no rational choice about driving across town. Even a one-in-a-billion chance of dying in a fiery crash is enough to stop any debate on the merits of the proposal.

This position is an infinite risk aversion, and its dubiousness is almost transparent. If the tiniest odds of conflict between two elements of personal good is enough to end any chance of ranking two prospects, as a practical matter it is completely impossible to rank any prospects whatsoever. Almost any action I undertake will expose me to marginally greater risks along some dimension of my personal good. If I spend the evening writing my book, there is a marginal decrease (I'm pretty sure) in my chance of making true friends. Had I spent the night out being sociable, I might have increased my chance of making true friends, but the odds are then considerable that I would not have advanced the cause of scholarship. As a practical matter there is nothing I can do short of total paralysis or complete irrationality that does not imperil at some level of risk some plausible component of my personal good. Infinite risk aversion, like the argument from ignorance against consequentialism, threatens to subvert not just utilitarianism but any tenable notion of rationality as well.

So suppose that a theorist of incommensurability backs down and confesses that the good of having more wealth and the good of some tiny risk to myself are commensurable, and that the risk may well be worth taking. Well and good, but then a paradox threatens. Suppose that we raise the risk a little, from one in a billion to two in a billion. Are the goods still commensurable? What about raising the risk to one in a million? To one in a thousand? Perhaps my hometown is full of bad drivers. We must remember that there seems to be an implicit premise that at least at the level of certainty no comparison is possible between the good of life and the good of wealth. As a matter of logic, then, it seems to follow that at some level of risk between one in a billion and certainty something magical happens and what were once commensurable goods become incommensurable.

But such an evaluative transubstantiation seems on reflection rather bizarre. At what level of risk does this occur, and what is magical about this level? It would seem that to avoid paradox, goods must be commensurable all the way up or there is a tricky argument to be made about something special taking place around some quantity of risk. If there is no such magical level, we have to accept full comparability, not just comparability about risk, since, after all, choices at certainty are just a limiting case of choices over risk.

A defender of the strong incommensurability thesis could claim that there must be something wrong with my argument. Surely the fact that there may be no detectable change in marginal transformations does not mean that there is no change when we cross a great distance. Even if there is no change in "mammalness" from one generation of mammals to the next, that is no reason for inferring that mammals are not the evolutionary descendants of nonmammals. It is fallacious to argue that since every mammal must have a mammal for its mother that, therefore, the chain of descent must be mammals all the way back. Likewise, it may be fallacious to argue that because goods may be commensurable at low levels of risk they must be commensurable at all levels. But this attempt at fallacy finding fails because the analogy between evolutionary descent and marginal changes in risk breaks down. It is relatively easy to imagine forms of animals that are intermediate between mammals and their nonmammalian ancestors. But what could it possibly mean for two goods to be partly incommensurable? That is surely no more coherent than to say that some number is partly prime. Unlike fuzzy notions of biological taxonomy, the von Neumann–Morgenstern conditions must, as a matter of logic, either be satisfied or not. Given the chaos that threatens when they are not, it seems to me far more plausible to insist that an adequate normative theory proceed on the assumption that rational agents will attempt to satisfy them.

What Is Really Wrong with Utilitarianism

Any number of intuitive objections, however, can be made to any theory that is indifferent to how the good is distributed among people. These objections are usually prompted by the exposition of imagined cases in which utilitarianism seems to recommend something seriously at variance with what we normally think of as moral. I must note that the use of imagined cases in moral philosophy is controversial. For some theorists, examples of the kind that follow are part of the stock in trade of moral thinking, a necessary clearing away of distracting detail to get at salient moral problems.[38] Others find their use deeply obnoxious and accuse those who use them of trying to base moral theory on the unrealistic and the bizarre.

Even if one is inclined to side with the latter group of theorists, there are still three reasons to take the following cases seriously. First, and as explained at greater length in the next chapter, there is reason to think that our intuitive moral sensibilities are not entirely disjointed from that which morality actually requires, so the fact that we have certain moral intuitions even in response to bizarre cases is at least prima facie evidence of a problem with a theory. To be sure, in instances of bizarre conditions one should be more skeptical of one's intuitive conclusions than in normal conditions, but it is at best difficult to draw the line between the bizarre and the normal with sufficient clarity to determine that certain intuitions have no probative value in moral theory building.

Second, while individual cases may seem bizarre, institutional cases are much less so. Individual agents may not take seriously cases (such as that about to be described) of sacrificing the one to save the many, but governments, for example, often face very similar choices when making allocations of resources or instituting criminal punishments.[39] But as argued in chapter 4, the dividing line between individuals and institutions is not all that hard and fast either. Without individuals who support, enforce, and carry out government policies, there are no such policies, so individuals are implicated in examples that may look bizarre. Therefore, a moral theorist may very well wish to clear away distracting details and consider intuitions as they apply directly to individuals who are interacting with one another.

Third, it so happens that a large number of people, professional philosophers and laity alike, will continue to be convinced by intuition-pumping examples even when other objections to utilitarianism are cleared away. If there is to be any hope of rationally persuading these people, account will have to be taken of these examples, however distasteful they may be to those who do not care for intuitions. Thus this discussion.

The first of these examples is the so-called problem of *utility monsters*. Suppose that there are some human beings whose personal good is raised by lowering the personal good of others. They may get pleasure or happiness by inflicting pain on others, or they may be able to achieve special kinds of perfection through the infliction of harm. Suppose further that the gains in the personal good of these utility monsters exceed the losses they inflict on others. Utilitarianism recommends that they should be allowed to engage in their monstrous activities. But the idea that some individuals should be allowed to prey on others strikes most people as deeply offensive. Few of us would be willing to concede that a sadist should be allowed to torture other people for fun, even if it could somehow be demonstrated that his or her gains outweigh losses to others.

Stated abstractly, this objection seems so farfetched that it is hard to imagine taking it seriously, but here is a way to make it seem more concrete: the case of the Roman arena. In the Roman arena, a few people suffer horrible fates (being eaten by lions, slain in gladiatorial combat, etc.) for the entertainment of a large number of people. These persons may enjoy watching the sufferings of others a great deal; indeed, this grotesque form of spectatorism may be their only relief from an otherwise dreary and difficult existence. If the number of spectators is sufficiently large, it is quite plausible that their utility gains, when aggregated, are sufficient to outweigh the great and greatly concentrated losses of those who are actually on the floor of the arena. And even if it is not possible to build an arena large enough to aggregate enough utility gains to outweigh the losses, casual sadists need have no fear. All that is needed is a technological innovation to change the balance. Once television is invented, it may be possible for millions rather than mere thousands to enjoy the sufferings in the arena. The viewing audience can function as a collective utility monster.

Since it seems unlikely that anyone will actually volunteer for death in the arena (at least, for the passive death of being eaten by lions), utilitarianism might seem to recommend thrusting some persons into the arena against their wills. Such a seizure seems the very nadir of injustice and immorality. And worse for the utilitarian, there is no dismissing this form of the objection on the grounds of sheer farfetchedness. Roman arenas and television are very much part of our historical experience.

The second of the problems to consider is that of *imposed sacrifices*. Suppose that you are a doctor in a hospital.[40] In room 1 you have a perfectly healthy patient who has come for a routine examination. In rooms 2 through 6 you have five other patients, all of whom are dying of various degenerative ailments: one is suffering heart failure; another, liver failure; yet another, degeneration of the bone marrow; another, advanced cancer of the lungs; and another, renal failure. You happen to know as a result of tissue-compatibility testing, which you have been performing on all six patients, that the organs of the healthy patient could be transplanted with a very high chance of success into the dying patients, thus saving their lives. But of course, doing so would require butchering the one healthy patient for his parts.

Assume for the sake of argument that if saved, the dying patients could be expected to make a full recovery and go on to live lives as full and productive as the healthy patient would live if he is allowed to leave unmolested. Assume also—for the sake of avoiding any unpleasant legal and emotional complications—that you have the opportunity to arrange for the healthy patient to die in an apparent freak accident within a fortunately short distance of an organ bank. What do you do? Utilitarianism appears to recommend killing the one healthy patient to save the dying patients. But doing so would be deeply repugnant to most people: it clearly is a violation of his rights, is using him as a means and not as an end, is prohibited by biblical injunctions against killing, and so on.

The third problem is that of *oppressed minorities*. There are any number of ways in which an insensitivity to distribution of the good among persons may be morally objectionable. For instance, it may be the case that having a vibrant capitalist economy unfettered by government regulation and redistributive taxation may produce a world of economic growth, technological wonder, and consumer satisfaction, which produces a great deal of personal good for most people but in which a perhaps not insubstantial minority of noncompetitive persons sinks into penury and despair. Such an arrangement might be endorsed by utilitarianism yet violate people's deeply held concerns about distributive fairness and the welfare of the worst off.

Other kinds of institutional arrangements might also produce great disparities between the relatively many and the relatively few. The serenity of untroubled beliefs and religious consolations may be part of the personal good of most people in some imaginable societies. The institution of a Church Universal could be a major benefit to most persons in such a society. And to see that people remain serene in their beliefs, a coercive apparatus—the Inquisition, perhaps—could be instituted for the sake of making sure dissenters from the Church Universal's teachings do not make themselves widely heard. That the genuine personal good of some persons consists in the unfettered individual pursuit of truth may be admitted—at least in the recesses of the Grand Inquisitor's heart—but the good of the many that outweighs the good of the few dissenters may be invoked as a utilitarian reason for silencing the latter. This reasoning offends against deeply held beliefs most of us have about justice and liberty.

A variation of the theme of oppressed minorities is *oppressed majorities*. It is possible that there may be some persons whose personal good has dimensions so vast that their enjoyments could outweigh even large numbers of people. The exquisite pleasures or the wonderful achievements of an elite high culture may be invoked as a utilitarian justification for institutions in which a majority, and not just a minority, enjoy very small portions of the personal good. Perhaps it was too bad that there had to be slavery in classical antiquity, but without it where would antiquity's great thinkers and artists have found the leisure necessary for their accomplishments? Too bad also about an industrial revolution in which eight-year-olds worked long days in factories and mines, but without the wealth generated by their activities, would the novel and the opera ever have come into existence? Perhaps not, but such elitism still strikes most people as morally repugnant.

A fourth and final problem is that of *moral alienation and the appeal to cost*.[41] It seems likely, given the great disparities of wealth in the world, that there are any number of things I could be doing with my time and energy that would advance the good of others a great deal while diminishing my own personal good by only a small amount. The dollar I spend in my neighborhood bar to buy a beer could buy a day's food for a starving child somewhere in the world. The beer I would miss only slightly; the meal would be of great significance to the starving child. Utilitarianism would recommend that I give the dollar away.[42] Indeed, utilitarianism would recommend that every dollar of my income that, when given away, makes a marginal increase in someone else's personal good greater than my marginal loss should be given away. In light of the amount of physical privation in the world, I would find myself reduced to a diet of rice and beans—and not much of that—quite quickly. Likewise, very little of my time would be my own. The small satisfaction I derive from taking a walk in the evening could be more than counterbalanced by spending that same time as a comforting companion to a lonely retiree in a rest home.

Utilitarianism would place considerable demands on me: since it is a universal theory of moral duties it would require me to do my part to maximize utility wherever possible. If I found myself as the healthy patient in the hospital example, it would require me to volunteer myself as a living organ donor. If I found myself in classical antiquity without the requisites to participate in high culture or even citizenship, it might require me to volunteer myself as a menial slave.

An extended version of this objection is that utilitarianism will require us to be relatively indifferent not only to our own fates but also to the fates of those who are nearest and dearest to us. If I find myself in a situation in which I am forced to choose between saving the life of my own child and that of two other children, utilitarianism seems to recommend the latter, even though it involves a tremendous sacrifice of my own well-being and a renunciation of my deepest personal commitments.[43]

Most people think that morality and justice cannot impose such stringent requirements on anyone. It is generally believed that a moral agent can be excused from performing certain actions if the cost to that individual is too high. Hence it is thought that there is an *appeal to cost* against the demands of morality.[44] If morality is too demanding on agents, they would regard it as something hostile and external—hence the notion of moral alienation. John Rawls reflects something like it when he discusses the strains that arise from commitment to a theory of justice. He believes that a problem with utilitarianism is that rational agents could not commit themselves to any theory of justice that imposes costs they might find too high to keep.[45]

It may not be immediately obvious how the possibility of an alienating morality stems from its indifference to distribution, but in fact the two problems are different faces of the same coin. Utilitarianism is an *alienating* theory of justice when looked at in the first person: one thinks of the case of the healthy hospital patient about to be sacrificed and imagines "that could be me."[46] Utilitarianism is a horrible theory of morality when looked at in the third person: one thinks of the case of the hospital, imagines oneself as either the doctor or as an outside observer, and thinks: "What's being contemplated for the healthy patient is wicked and iniquitous."

Both horribleness and alienation seem to share a common structure in that they are both facilitated by distributive indifference. It is only when we find it acceptable to make the lives of some persons go very badly for the sake of making the lives of other persons go better that we can accept the horrible or alienating acts. Only if we are indifferent about how personal good is to be distributed among persons would we be prepared to make one person suffer the agony of being eaten by lions, while the crowd goes wild in the Roman arena, or force the heretic to suffer oppression, while the rest of the populace enjoys the tranquility of religious consolation untroubled by skeptics.[47] It is also only when we are indifferent about whether we are doing our "fair share" to alleviate the misery in the world (as opposed to doing as much as possible to alleviate that misery) that moral alienation becomes an acute problem.

The problems stemming from the alleged injustice of distributive indifference make a fairly damning indictment of utilitarianism. Can it be saved?

Living by the Rules

A common line of rebuttal is to claim that these examples of intuitive horribleness and violations of commonsense morality lack the bite they initially seem to have because relatively few agents find themselves in the godlike position of being able to make utility calculations for the consequences of specific acts. For the most part, utilitarians hold, our very inability to make precise calculations about either causal consequences or the kinds of personal good that attach to those consequences requires us to make use of rules and heuristics for the purpose of making correct decisions. While a perfect being might make the "horrible" utilitarian decisions previously cited, we would have to make rather different decisions. We would have to make decisions indirectly; that is, utilitarianism would give us general principles, which we would use to make specific decisions.

A typical example of such a *two-level* utilitarian view is that of Richard Hare.[48] He asks us to imagine two different kinds of beings. The first is the "archangels," who have the ability to make interpersonal comparisons quickly and easily, who have instant access to vast and reliable sources of information about the world, and who can make causal calculations of consequences with great ease. The second class is the "proles," who have none of the advantages of archangels. The proles are very much like the rest of us in that they are poor at making interpersonal comparisons and estimating consequences and have highly limited and imperfect information about the world.

Proles who are faced with the case of forcible organ donation would have to take into consideration a variety of uncomfortable facts: their information about the relative states of health of the patients is likely to be highly fallible; they cannot give anything like a guarantee that they can create an accident in which the healthy patient will die in an unsuspicious manner; they cannot know that their actions will not create a moral hazard for future patients; and so on. Given all the problems the prole doctor faces, he or she may actually bring about the best possible state of the world not by trying to maximize utility directly but by sticking to the old Hippocratic injunction *primum non nocere*. Likewise, since we proles are unlikely to be able to make precise interpersonal comparisons of utility for every possible case, we should not give in to utility monsters—for how can we really know from case to case that torturing one person will benefit another in a maximizing way? Better for us to stick to some system of rules that requires the integrity of persons not to be violated.

Consequentialists, Derek Parfit in particular, have also advanced arguments against the alienating effects of morality by claiming that we should not direct our attention to the acts of individuals considered one by one but to the entire set of acts of all agents.[49] If I alone were the only benevolent person in the world, I would certainly ruin myself if I redistributed my time, my income, and my energy in a utility-maximizing way. There is simply too much suffering in the world, and my resources alone are hardly ample enough to make more than a small dent in the problem. But if every agent acted in a benevolent manner and donated an appropriate amount of income, time, and energy to the relief of hunger (and privation more generally), the individual donations that would be required might be quite modest, leaving each of us with considerable time and energy with which to pursue our own projects. Everyone's resources amount to a great deal and could probably eliminate most of the world's privations if applied in a coordinated and intelligent manner.

The arguments that might be made by using two-level views and collective views can ameliorate the situation of utilitarianism somewhat, but as they stand they suffer from three fairly strong objections.

First, they can properly be accused of *underdevelopment*. The stories that might be told in support of rules like "respect people's rights" and *primum non nocere* seem fine as far as they go, but how are we to know that rules like these are really the rules we should apply? Might it not turn out, on more careful examination, that if we think critically enough about the rules we will in fact end up with rules, justified by utilitarianism, that support the involuntary transfer of organs from one individual to others, at least in some cases? And might it not in fact turn out that many of the noxious political and economic institutions about which I worried previously would be supported by utilitarian rules?

As for collective utilitarianism, the fact is that many people will not comply with a utilitarian program for the relief of privation or whatever seems to be a serious problem. It would be truly excellent if all were willing to give up a fifth of their incomes to eliminate starvation, but since many people are selfish it seems unlikely that this will occur. What is a good utilitarian to do under these circumstances? Does one abandon one's utilitarianism by refusing to impoverish oneself on the grounds that others are not doing their fair share? It might seem so since the notion of a "fair share" hardly appears to be at home in a theory that is indifferent to how shares are distributed. But if the individual does not thus abandon utilitarianism, one is stuck again with the problem of alienation. Parfit has no theory of partial compliance—of what a utilitarian should do when others are not doing what they should. Utilitarianism needs such a theory. It will not do for the utilitarian to make oracular pronouncements about ideal rules from on high. Utilitarianism is a theory that commands us to live in the world that is and to work with the materials that come to hand.

There is a second plausible accusation against rule-based accounts, that of *rule worship*. One of the virtues attributed to utilitarianism in this very chapter is its sensitivity to changing empirical circumstances. But the proles are stuck with rules, and the rules may be considerably stickier than the circumstances to which they are supposed to be adaptions. A rule like *primum non nocere* originated in an era when medical knowledge and technology were relatively crude. In an era of no antisepsis, no anesthesia, no reliable theory of disease, and no understanding of the biochemical basis of physiological processes, it almost certainly was the case that patients would be more likely to make a recovery with only the limited and cautious interventions that this rule would allow. It is not quite as clear that such a blanket rule is a good thing today, when medical knowledge is far more comprehensive. If such areas of knowledge as psychopharmacology or genetic engineering advance considerably in the future—and they probably will—the rule may become more of an impediment to human flourishing than otherwise.

What is true of medicine is no doubt true of every other area of human activity. Human capacities change and empirical circumstances change, and therefore the rules that would be utility maximizing also change. But the changing of the rules raises no end of problems. Who is to change the rules? If the answer is just anyone, according to his or her own best understanding, we have tacitly given up on the idea of having rules at all. If doctors could decide to abandon *primum non nocere* the minute they encountered some (possibly transitory) circumstance that they thought was different from that in which the rule was justified, we might very well find lots of nasty business—forcible organ transfers and worse—going on under the banner of utilitarianism. But if rules are to be rigid and inflexible, it seems that utilitarianism loses its virtue of being able to adjust to changing empirical circumstances. The inflexibility of rules would lead to a charge of "rule worship," of fetishizing rules in a way contrary to the consequentialist spirit of utilitarianism.

One possible response to this problem would be to appoint an elite of moral philosophers and policy scientists to keep in touch with changing empirical conditions and change the rules as needed, but this response raises the problem of what Bernard Williams calls "Government-House Utilitarianism."[50] Williams holds that the idea of being ruled by such an elite is deeply offensive, and many of us would agree with him.

Finally, even rule-based accounts cannot by themselves defeat the position of *hard-core deontological intuitionism*. Even if it can be shown that the rules that utilitarianism would recommend to us would not have the same counterintuitive implications that the parade of horrible examples seems to show, and even if we could clear up the puzzles surrounding the concept of rules, there would still be the objection that utilitarianism would under some circumstances be willing to countenance horrible acts, massive injustice, and severe moral alienation. Hard-core deontological intuitionism holds that we can morally reason about any kind of factual universe, even really bizarre ones that contain such improbable creatures as archangels, utility monsters, high-tech Faustian physicians, and what have you. Were such creatures to exist, this position holds, utilitarianism would recommend that they do terrible things and that we submit to their doing terrible things. The very logical possibility of such horrible acts, in this view, is enough to discredit utilitarianism, no matter how mild and benign its this-worldly recommendations.

An example that provokes some people to this extreme deontological view is spun out by William James:

> If the hypothesis were offered us of a world in which Messrs. Fourier's and Bellamy's and Morris's utopias should all be outdone, and millions kept permanently happy on the one simple condition that a certain lost soul on the far-off edge of things should lead a life of lonely torture, what except a specificial and independent sort of emotion can it be which would make us immediately feel, even though an impulse arose within us to clutch at the happiness so offered, how hideous a thing would be its enjoyment when deliberately accepted as the fruit of such a bargain?[51]

This is an upsetting story to be sure, even if it invokes factual conditions that seem a mite implausible. I doubt that utilitarianism could find within itself the resources not to recommend that the lonely soul be left to his or her fate.[52] Faced with this conclusion, at least some people will think that if utilitarianism could recommend that fate under any circumstances, it must be a horrible doctrine.

What Is to Be Done?

If utilitarianism is to be defended along the lines presently held by Richard Hare and Derek Parfit, three tasks must be undertaken.

1. *A theory of what moral intuitions are must be provided.* I must show that the fable of the lonely soul lacks the force that some people think it has. This is a task that requires a discussion of moral reasoning, which will follow in the next chapter.

2. *Some claims about what utilitarianism actually recommends must be advanced and defended.* In this respect my project is very similar to that undertaken by Russell Hardin in his excellent *Morality within the Limits of Reason.* The institutionalist core of the book differs from his project primarily because it uses some novel theoretical apparatus. That will be the task of a theory of institutions, which appears in chapters 3–6. Chapter 3 advances and defends a general principle that this-worldly institutions must satisfy: a utilitarian nonexploitation principle. Chapter 4 discusses how institutions and rules can be expected to work in the abstract. Chapter 5 is a discussion of the institutions of the optimal political economies of different factual universes, as well as the rights and duties that inhere therein. Chapter 6 discusses redistribution. The theory advanced throughout is an attempt to make utilitarian rules endogenous, to explain why this-worldly agents, with the preferences they are in fact likely to have, would comply with the rules and live in the institutions they create.

3. *Some puzzles about institutions must be discussed.* The question of when and how institutions can be changed to deal with changing empirical conditions is discussed briefly in chapter 7. I then return to my parade of horribles and see how horrible it looks at the end.

If all these things can be accomplished, a plausible defense of utilitarianism will have been made. I remain well aware, however, that I cannot hope to convince all readers. I have to rely on a number of complex arguments, as well as a number of empirical premises, that may not be well founded. So before moving into the argument itself, I should say a few words on what I hope to achieve other than a vindication of the plausibility of utilitarianism.

In the end, some readers may feel that I have still slighted the worst off in the world too much and that my indifference to the distribution of the good leaves me still too open to a charge of supporting oppression and poverty. If that be the case, I can at least pose the question like the following: given what I have just said about how institutions and rules realize moral principles in practice, how much weight would we have to give to equality or priority to the worst off in order to quash our remaining queasiness? If we must give it some weight, some understanding about how institutions are actually to work may make somewhat less arbitrary the weighing of equality or priority we need to satisfy our consciences.

TWO

Reasoning about Right and Wrong

The Need for a Metaethics

A central task of political philosophy is to provide a coherent explanation of how individuals are related through moral duties to political institutions. This task cannot be avoided by any political theory, although in the case of utilitarianism it is particularly pressing. It is not pressing because the classical founders of utilitarianism—Bentham and the Mills—were themselves deeply interested in institutional questions in a way other moralists may not have been. My purpose should surely be greater than simply honoring past practices. Nor is it pressing just because it has often been claimed, by Brian Barry, for example,[1] that utilitarianism is somehow better suited for making decisions about affairs of state than it is about one's personal life. After all, decisions about affairs of state will ultimately affect one's personal life, often in intimate and painful ways. Rather, my claim in this book is that if we think seriously and carefully about the kinds of institutions that real-world utilitarians will create, that utilitarianism becomes a much more palatable theory than it has hitherto been represented as being.

Thus, my primary task is to show what kind of institutions utilitarians will try to build in an imperfect world and, in turn, to show how those institutions reflect back on personal duties. I hope to prove that the resulting duties are not as obnoxious as the opponents of utilitarianism seem to think they are. Given the amount of criticism that utilitarianism as a theory of justice has taken over the last few decades, however, it is incumbent on me to provide at least some prima facie evidence of its plausibility. To a limited extent I have already begun to do so by arguing in chapter 1 that utilitarianism has a number of highly desirable theoretical attributes. But the parade of horribles should have given us pause. It makes utilitarianism look very bad in the light of our moral intuitions.

At this point readers of whatever moral persuasion may simply feel more of a sense of bewilderment than anything else. They should be wondering what really counts as evidence in this argument and how that evidence is to be weighed. Hence, I devote a chapter to a discussion of the methods of ethics and their relation to foundations of utilitarianism. While I can in no way hope to demonstrate the principle of utility beyond question, at least I can show that a number of arguments offered against utilitarianism in the past few decades do not immediately knock it down.

Almost anyone who has thought about and discussed moral issues has experienced either uncertainty or conflict or both. Uncertainty exists within persons. It crops up whenever we suspect, given a choice between acts or rules or dispositions or institutions, that we might choose rightly or wrongly but do not know which of a set of options would be right or wrong. Conflict exists between persons. It can be found whenever one person claims that to choose a given act—or whatever—is right and another claims that it is wrong. The aim of ethical theorizing is to articulate principles to which we can appeal in hopes of reducing uncertainty or conflict.

The existence of moral uncertainty I take to be an indisputable psychological fact for most people. If any of my readers can honestly claim never to have felt it, they would be well advised to put this book down now, for it will be of little use to them. Moral conflict, however, presents a different problem, for it may seem that what appears to be moral conflict is perhaps nothing of the sort. It is not necessarily the case that if I affirm that X is right and you affirm with equal vehemence that X is wrong that we are disagreeing on a moral principle. Perhaps we are disagreeing on either material or metaphysical facts.

Let us take a not-too-implausible example. Perhaps you and I agree on the moral principle "One ought never to act in such a way that one deprives an innocent person of life." I am practice shooting outside one fine afternoon, and just as I am about to shoot an old garbage can on my isolated property, you approach and say, "Stop! A child has crawled into the can." Am I morally permitted to shoot? I believe that the can is full of garbage and that I may shoot. If it is in fact the case that there is someone in the can, then I may not. But my disagreement with my neighbor is not one of moral principle.

There are other cases—less trivial and, indeed, seriously important ones—in which moral disagreements turn on factual rather than moral questions. Note, of course, that some of these facts might be metaphysical. The cruder attempts at moral persuasion by the prolife movement exploit vivid demonstrations of physical facts about fetal development and the procedure of abortion in hopes of convincing persons of the wrongness of this practice. Of course, some may not be moved by such persuasion; in response to the antiabortionist's moral complaint that "abortion stops a beating heart," one can respond, not without justice, "So what?" Those who do not object to the practice of abortion can claim that there is per se no moral significance to stopping a heart; we can thus easily acknowledge all the material facts about fetal development and the practice of abortion and still countenance it. But a more sophisticated opponent might be able to produce a metaphysical argument, showing that moral personhood emerges in a fetus prior to birth. Since many moral rights are commonly thought to be attached to one's achievement of a metaphysical state called personhood in a way that they are not attached to merely having a beating heart, we might thereby become convinced of the wrongness of the practice of abortion.

Might it be the case that all moral conflict is really factual conflict? Such an hypothesis is intriguing and perhaps even attractive; were it true, moral philosophy would not need to exist as an autonomous discipline. Moral conflict and moral uncertainty could be resolved by the right application of the sciences and of metaphysics. Unhappily, the hypothesis that moral conflict is really factual disagreement is false, as a look at a few other cases should show.

Let us consider a serious moral question. Is it right to put murderers to death? While it is certainly the case that much of the dispute about the moral rightness of the death penalty arises out of disputes about empirical issues, such as the question of whether it does or does not deter crime or whether it is or is not a cost-effective means of punishment, a resolution of these issues will not resolve the disputes about the morality of the death penalty. Even if it could be demonstrated beyond a reasonable doubt that the death penalty had a dramatic deterrent effect on murder or other brutal crimes, and even if it could be administered efficiently and fairly, not all morally sensitive persons would support it. Some people think that the sanctity of human life overrides any premeditated destruction of a defenseless person. Likewise, even if it were shown beyond a reasonable doubt that the death penalty had no deterrent effect whatsoever and that it was costly and unfairly administered, not all rational persons would oppose it. Many people strongly believe in retributive just desserts and thus in the moral requirement of taking a life for a life even when so doing achieves nothing more than a dead criminal.[2]

Around the death penalty and around any number of hot issues in morality, public and private, there seem to be genuine differences of moral principle. Some take "thou shalt not kill" as an absolute, not to be abridged or compromised by even a socially acceptable purpose such as the reduction of the rate of brutal crimes. Others want an eye for an eye, even when there is a hefty moral price to be paid for getting it.

These differences call out for resolution. It is obviously not just a matter of different principles being logically contradictory. They are also pragmatically incompatible. But some effort must be made if the proponents of different principles are not to come to blows. Moral theorizing thus gets its impetus from the conviction that thinking and talking with one another are better than deadlock or civil conflict.

The question then arises, though, of how it might be possible to resolve differences in moral principle. Other disciplines provide two models for rational inquiry. These I call the scientific and the mathematical.

Is Ethics a Science?

By a science, I mean a form of disciplined enquiry with the purpose of discovering regularities among facts that we discover through some means. In the physical sciences, these means are our ordinary senses. In the human sciences, we may add our capacities to interpret the meanings of human acts and artifacts. Theories attempt to explain existing regularities and predict novel ones. The project of understanding ethical theorizing as a science is a doubtful one for two reasons. First, it's far from clear exactly what "facts" are in ethics. Second, neither is it clear what "explanation" or "prediction" means in ethics. There are certain facts about our psychology that might be advanced as candidates for moral facts. The fact that we feel guilt or anger or contempt or any other of the "moral" emotions in certain circumstances might, for instance, be thought to be such facts. But why should not these facts be simply facts about our psychology and nothing more? What grounds do we have for believing that they have anything to do with morality? The fact that I am angry with someone for something that person did might simply be a reflection of my upbringing; from a different psychological standpoint, my anger would be wrongheaded or even morally unintelligible.

A defender of the view that there are moral truths to be found in psychological phenomena might claim that there is something special about the feelings that we call "moral" that distinguishes them from those that are not. I can be pleased or angry without imagining that there is a moral issue at stake, but there are certain issues in which I am convinced that my pleasure or anger seems moral; in this view, only if one feels the desire that someone should be punished or rewarded for something do psychological phenomena count as moral phenomena.

But this view—that a desire to punish or reward constitutes a moral fact—cannot survive serious reflection. For one, it seems far from clear that this desire is constituted in any way other than our other desires; it is the product of our evolutionary experience and our socialization. Unless we take a metaphysically extravagant view, all our desires can be produced only by mundane causal means. But surely not all our desires are for things that are morally right. Indeed, surely not all our desires to see someone blamed or punished are right. I should hope that anyone reading this book would admit that there are or at least have been many persons who have had desires to see others punished for acts that to us are in no way wrong, such as engaging in a heterodox form of religious worship according to the dictates of their consciences. Likewise, many persons have felt compelled to single out for reward those who have performed deeds that most readers will find horrible; no doubt even efficient administrators of extermination camps have received the gratitude of some. Thus, psychological phenomena of anger and gratitude are psychological only, not moral. Without independent criteria of rightness and wrongness, there can be no assessment of them as moral or not.

I must add a qualification at this point, however. I do not mean to suggest that the psychological phenomena that are grouped together under the label "moral intuition" necessarily have nothing to do with morality. These phenomena admit of at least two different interpretations, in one of which they do have something to do with determining right and wrong. I discuss these interpretations in following pages.

Certain vulgar popularizers of science have advanced the proposition that biological facts might play a role as moral facts.[3] "Pop sociobiology" has advanced the thesis that morality is a ruse of evolution, a means that selfish genes use for the more efficient propagation of themselves. It may be the case that certain moral rules do in fact promote the propagation of certain genes. It can be shown, for example, that under specific evolutionary conditions, those individuals who possess genes coding for behaviors that take account of the welfare of other creatures will be more likely to leave descendants than individuals who behave "selfishly." Consequently, such genes will be selected by evolution. But are those behaviors justified by their mere survival? It might very well be the case that for a sufficiently strong and wily fellow, the rules of morality interfere with his leaving as many descendants as possible. I rather doubt that many people would think him released from his obligation not to murder or enslave others. The premise "That which will get your genes duplicated is right" is also absurd. There is no general relation between evolutionary success and good conduct. It will sanction murder just as easily as altruism.

Readers should not assume, however, that evolution has nothing to do with morality. Consequentialists of any kind do have a reason to be concerned with questions of evolutionary survival—a point I try to make in the next chapter. The problem with pop sociobiology is not that it is concerned with evolution but that it gets the relationship with evolution and morality backward. Pop sociobiology attempts to derive moral principles from evolution. Moral consequentialists should be interested in evolution, but they should put moral principles anterior to it, as we shall see.

Perhaps there are metaphysical facts that seem to be better candidates for "moral facts." The will of God, for instance, might be a discoverable metaphysical fact that would also be a moral fact. Unfortunately even this thesis seems to be false. Philosophers have known since at least the time of the *Euthyphro* that what is good is not good because God loves it but that God loves it because it is good. Those who think differently ought to ask themselves, "If God loved the act of torturing small children—assuming that this would be a discoverable metaphysical fact—for the sheer fun of it, would it thereby become right?" Surely any sane person would answer this question in the negative. The thesis "What God wills is always right because He so wills" is thus absurd.

Of course, there would seem to be theses about what is right that are not absurd, but there seems to be no way of getting at them through mere facts. There is a rule in moral theorizing called (by some) Hume's Law: one is not to derive an *ought* from an *is*. "Is" statements may have bearing on "ought" statements, but only when conjoined with some original "ought" statement.[4] Given that Hume's Law seems to have stood the test of time (it is now over two centuries old) and has not been very seriously challenged, it would seem that ethics as a science is a dubious project.

Is Ethics a Mathematics?

Not all reasoning is about determining facts; some of it is about manipulating tautologies.[5] Some disciplines—mathematics is a prime example—proceed on a purely deductive basis. Readers should not, however, assume that a purely deductive basis is a purely algorithmic basis. As any good mathematician will tell you, imagination, intuition, and creativity are indispensable components of mathematical inquiry (although results in such an inquiry are only justified if they can be checked algorithmicly).[6]

Beginning with certain specific principles—the law of noncontradiction, the axiom of choice, and certain axioms of set theory—one can create a mathematics. Of course, which principles are chosen must to some extent seem arbitrary. Intrinsic plausibility no doubt plays an important role (it is not easy, and may not even be possible, to imagine how we could dispense with the law of noncontradiction). Other axioms may be chosen for the purpose of making the enterprise interesting and rich. Mathematics has been quite successful in working for a pretty miserly axiomatic basis. Mathematical economics has also done interesting things from small beginnings.

Might we attempt to elaborate moral principles in a way similar to that in which we derive mathematical theorems? It will be by no means as "easy" as mathematical reasoning. But perhaps there is a line of thought worth pursuing here. It may be too much to ask of ethical theories that they produce truth; but it surely is not too much to ask that they be coherent and plausible.[7]

Fundamentalist Utilitarianism

If we proceed with a kind of ethical theorizing in which ethics is a mathematics, there is a temptation to choose just one grand axiom from which, in conjunction with the sum of our empirical knowledge, we can derive every ethical imperative. Such a position is attractive for its generality, for it seems to yield a simple way of covering all cases and thus putting an end to uncertainty and moral conflict. It is also attractive for its coherence, for if the system contains only one moral axiom there can be no question of this axiom being contradicted by other moral axioms. Small wonder that the classical utilitarians, especially Bentham, thought they had a most remarkable discovery in the principle of utility. It was a single principle that, when conjoined with appropriate factual statements, did indeed seem to yield a coherent, rich, plausible system of ethics. For many early utilitarians, the principle of utility was taken to be simply self-evident, a principle for which no further proof was either necessary or possible. I call this position *fundamentalist utilitarianism*.

In the first chapter of his *Introduction to the Principles of Morals and Legislation*, Bentham, after providing us with a brief explanation of the principle of utility, denied that there could be any ultimate defense of it:

> Has the rectitude of this principle been ever formally contested? It should seem that it had, by those who have not known what they have been meaning. Is it susceptible of any direct proof? It should seem not for that which is used to prove every other thing else, cannot itself be proved: a chain of proofs must have their commencement somewhere. To give such a proof is as impossible as it is needless.[8]

Bentham reasons as a mathematician might—or rather, might not. Asked to give a "demonstration" of the truth of the law of noncontradiction or the axioms of set theory, the mathematician would no doubt rightly throw up his hands and respond that such a demonstration would not be possible in mathematics. Rather, such rules would be constitutive of mathematics, the basis for all possible demonstrations.

To be sure, Bentham does not stop with a pure ipse dixit. In the second chapter of his famous *Principles*, he does attempt to give some evidence for the principle in an indirect way, by attacking other proposed principles of morality. In a short discussion, he disposes of principles he calls "asceticism," "sympathy," and "antipathy," and then in a discussion of even more breathtaking speed, he does in moral sensibility, commonsense morality, natural law, and divine inspiration. Bentham assumes that the principle of utility is the only principle left standing and, as such, wins as the least absurd. Doubtless it does, but only because of feeble competition.

John Stuart Mill is perhaps more subtle in his metaethics than Bentham, but only slightly so. In the fourth chapter of his *Utilitarianism*, he discusses the issue of to what proof the principle of utility might be susceptible. It is not one of his more convincing arguments. His position seems to rest on the thesis of psychological hedonism: only happiness is desirable as an end in itself. Since ethics is concerned with the general ends to which human conduct is to tend, the general end of human conduct is to bring about as much happiness as possible—hence utilitarianism. Anything else would just seem absurd.

If anything else were absurd, perhaps fundamentalist utilitarianism, the assumption that only the principle of utility and nothing else can be the basis of ethical reasoning, would be a viable philosophical position. To be sure, the principle of utility is not—or at least does not seem to me to be—an implausible principle. But it is surely not the only plausible principle on which one could found a coherent ethics. It is simply not the case that anything else is simply absurd. Axioms other than the principle of utility need not lead to absurd deductions, and some of these might well be more plausible to many people than the bare principle of utility.[9] A few candidates have already been hinted at, so I here confine myself to some additional illustrations.

Some morally sensitive people find an axiom of the "sacredness" of persons to be important; they might add such an axiom to the principle of utility—indeed, give it lexical priority over the principle of utility to avoid conflicts between it and that principle—and thus derive a vastly different ethics. In a system such as this two-axiom one, persons would be morally required to pursue the greatest happiness but would face constraints in doing so; they would not be permitted to sacrifice the lives or well-being of innocent individuals in their efforts.[10] Others may wish to junk the principle of utility altogether, replacing it with a principle that divides the world into different entitlements and forbids everyone from interfering with those entitlements—as does Robert Nozick.[11]

A restricted utilitarianism, a libertarianism, and many other possible systems might have a deductive coherence. None of them is necessarily absurd; all of them are based on principles that would have some intuitive plausibility. It seems, unhappily, that we have traded an intractable shouting match over moral issues for an intractable and confusing shouting match over moral axioms. How are we to sort out their competing claims?

Intuitions

It is believed both by ordinary people and many philosophers that we possess some kind of faculty of moral judgment, which functions so that whenever we are presented with a real or hypothetical moral problem, some answer comes to the fore. This answer is called a *moral intuition*. Thus, if someone asks me if she may use deadly force to ward off a deadly and unprovoked attack, it just seems obvious to me that she may. If someone asks me if he may murder his rich uncle to get early access to a generous inheritance, it just seems obvious to me that he may not.

It is not deeply mysterious that persons should have this capacity, either within the domain of morality or not. Persons who have had sufficient experience with all sorts of matters often acquire the capacity to make judgments without conscious calculation. Some mathematicians, for example, manifest such abilities. They can "see" their way to the end of problems or proofs without having to work through the intervening steps; the solution to the problem, the deductive result or the validity of the proof, simply presents itself to their minds without any conscious awareness.[12] Of course, such intuitions are not limited to areas of abstract cognitive activity. We have intuitions about the behavior of physical objects and can accurately predict where a thrown object will land without consciously solving differential equations in our heads, and we have intuitions about the mental states of other people from their behavior without resort to any body of scientific psychology.

There is nothing spooky about how mathematicians or ordinary people manage to do what they do. No angel sits on our shoulders, whispering the answers in our ears. It is simply that our long experience with our respective fields of expertise gives us a great store of tacit knowledge and little mental shortcuts that enable us to get through problems. I say "tacit knowledge" because none of us seems capable of fully articulating what we know; we simply *know*.

It has often been claimed that by resorting to our moral intuitions we can sort out competing moral claims and competing moral principles. We can, for instance, ask ourselves about difficult moral cases. We can compare how different principles would resolve these cases and compare our intuitive judgments to these solutions.[13] Those principles that produce the intuitively "right" answer most often are, according to this line of reasoning, the better principles.

The question then arises: just what are we doing when we are digging up moral intuitions? There are at least two possible answers: (1) we are somehow directly perceiving the truth of moral propositions, the *perceptual* view, or (2) we are engaged in a sub- or semiconscious act of applying some set of principles—along with a large amount of tacit empirical knowledge—to different problems, the *inferential* view.

The perceptual view may seem initially plausible, but it cannot withstand serious scrutiny. It seems suspiciously close to the position that our psychological phenomena are moral "facts," a position that has already been refuted. Moreover, it is entirely unclear exactly how we could be perceiving anything. We see with our eyes and hear with our ears, but even the most subtle anatomist has yet to find an organ the function of which is to perceive moral truths. The doctrine that we have a moral sense might be a bit less embarrassing if it were the case that we all perceived the same moral truths. But as we have seen in the first section, it is most emphatically not the case that we perceive the same truths.

In ordinary, mundane cases of intuition, we can speak of certain people having "good" and "bad" intuition. Some of us are astonishingly good intuitive mathematicians, but most of us can solve problems only the hard way. Might conflicts in moral intuitions indicate that some people have a good and bad moral sense? Such a position would be seductive for theorists of moral perception (and a boost to their egos since, at least in my experience, it is a rare moralist indeed who is not convinced that he or she is surely better than one's neighbor in making determinations about what is right and what is wrong.)

Unfortunately, it is utterly unclear what criterion we might appeal to in sorting out who is a good and who is a bad moral intuiter. We can tell whether a mathematician is good at mathematical intuitions by actually doing the hard work of actually going through the steps in a proof or a problem and seeing if his or her intuition squares with generally accepted canons of mathematical reasoning. But in the case of moral intuitions, we come around the stumbling block of the apparent lack of moral facts.

Too often, the debate about who has good moral intuitions can be reduced to nothing more than "X agrees with my positions a lot, so it's clear he is a good man with sound moral sensibilities, whereas Y has the bad taste to disagree with me so obviously she has a corrupt mind and perverted moral faculties." What started as a shouting match becomes an exchange of argumenta ad hominem. Or perhaps the argument turns to metaphysical or theological extravagance. The angels whisper in my ear, Satan in yours—hence our disagreement.

Rather than prepare a pyre on which to burn our moral opponents, let us turn to the inferential view. The view that moral intuitions are a process of using tacit knowledge in conjunction with moral principles is not embarrassing at all. Not only does this make the phenomenon of moral intuition similar to that of intuition as studied by psychologists,[14] but it also gives a perfectly mundane account of the phenomenon of conflict between the intuitions of different persons. It seems clear that different persons will have different stores of tacit knowledge and be better or worse at making use that knowledge. But what has this observation to do with utilitarianism and the search for moral principles generally?

If we view our moral intuitions not as infallible guides to moral truth but merely as possible clues to a coherent morality, we might choose to engage in what moral theorists call *reflective equilibrium*. In this process, we choose principles that seem to "fit" with our intuitions. Knowing full well that it is probably impossible for our intuitions to fit those principles perfectly, we try to revise the former appropriately. We then reflect back on those principles and see how well they finally do fit. We thus attempt to serve two ends at once: we try to hold onto as many of our intuitions as possible while still attempting to obtain the coherence and richness we might want from a moral "mathematics."

This process of reflective equilibrium is a common way of proceeding in moral philosophy. Most moral theorists are wary of throwing out too many of our intuitions in an attempt to get coherence and power, even though the process of critical reflection would make such radical surgery a logical possibility. As we saw in chapter 1, there are a number of cases in which utilitarianism seems to offend so strongly against our intuitions that such radicalism would seem to be required of utilitarians. Hence, many theorists think that the method of reflective equilibrium makes utilitarianism highly doubtful.

If it is the case, however, that our intuitions are merely our use of tacit knowledge in conjunction with some set of (perhaps only vaguely understood) moral principles, then the business of showing that utilitarianism is really a radical theory that requires us to throw overboard many of our intuitions is not so easy as it may seem. There is no end of "refutations" of utilitarianism, which run something like this: "In case X, utilitarians would require us to do such-and-such. My deepest moral intuitions are offended by such-and-such. Therefore, we have to chuck utilitarianism." The fault of this argument often turns on its major premise. It may in fact be the case that if utilitarians reason by using the same general tacit knowledge that the intuition holder uses sub- or semiconsciously, they will not conclude that we should do such-and-such. And thus just like M. Jourdain, who had been speaking prose all his life without knowing it, our intuitions could well be fundamentally utilitarian without our really being aware of the fact.

Antiutilitarian intuition holders may of course object that they can construct examples in such a way that the use of certain kinds of tacit knowledge is ruled out. Their confidence is unwarranted. It seems far from clear that they can ever reason intuitively without background knowledge. If they could ever truly eliminate it, they would simply be at a loss; they would in such a case have *no* intuitions. Perhaps they have some spooky metaphysical theory about where our intuitions come from that does not appeal to tacit knowledge. If they do, it is up to them to produce it.

The chapters that follow attempt to show that in general the world is such that we would have the kind of tacit understandings that would make apparently anti-utilitarian intuitions not only possible but also likely. If I can show that, I have won half the battle. To win the whole battle, though, I should try to show that utilitarianism does have some greater plausibility than just that of fundamentalist utilitarianism. For if our intuitions result from the tacit application of background knowledge in combination with moral principles, then with slight alterations in that background knowledge we might be able to square our principles with a great variety of different intuitions.

The enterprise of arguing for a certain kind of tacit knowledge is necessarily rather speculative. So, rather than simply trying to show that utilitarianism could be consistent with our intuitions, I should also attempt to do a better job of showing that the principle of utility is itself highly, rather than just barely, plausible. Utilitarianism needs a better mathematical foundation than can be had by fundamentalism. This foundation can be obtained by using a form of moral reasoning that is at once currently very popular and often thought to knock down utilitarianism: contractualism.

Contractualism

Contractualism in General

In the last twenty-five years, in an attempt to avoid the pitfalls of both fundamentalist utilitarianism and out-and-out intuitionism, philosophers have revived a notion that dates back to the sophists and has found its original modern expression in Hobbes and Locke. This is the notion that if we adopt certain strictures on our reasoning, it might be possible to find principles on which all rational persons would agree. These principles can serve as our principles of justice; since all reasoners would agree to them, they are assumed to have a morally binding force.

This theory is called contractualism because the inferential method involved often makes use of hypothetical agreements, which we would strike in light of constraints on our moral reasoning that seem acceptable. Contractualism is thus an extended thought experiment. There is, of course, no actual contract; the contract is a metaphor for those rules that we could all accept.[15] We attempt to isolate certain elements that we think are indispensable to an acceptable theory of the right and see if they entail anything.

John Rawls, in what is surely the most famous piece of contemporary contractualist theorizing, suggests a set of five conditions that any acceptable theory of the right will have to meet: (1) generality, (2) universality, (3) publicity, (4) ordering, and (5) finality.[16] I do not have too much to say in either explanation or defense of these five principles since most sane theorists are in agreement with them, but I do attempt a few remarks.

The generality condition requires that a proper theory of justice will make no use of proper names, indexical references, or "rigged" extensional descriptions. One is not allowed to have a theory that holds, "Everyone must do what I say." Nor is one allowed a theory that requires everyone to do what a person extensionally identical to oneself says.

The universality condition requires that no one be exempt from the principles of the right, whatever they may turn out to be. No person is allowed to ride free on the general observation of rules or benefit from them except insofar as one contributes to them and observes them oneself. Moral anarchy would thus seem to be ruled out as a viable theory of the right.[17]

The publicity condition requires that whatever rules of justice there are to be publicly knowable; they are to be complied with by agents who apprehend them directly. There are to be no Platonic guardians and no utilitarians hidden in Government House, sneakily manipulating us into doing the right thing. This third requirement might be disputable, especially on utilitarian grounds, although it is strongly in accord with the intuitions of almost all of those who have grown up in open societies. In chapters 5 and 7, I provide some arguments for why utilitarians in this world should share those intuitions.

The ordering condition suggests that knowledge of the principles of right should enable us to rank states of affairs from more to less just; it seems to be pretty much a requirement that any rational person would want, especially when faced with the question "what ought we to do." One rationale for this principle may well be that since we shall surely not be able to bring a completely just world into existence, we must choose to marshall our resources in such a way that we make it as just as possible. Otherwise, we might find ourselves stuck in an all-or-nothing position, one that we might well find self-defeating.

Finally, the finality condition requires that the most fundamental principles of justice, once arrived at, must be conclusive as a final court of appeal in moral reasoning. They are to override considerations of prudence and self-interest, although such considerations can be taken account of in formulating them.

Is it possible to have a utilitarian theory that satisfies these conditions? It has already been done.

Harsanyi's Utilitarian Contractualism

The great welfare economist John Harsanyi, in the middle 1950s, provided a version of a derivation of utilitarianism from a few simple criteria.[18] He later was able to derive utilitarianism as a formal theorem from a few axioms of welfare economics.[19] Readers interested in Harsanyi's technical proof should read it at the source. For readers not interested in the technical details, I offer the following, rather literary gloss on his results.

For Harsanyi's argument to work, we must accept four principles, or more accurately, four sets of principles. These principles are (1) that moral rules should be the object of rational choice, understood as the intelligent maximization of well-being;

(2) that moral choices are made impartially with respect to all agents and patients of moral action; (3) that Baysian rules of inference are appropriate to moral decision making; (4) that cardinal interpersonal comparisons of welfare are possible.

Principle 1, that moral principles are proper objects of rational choice, is accepted by all proponents of contractualism. It seems just too odd to think that if moral principles depend on the ideal consent of those who are subject to them, that said consent should rest on errors of fact or of inference or on erroneous judgments of value. There might be those who reject contractualism and also reject principle 1. Proponents of some extreme versions of intuitionism or of certain kinds of divine command theories of ethics would deny that moral principles are properly the object of human rational choice. If we just see moral truths or if moral truths are part of revealed religion, one might believe that rational choice has nothing to do with morality. But if my argument in the section "Is Ethics a Science?" is correct, such theories would be in clear violation of Hume's Law, and are thus unacceptable.

It is, of course, possible to deny that the intelligent maximization of personal good is the proper end of rationality. Those who subscribe to the strong incommensurability thesis might deny that maximization is the central feature of rationality at all, whereas an objective-good-consequentialist, like the courage-consequentialist in the previous chapter, may defend maximization but reject the notion of a personal good. But we have already seen that the strong thesis of incommensurability leads to nigh-intolerable paradoxes. Others might reject principle 1 because they are simply irrationalists. Against such a latter group, obviously, arguments are necessarily unavailing.

Principle 2 contains the various requirements of full impartiality. They seem at once to have intuitive support and to fall out of an analysis of the concept of justice. We would rightly hesitate to call just a judge who acted partially to certain kinds of petitioners before his or her court. We would further hesitate to call just a law that created privileges for some and disabilities for others for no readily discernable reason. Furthermore, the requirement of full impartiality may be necessary to get any kind of moral contract together; for if each person is allowed in a hypothetical process of bargaining to favor his or her own interests, the result might well be either deadlock or nothing other than would have resulted in a Hobbesian state of nature anyway since each contractor would be able to bring his or her own threat-advantage to the parlay. Finally, impartiality does seem to have nearly universal assent among persons who think about justice, almost to the extent that when someone rejects impartiality as a requirement for justice, we do not say, "This person believes in a theory of justice without impartiality" but "This person doesn't believe in justice at all."

There are exceptions to this consensus. Postmodernists and communitarians often argue that the notion of impartiality is incoherent or wrongheaded.[20] Their claims usually stem from a rather murky philosophical argument that there are no claims that can meaningfully be made from anywhere but the parochial standpoint of a particular person. There are in this belief no "objective" views, no views from nowhere.[21] These theorists are perhaps correct in this belief, but it is irrelevant if they are. The notion of impartiality I use here does not depend on any metaphysical notion of a view from nowhere, much less on a concept of an "objective" view. The theory here, as well as Rawls's theory of justice as fairness, advances the concept of impartiality as a view that takes seriously the possibility that one can imagine what it would be like to be another person. And it is not hard to imagine how one could take such a view, especially if the concept of interpersonal comparisons of well-being (what is it like to be person X in situation S) has any validity.

It should also be noted that the first two formal constraints that Rawls identifies on a theory of the right, generality and universality, jointly entail some form of impartiality. The requirement of generality prevents the singling out of a particular person or set of persons who are to be specific beneficiaries of a system of rules that govern behavior. The requirement of universality prevents specifying persons who have special exceptions to the rules.

Principle 3 assumes the validity of Baysian rules of inference in moral deliberation. The practical upshot for Harsanyi's contractualism is that when we lack any background information about the probabilities of different outcomes, and these different outcomes are reasonably well defined, we assign equal[22] subjective probabilities to each of them. To defend principle 3 is to enter into a real philosophical thicket. Some decision theorists think that Baysian rules of inference are the only rules that rational decision makers would use under conditions of ignorance; others think that they are little better than a form of superstition.

It is on principle 3, as we shall see, that Rawls and Harsanyi fundamentally disagree. Rather than thrash around at the heights of abstraction, I delay my discussion of it until I have discussed Rawls, so that readers may see for themselves exactly what is at stake. I then offer some examples in an attempt to explain my intuition that this principle is acceptable.

Finally, Harsanyi assumes principle 4, the meaningfulness of cardinal interpersonal comparisons of well-being. Harsanyi assumes that we can with at least some reliability attribute a truth value to the statement that "It is better to be person X in situation A than it is to be person Y in situation B." Indeed, he further assumes that it is meaningful to state, "It is better to have probability p of being person X in situation A than it is to have probability $1 - p$ of being person Y in situation B." Needless to say, such claims do bring about a great deal of skepticism both from ordinary persons and from professional philosophers.

The literature on interpersonal comparisons is large and difficult.[23] I think, however, that a few examples should show that interpersonal comparisons of well-being do not run contrary to moral common sense. To the philosophical skeptics I am not sure how to respond, except to remark, with Rawls, that given our commonsense assumptions and moral beliefs, throwing out the possibility of interpersonal comparisons seems to throw out the possibility of much of what passes for our moral reasoning altogether.[24]

Most human beings have the twin gifts of imagination and sympathy. To be sure, both these gifts are limited in almost anyone—a fact that will take on considerable importance later in this book—but few would doubt that we can and do exercise them. We often decide whether something would be good or bad for someone by asking whether it would be good or bad to be a certain person in a certain situation.

Since many of us also possess the virtue of benevolence to some degree, and admit of a moral duty to take some regard of the needs of strangers, we can think about the following two hypothetical cases:

1. As you are about to go out for a pleasant drive in the country, you discover that your car has been taken without your knowledge or permission. Your afternoon is ruined. Early that evening, your neighbor returns with your car, and explains—in a manner that satisfies you that he is telling the truth—that he had no choice but to take your car in order to get medical assistance for his desperately ill child, without which the child would have suffered greatly. Your neighbor regrets that because of circumstances beyond his control he cannot compensate you for your loss.

2. As you are about to take a pleasant drive in the country, you discover that your car has been taken without your knowledge or permission. Your afternoon is ruined. Early that evening, your neighbor returns with your car and explains to you—in a manner that satisfies you that he is telling the truth— that had he not taken your car, he would have missed a chance to save some small amount of money at a one-day-only sale at the local mall. Your neighbor regrets that because circumstances beyond his control he cannot compensate you for your loss.

How are we to react to cases 1 and 2? It seems that one should be quite forgiving of the neighbor's transgression in case 1 but can rightly be rather irritated in case 2. How are we to understand this difference? In both cases a theft was committed—surely to insist otherwise would be sophistry. In both cases one has suffered a loss for which one cannot be compensated. It seems that the most plausible and natural way to understand the difference between the two cases is that in case 1 something very important was at stake—the welfare of both a child and its parent were seriously endangered by the child's illness. But in case 2, the danger or loss to the neighbor from missing a minor sale seems quite trivial.

Have we not, in making this judgment, made an interpersonal comparison? After all, even if we have no children we can surely conceive that it would be a very bad thing for a child to suffer and for a parent to see a child suffer. And no matter how much we like shopping, even with the fullest extension of sympathy, we are unlikely to understand how for anyone a sale would outweigh in importance our good afternoon. One who would consider case 1 just as much a transgression as case 2 would be completely lacking in either imaginative sympathy or the simple virtue of benevolence.

Of course, in comparing cases 1 and 2 we may only be making a judgement of ordinal utility, such that the utility of a child getting medical help is greater than the utility of my getting a pleasant drive in the country, which is in turn greater than the utility of my neighbor getting to the sale. We can, however, probably come up with cases in which interpersonal cardinal utility is needed to render a judgment. We might, for instance, assign probabilities to the neighbor's veracity. Perhaps he either needed to take his child to the doctor or wanted to go to the sale. If the probability that he needed to take his child to the doctor was, say, around 0.9, we might still be indulgent with him. If it were around 0.5, we might be a bit irritated. If it were only around 0.05, we might become distinctly resentful. If these judgments still depend on interpersonal comparisons of well-being, these comparisons must be cardinal in order to work with numerical probabilities.[25]

We can consider another case, this one involving a choice of your own. Assume that you have two children whose welfare you care about equally. You are quite poor, and after providing basic subsistence for yourself and your children you have very little left over. One of your children is sick and suffering. Fortunately, your family budget is such that there is just enough income to buy the drugs necessary to enable the child to recover. The other child not only is in robust health but has considerable musical gifts. If this child were to be trained in music, the child's life and the lives of others would be filled with great joy, which would otherwise be lost. Unfortunately, you are so poor that buying both medicine for one child and musical training for the other are simply out of the question. It seems highly doubtful that, trading on certainties, readers will trade the recovery of the one child for the musical education of the other.

But what was said about cardinalizing utility in the first pair of cases seems to hold for this case as well. Suppose that the drugs in question would not provide a certain cure for the sick child. We might be willing to buy them if the probability of their working successfully fell to 0.5, to 0.1, perhaps even to 0.01. But what if the chance fell to 1 in a million or lower? There would seem to be some point—for rational parents at least—at which we might think that a tiny chance of curing the first child would not merit sacrificing the certain happiness of the second. Such an estimation, of course, implicitly depends on cardinal, interpersonally comparable utility. So it would seem that either we really can make judgments of cardinal interpersonal utility or there is something deeply wrong with moral common sense.

From principles 1–4, Harsanyi is able to derive utilitarianism. How? Beginning with the assumption that moral rules are to be rules of rational choice (1), Harsanyi next needs to come up with some device to ensure that those who decide on principles of right do so in an impartial manner (2). For this purpose, he introduces (through a mathematical formalism) a device that Rawls was later to appropriate: the veil of ignorance. Choosers are to know that they are to live in a society governed by the rules that they choose, but they are not to know which person in that society they are to be. They thus have no choice but to find some way of being impartial among different kinds of persons with different personal attributes; to do otherwise would be to choose irrationally. Using Baysian rules of decision (3), they assume that they have an equal chance of being any person. If they are rational—assuming as I do that rationality means the intelligent pursuit of well-being—they will choose those principle that will yield the greatest expected average well-being.

Rawls charges that such a decision procedure may be incoherent[26] because it relies on treating the utility functions of multiple individuals as if they could be derived from a simple amalgamation of individual utility functions derived from individual consumption preferences. The incoherence in such a method comes from the fact that, as Rawls points out, the preferences of different individuals are not necessarily part of a single system of ends.

While it is true that in his original presentation of the theory, Harsanyi perhaps rather naively added up a set of von Neumann–Morgenstern utility functions into a single social welfare function of dubious coherence, this flaw is not necessarily fatal to his argument. If we make interpersonal comparisons of utility possible not just through mathematical operations but also through the use of sympathetic imagination of what it would be like for an individual to be person *X* in situation *A*, then this incoherence does not follow; and potential contractors can reason, for any set of individuals *i* and situations *s*, what rule would maximize one's well being. Harsanyi, it should be noted, explicitly did modify his theory after the publication of Rawls's *Theory of Justice* to give imaginative sympathy an important role in rational moral deliberation.[27]

Thus, under the conditions Harsanyi specifies, the principles of right that are decided on will be utilitarian. This conclusion follows mathematically since there is no way to maximize one's own expected utility when one has an equal chance of being anyone without maximizing the aggregate utility of a given population.[28]

Harsanyi's proof and the argument attached to it are very elegant. Not only do they derive utilitarianism from principles that may have more general appeal than the fundamentalist utilitarian version of the theory, but also they force opponents of utilitarianism to nail their colors to the mast. For since it is the case that principles 1–4 jointly entail utilitarianism, anyone who rejects utilitarianism must, through the *modus tollens*, reject at least one of the principles. If one rejects a plausible principle, it follows that one risks coming up with an implausible theory. Rawls, as we shall see, explicitly rejects principle 3.

Another virtue of Harsanyi's contractualism is that it closely parallels and perhaps manages to make explicit another form of moral reasoning, that of R.M. Hare. Hare has made an analysis of moral language in which he claims that moral statements are prescriptions that a speaker can rationally universalize.[29] A prescription in general is a sentence of the form "Let *S* do *A*." Hare claims that prescriptions, while not statements of fact, are subject to rational evaluation. Thus, if I prefer ice cream to cake and I am offered a choice between the two, it is rational for me to prescribe, "Let me choose ice cream" and irrational to prescribe, "Let me choose cake."

Prescriptions are universal when they take the form "In circumstances *C*, let everyone do *A*." Hare's claim is that we can make rational evaluations of universal prescriptions. The putative moral rule "Thou shalt not kill" can be rewritten as a prescription: "In all circumstances, let everyone not kill." Our evaluation of that prescription—if we do so universally—requires us to weigh not just our own preferences but also those of all other persons since in the act of universalizing our prescription, we consider whether on balance it would be rational to accept it, not just if we are the people whom we happen to be but also if we might happen to be anyone.

Hare's form of moral reasoning is thus strongly Kantian. We should act according to maxims that we can rationally will to be universal laws.[30] We should consider "In all circumstances, let everyone not kill" both from the perspective of those who might have a reason to kill and those who have a reason to want not to be killed.[31]

Hare thinks that only by weighing all preferences can we come up with universally rational prescriptions. I do not attempt to defend his analysis, sympathetic though I am to it. I do, however, wish to point out that Harsanyi's contractual reasoning gives us a means of thinking about how one might universalize a prescription. If we imagine that we might be anyone, our perspective on what is rational and not rational to prescribe seems to become clearer.

Hare claims not to rely on moral intuitions but only on linguistic analysis in arriving at his conclusion. I do not venture a speculation on whether this project succeeds. His theory, like Harsanyi's, explicitly depends on our ability to make valid interpersonal comparisons of well-being, and it is possible that such comparisons may ultimately depend only on intuition. Likewise, the theory of rational choice on which we are to rely in evaluating proposed universal prescriptions can be challenged, and it, too, may rest on an intuition. Should either of these possibilities be actual, Hare's brave attempt to provide a moral theory free from the contamination of appeals to intuition does not completely succeed.

Hare's is an intriguing theory nonetheless, and to the extent it does succeed, it would seem to point to utilitarianism of a Harsanyi-like kind.

Rawls's Justice as Fairness

If one had to summarize John Rawls's magisterial *Theory of Justice* in just a few words, one might do so by saying that he sets up his thought experiment much like Harsanyi's, except that he claims that persons behind a veil of ignorance will reason differently than Harsanyi does. Rawls believes that it would be irrational for choosers to use Baysian rules of decision, that is, to choose as if they had an equal chance of being anyone. He proposes that individuals instead should choose by using a *maximin* rule. Rational choosers would look to the position of the worst-off representative person in a proposed scheme of choice and attempt to make that person as well off as possible.

I am aware that this characterization is an oversimplification of Rawls's theory. A reader unfamiliar with Rawls might conclude from the exposition so far that he is a kind of utilitarian sensitive to the distribution, as well as to the average level, of well-being. As readers of Rawls know, he nothing of the sort. He is not directly interested in the distribution and production of utility; rather, his principles of justice are concerned with what he calls "primary goods," those things that, supposedly, any rational person would want in carrying out a plan of life.

I do not reproduce Rawls's reasoning for the use of primary goods rather than utility as an index for ordering different schemes of collective life since that ground is already well trod. It should suffice to say that his disagreement with Harsanyi on the correct principle of choice from behind the veil of ignorance leads to two quite different theories. Rawls proposes two principles of justice: (1) each is to enjoy the maximum possible liberty consistent with an equal liberty for all; and (2) the distribution of the primary goods of wealth and income is to be such that the worst-off representative person is made best off.

Much has already been written on Rawls, so let us be as brief as possible. The question that must be posed is the following: what possible grounds can we have for rejecting Baysian rules of decision and replacing them with a maximin rule for making moral decisions? The formal constraints on a theory of justice are no help since any form of utilitarianism meets them just as much as does Rawls's principle of justice as fairness. Any requirement of impartiality will do no good either since Harsanyi's form of utilitarianism is gloriously impartial. The most Rawls has achieved has been to provide an account of a different theory that is also impartial—or, perhaps, *might* be since one could argue that his theory is partial to those on the bottom of a social order. One can thus criticize maximin as a principle of moral choice on two grounds: (1) that it is dubious in itself and (2) it leads to a theory of dubious impartiality.

When we look at Baysian principles and the maximin principle in themselves it hardly seems clear that maximin is a superior principle. Let us consider a thought experiment. You are to be a survivor, with three others, in a lifeboat. It is to be a very small lifeboat on rough seas. Consequently, its occupants have two choices about the crew. If one person—the one with the worst seamanship skills—is allowed to drown, the other three members of the crew will almost certainly survive.[32] If all four attempt to crew it, there is a large chance, a probability in excess of 0.5, that the boat will founder and be lost with all hands. You, the chooser, do not know how well your seamanship skills stack up against the other three potential crew members of the boat; perhaps you are an old salt; perhaps you have never been out of sight of land in your life. Maximin requires you to choose a four-member crew, whereas Baysianism suggests a three-member crew. Many people, when pressed, admit that the three-member crew is the best option.

It is important to note that maximin would require a chooser to select the four-member crew no matter how small the chance of survival becomes. Even if a four-member boat had only one chance in a hundred of making it safely to shore, maximin would require us to choose the larger crew under conditions of uncertain choice. Needless to say, it would seem that maximin sanctions something quite counterintuitive in this case since it could potentially require three lives to be placed in serious jeopardy. An impartial observer might therefore be inclined to think that maximin —and a theory of justice that stems from it as a principle of choice—stands on doubtful ground.[33]

In section 30 of his *Theory of Justice*, Rawls discusses the possibility that an ideal observer might prefer some version of the principle of utility to his two principles of justice on the grounds that the former better satisfies the requirements of impartial benevolence. His response is that while utilitarianism might well satisfy those requirements, a benevolent observer would not prefer it because—as he charges in an earlier section—it refuses to take seriously the separateness of persons. In our lifeboat example, for instance, the loss to an individual thrown overboard could not be compensated for by the gains made by the survivors. In society at large, the losses made by the persons who might fare badly under utilitarian institutions could not be compensated for by the gains made by persons in general. Rawls thus charges utilitarianism with confusing impersonality with impartiality.[34]

The response to this "separateness of persons" argument is a tu quoque. Rawls's theory and theories like it also ignore the separateness of persons when they find it convenient to do so. To see how they do so, let us consider the following moral analysis of the concept of separateness: if *A* is a separate person, then no other agent is morally permitted to redistribute well-being from *A* to any other agent, so long as nothing *A* does makes any other agent worse off. After all, *A*'s separateness means that gains to other agents are not compensated for in his or her own life. Now suppose we have a society consisting of *A*, *B*, and *C*. *A* and *B* engage in wealth-creating trades with each other. These trades improve their situation relative to *C*, leading to an inequality of wealth. Assuming that redistribution would not create perverse incentives for *A* and *B*, Rawls's difference principle would require redistribution of some of the newly created wealth from *A* to *B* since *C* would now be the worst-off person in society. But these redistributions, if that wealth has positive utility for *A* and *B*, would be a breach in their separate personhoods since they would lower their well-being for the sake of improving that of another, without compensation in their lives.[35]

If Rawls himself rejects separateness of persons, it cannot be an objection against utilitarianism that he does so. Libertarians like Nozick and Gauthier would argue that the rejection of separateness of persons is a fatal flaw in both justice as fairness and utilitarianism. The proper response here is that if one really accepts separateness of persons, one puts in jeopardy the requirement that moral theories be genuinely impartial among all persons. Insistence on the separateness of persons can with some justice be accused of being a form of moral favoritism of the talented and the lucky, of consequentially giving greater weight to the well-being of those who have the greatest talents, wealth, or skills to trade. In the example just given, *A* and *B* have no perfect moral obligations to *C* and would be morally permitted to let *C* remain poor, even if the sacrifices on their part for preventing this outcome were trivial. If this is not an acceptable moral outcome, the real moral debate should be between those forms of moral theory that do accept a form of consequential impartiality.

The probable reason for why Rawls and Rawls-like theories have been so successful is that in providing an alternative to utilitarianism that is or at least seems to be impartial, Rawls had provided an outlet for all those who somehow had intuited that utilitarianism is "wrong" but had hitherto lacked such an alternative. Thus, since utilitarianism is "wrong" and Baysian principles lead to utilitarianism, they too must be "wrong." But, of course, one should not simply allow intuition to pick the winner in advance. Either such a selection is arguing in a circle or it renders the whole apparatus of a contract superfluous. If the latter, why not simply rely on intuitions *tout court*?

Form and Substance

Russell Hardin has suggested[36] that the proper way to deal with the problem of intuitions is to partition those we have into formal and substantive intuitions and give evidentiary weight only to the former. *Formal intuitions* are those intuitions we have about what formal properties an adequate theory of justice must possess. *Substantive intuitions* are intuitive judgments about particular cases, such as those in chapter 1's parade of horribles.

We can explicate this distinction by making an analogy to mathematics. The intuitions mathematicians have about the formal requirements of noncontradiction, the validity of the axiom of choice, and the axioms of set theory are formal intuitions. The intuitions they have about the truth or falsity of, say, Goldbach's conjecture are substantive intuitions. In developing a mathematics, they allow only their formal intuitions to have authority over what is and what is not part of mathematics. If they arrive at a contradiction between their substantive intuitions and what they can derive from formal intuitions, they simply abandon the former. But in the method of reflective equilibrium, this is not the case. If our commitment to Baysian decision theory yields distributive indifference about the good and that distributive indifference leads to the conclusion that we are obliged to do horrible things, we may reason backward and throw out the Baysianism instead.

Hardin suggests that this kind of reasoning is nonsense, that it is the tail wagging the dog. No mathematician would dream of throwing out the law of noncontradiction just to save an intuition one has about the truth of some substantive result. Why should moral theorists do the same? Can we not just dismiss our substantive intuitions as "errors" if they conflict with our formal intuitions?

Although Hardin's views on the matter are not without their attractions, I proceed on the assumption that it is the wrong way of going about things for the following three reasons. First, one should worry about the potential it raises for arbitrariness. Second, there is a tension between a position that would require us to derive our moral considerations exclusively from first principles and the account of moral intuitions given in this chapter. Third, even if we endorse it, we may bring up other formal problems.

The worry about arbitrariness has the following content: all the moral intuitions we have, whether they are about formal properties of adequate theories of justice or about the correct resolution of substantive cases, may rest on nothing more than the solidity of our convictions. As I have argued, it is far from clear that there are any moral facts of any matter, and there seem to be no objective natural or metaphysical facts that can stand in for moral facts. But if that is so, what coherent reason might we be able to give for accepting one set of intuitions over another?

Mathematicians can answer this question. A mathematics in which formal intuitions govern is much more likely to be aesthetically pleasing and pragmatically useful as a formal tool for sciences and engineering. But it is not clear that a moral theorist can give the same answer. There is something rather odd about choosing moral principles on grounds of aesthetic neatness. And it is unclear what it could mean for a moral theory to be "successful" since there is no obvious way to specify what counts as success independently from some theory of good or right outcomes—which is precisely what a moral theory is supposed to provide.

The second worry has to do with the relation between this account of moral theorizing and the inferential account of moral intuitions given here. We have a lot of tacit knowledge of the world, and the fact that many of us do manage to get through life suggests that much of it is at least approximately correct. If we assume that our moral intuitions reflect the not fully conscious conjuncture of moral principles with tacit knowledge, any disjunction between what those principles would consciously require and what we intuitively think is necessary is at least a minor anomaly. To be sure, such disjunctions can and doubtless do happen because our tacit knowledge can be mistaken, partial, and biased, and it may be especially fallible in "bizarre" cases distant from ordinary experience. But it is not enough simply to dismiss anomalies with an automatic assumption of mistake, partiality, or bias. Since there is no hard-and-fast rule that distinguishes the bizarre from the ordinary, there must at least be some kind of account of the disjunctions.

The final worry is a worry about pragmatic consistency. If Rawls's requirement of "finality" is a formal property of an adequate theory of justice, and if utilitarianism often and seriously offends against our deeply held moral convictions, there is an internal tension in our practical reasoning, for it is doubtful just how final a moral theory can be that prescribes to individuals acts that they find alienating and oppressive. The strains of commitment to a theory that requires us to build Roman arenas and run the risk of being used as organ donors against our will may simply be too great to allow that theory to actually be instantiated in a social order. Considerations of prudence and self-interest could swamp morality. This tension may force us to junk one or another of the formal principles from which we derive a moral theory, and the Baysian decision rules—and with them utilitarianism—may be what goes. Our arguments for utilitarianism may fail because they fail to rebut the presumption, which its critics hold in all sincerity, that there are acts that ought not to be performed even when they maximize utility.

Given these worries, I believe that the best theoretical choice is to try to reconstruct that background knowledge that could lead us to have those "counterutilitarian," substantive moral intuitions, even if the deep underlying principles of our morality are in fact utilitarian. The aim is not to reconcile all of our intuitive difficulties with utilitarianism, for some gaps will remain between our intuitions and the most carefully calculated utilitarian results. The aim is rather to show that given the world as it is, it is consistent with utilitarianism to have something like commonsense morality.

THREE

Nonexploitation as a Rule of Thumb

Exploitation in a Simple Game

A number of general empirical conditions obtain in virtually any world with which we are familiar. Our background knowledge will be shaped by these general conditions, and the moral intuitions we are likely to have will be thereby constrained. In this chapter I use an evolutionary model to show that even if our moral convictions are at their base utilitarian, many of our concrete moral judgments are just as "selfish" and "partial" as our ordinary moral intuitions and commonsense moral beliefs appear to be, insofar as they permit us to take greater heed of our own well-being than that of others. Thus the alleged gap between moral common sense and utilitarianism can begin to be narrowed. The aim here is to give not a comprehensive theory of the evolution of norms but rather a rational reconstruction of why it is that certain norms, which might appear to be ways of instantiating utilitarianism in the world, are in fact likely to be self-defeating.

Ordinary self-interest requires one to act in such a way as to maximize those benefits that accrue to one personally. The principle of utility requires one to maximize benefits generally and impartially. A central principle of game theory is that if one is in an interaction in which one has a dominant strategy—that is, a strategy that will improve the achievement of one's objectives no matter what other players do— then one ought to use it.

The game known as the Prisoner's Dilemma[1] is so famous that it hardly needs an introduction here.[2] In a simple version, there are two players. Each independently chooses one of two strategies, commonly known as either "cooperation" or "defection." The payoffs received by each of the two players depend on the combination of the strategies they used. Two facts define the game as a Prisoner's Dilemma: (1) if both players cooperate, both receive higher payoffs than if both defect; (2) defection is a dominant strategy for both players. A sample Prisoner's Dilemma and its payoffs are illustrated in table 3–1.

Table 3–1.   Simple Prisoner's Dilemma

Alpha

	Cooperate	Defect
Cooperate (Beta)	3 3	5 0
Defect (Beta)	0 5	1 1

When the game is played between self-interested players, it leads to a perverse result: both players will defect. Although each player would prefer mutual coopera-tion to mutual defection, each knows that defection is a dominant strategy, and each will choose it over cooperation. For the players to do so is only rational; it is required by the dominance principle. If one manages to defect while one's opponent cooper-ates, one gets a special prize which is often called the *temptation* (*T*) payoff. Cooper-ating while the other player defects leads to the *sucker's* (*S*) payoff. Between tempta-tion and the threat of being played for a sucker, the incentive that a self-interested player has to defect is quite strong. The existence of such games indicates that pure self-interested rationality is self-defeating in some instances. The outcome in which both players defect ·· ιn technical terms, *Pareto inferior* to that in which both cooperate.[3]

The Prisoner's Dilemma has fascinated theorists of games and social interaction for many reasons. Two primary ones are its ubiquity and its perversity. Prisoner's Dilemmas in either two-player or many-player forms show up all the time in social life. Paying taxes for the provision of public goods is a common example of a many-player Prisoner's Dilemma. Everyone would prefer a world in which each pays one's fair share to support public services to a world in which no one pays and consequently no public goods are provided. But, of course, it would be in one's own personal inter-est to allow everyone else to contribute while one rides free on everyone else's contri-bution. And it would be worst of all if one contributes alone while everyone else at-tempts to ride free. Hence, we are threatened with a world in which no one contributes.

Prisoner's Dilemmas underlie problems of personal security. If every man com-mits an aggression against his neighbors, we will all be badly off; we would live in the nightmare world of Hobbes's state of nature, in which life is solitary, poor, nasty, brutish, and short.[4] The problem is that it would often be in any given person's rational self-interest to commit crimes while everyone else remains law-abiding. Worse yet, to remain law-abiding while everyone else commits aggressions would seem to put one on a short list for imminent extinction—a real sucker's payoff.

Even within the more benign areas of social existence, such as the creation of wealth through mutually beneficial exchange, Prisoner's Dilemmas lurk. Russell Hardin[5] shows that we can think of every exchange as involving a kind of Prisoner's Dilemma. To see how, I introduce a little shorthand. Define the expression V(Person,Object) to mean "The value to a given *person* of the control or use of a given *object*, measured in cardinal utility that is comparable to the cardinal utility of another person."

Now let us suppose that I am in possession of a bicycle and you are in possession of $100. I do not often ride the bicycle, although I do get occasional enjoyment out of it. I might well get greater enjoyment out of something else, such as collecting comic books—a pastime I could pursue more easily if I had more money. You, however, would get great enjoyment out of the bicycle. For the sake of this example, we might assume V(Me,Bicycle) = 1, V(You,Bicycle) = 3, V(Me,$100) = 3, and V(You,$100) = 1. We must also assume for the sake of completeness that V(Me,No Bicycle and No Money) = 0 and that, likewise, V(You,No Bicycle and No Money) = 0. Should all these facts obtain, you and I are in the game described in table 3–2.

Analysis of the game matrix shows the game to be a classic Prisoner's Dilemma. Keeping what we own is a dominant strategy for both of us. No matter what you do, I will always be better off if I keep the bicycle; the converse also holds. But the equilibrium outcome of the game is Pareto-inferior to our mutual cession of what we own.

Prisoner's Dilemmas are also fascinating because of their perversity. Starting with an assumption that agents rationally maximize their well-being, we generate at once

Table 3–2. Exchange as a Prisoner's Dilemma

	I	
	Cede bicycle	Keep bicycle
You Cede money	3 · · · · · 3	· · · · · 4 · · · · · 0
You Keep money	0 · · · · · 4	· · · · · 1 · · · · · 1

a normative and an explanatory problem. The normative problem stems from the fact that in the case of a Prisoner's Dilemma, rationality and self-interest seem self-defeating because they lead to a worse outcome than that which both agents would prefer.[6] The explanatory problem stems from the fact that we do not live in a Hobbesian state of nature in spite of the ubiquity of implicit Prisoner's Dilemmas in social life. Why does life not collapse into a mess in which no one pays taxes, all commit aggressions against all, and even simple exchanges are not realized? The Prisoner's Dilemma is thus a most useful analytic device for political philosophers because it poses problems of cooperation and conflict in a particularly stark way. So if a moral analysis cannot give us purchase on this problem, it is probably not worth the paper it is written on. Much of the analysis that follows is thus of this simple game. It is, though, worth stressing that one should not think that life is all or even mostly Prisoner's Dilemmas, even if these interactions are ubiquitous.

One of the central problems in explaining the emergence of cooperation lies in assuming that the players are egoists, that they are calculatingly interested only in their own well-being. Such an assumption is common and unremarkable in conventional rational choice explanations of human behavior, but we should not be thus led into believing that it is always helpful or realistic. While a healthy skepticism about the degree to which individuals behave as anything other than selfish maximizers is not unadmirable, both ordinary introspective experience and psychological evidence indicate that not all of our conduct can be quite so simply construed. The very fact that we both have and act on moral intuitions—that we refrain from violating what we believe to be the rules of morality even in cases in which rational reflection would indicate that doing so would be to our advantage—would seem to indicate that a more complicated story needs to be told about human motivation than that which a simplistic kind of rational choice theory is willing to allow. Ordinary persons might be rational without being narrowly self-interested. They may subscribe to norms, which make an escape from a Prisoner's Dilemma considerably less difficult.

In the section that follows, I discuss how norms can transform the problem of cooperation. The discussion is simplified by making what is an unrealistic assumption about norms. I write as if normatively driven behavior is qualitatively different from self-interested behavior, as if one is either self-interested or morally motivated. In chapter 4 we relax that assumption by showing how following norms under realistic conditions actually serves self-interest.

Norms: Minimalist and Utilitarian

The principle of utility, which tells us to maximize benefits to all persons, is a kind of norm. A different kind of norm, which I call *minimalist*,[7] might be as follows: "In those cases in which pursuit of the dominance principle will lead to a Pareto-inferior outcome, abandon that principle in such a way that it will lead to a Pareto superior outcome, if it can be rationally anticipated that your opponent will do so, conditional on your own cooperation." Thus a minimalist links his or her choices to those of other minimalists; one's choice is concerned not just with one's own goals but also with those of others. At the same time, the minimalist takes no direct interest in the well-being of others, as a utilitarian would.

For utilitarians, the Prisoner's Dilemma is actually a fairly trivial game to solve. If we assume that the numbers in the first version of the game, in table 3-1, represent cardinal, interpersonally comparable utilities, we get the game played by two utilitarians in table 3–3.

It is a rather trivial coordination interaction. Since cooperation is a dominant strategy for both players—and since nothing in utilitarianism precludes the use of dominant strategies—the game has a strong Nash equilibrium of cooperate-cooperate.[8]

For followers of minimalism, if both pay attention to the minimalist norm, they will agree on reciprocal cooperation in order to achieve the Pareto-superior outcome. Now what would happen if a utilitarian were to meet a minimalist? We might find a payoff matrix something like that in table 3–4.

For the utilitarian, cooperation remains a dominant strategy. The minimalist faces the same incentive to defect. Furthermore, it is not the case that the latter's use of the dominance principle in this case would result in a Pareto-inferior outcome, so the minimalist principle does not preclude his or her defection in this instance. Consequently, the equilibrium outcome of this game will be for the utilitarian to cooperate and the minimalist to defect.

The outcome of this game should make utilitarians rather wary. After all, the personal welfare of the utilitarian turns out to be 0; that of the minimalist, 5. The outcome seems unfair; it seems to impose an excessive cost on the utilitarian, and thus seems to be a toy instance of the perverse overdemandingness of utilitarianism. Why should I be a utilitarian if I am to allow this sort of thing to happen to me? It seems wildly counterintuitive and, therefore, telling against utilitarianism.

Let us use the following definition of the phenomenon of *utilitarian exploitation*. A utilitarian (*U*) is exploited in any game in which there are at least two definable

Table 3–3.   Two Utilitarians in a Prisoner's Dilemma

	Alpha	
	Cooperate	Defect
Cooperate	6 6	5 5
Defect	5 5	2 2

(Beta labels the rows: Cooperate, Defect)

Table 3–4.   A Utilitarian and a
Minimalist in a Prisoner's Dilemma

	Utilitarian	
	Cooperate	Defect
Cooperate	6	5
	3	0
Egoist	5	2
Defect		
	5	1

outcomes A and B and (1) the aggregate well-being in A is less than that in B; and (2) U is worse off in A than in B; and (3) given the norms of the players, A comes about rather than B. Such exploitation exists in the game presented in table 3–4. Although mutual cooperation is better in aggregate terms and would be better for the individual utilitarian player, the outcome is not mutual cooperation but unilateral defection.

Considerations of fairness aside, utilitarians must be concerned with the problem of exploitation. If utilitarians allow exploitation to occur, utilitarianism is failing even its own terms. In a world of minimalists, all would cooperate with one another and realize greater aggregate welfare than a world in which utilitarians and minimalists exist and the latter exploit the former. Thus, if there are not utilitarian reasons for avoiding exploitation, utilitarianism would seem to face an internal pragmatic inconsistency.

One quick response to this inconsistency is simply to argue that utilitarians should simply avoid getting into interactions that are self-defeating. This bit of tautological advice can be useful in those circumstances in which there is no conflict between resisting exploitation and designing institutions, and often in the account of institutions that follows I rely on it directly. But in some instances utilitarians may face a situation in which in the short-to-medium run they can either bring about the larger aggregate of utility at a considerable cost to themselves or bring about a smaller aggregate while doing somewhat better for themselves. A one-shot Prisoner's Dilemma played against an egoist is a toy illustration of such an interaction, but there can be more complicated ones. As we see in following chapters, the choice of which institutions to foster may often lead to the dilemma of having to choose between suffering exploitation for the sake of short-run maximizing and resisting exploitation. A naive view would hold that one should opt for short-run maximizing. This chapter is an argument that long-term maximizing requires resisting exploitation.

Many students of strategy think that problems of cooperation can be solved by making commitments.[9] There are many cases in which individuals may want to make an arrangement to take (or refrain from taking) some action, but they cannot convince others that they would be willing to take that action because when the moment for action comes, it would be irrational for them to actually take it. The classic example given by Thomas Schelling is the following:[10] a criminal has kidnapped someone, only to find that for some reason the criminal has no hope of collecting a ransom for the victim. The kidnapper has a choice of either killing the victim or letting him go. Not being an entirely wicked sort, he would ceteris paribus let the victim go. Unfortunately as is so often the case, the ceteris is not paribus, for if he lets his victim go, the victim would be able to identify the kidnapper to the authorities, which would likely lead to the latter's arrest and punishment.

To make this story work, we should assume that the victim resents the kidnapping and would therefore get at least some satisfaction out of revealing the kidnapper's identity. We should assume further that the victim, once released, would face no credible threat of retaliation from his former captor. Thus at the moment when he would have the opportunity to reveal his identity, he would have no reason to refrain from doing so. The kidnapper thus reluctantly concludes that he must kill his victim.

This facts given by this story constitute a dilemma for both the kidnapper and his victim. How is it to be escaped? Schelling proposes that if the victim has some secret that might do the victim considerable damage should it come to light, the victim could disclose that secret to his kidnapper as part of a promise not to reveal the kidnapper's identity once he is freed. In giving the kidnapper a credible means of retaliation should the victim go back on his promise, the victim gives himself a reason not to go back on his promise. His disclosure of the distasteful secret is thus a device by which he commits himself to silence.

Strategic theorists have proposed a variety of commitment devices so that persons who make promises give themselves an incentive to keep them. To make a promise credible to a second person, one might give a security bond to a disinterested (and presumably honest) third party, on the condition that the bond will be forfeit should the promisor default. Or one might bring in a third party as a direct enforcer, with the capacity to do violence to oneself should one not be as good as one's word.

We have seen that utilitarians have a problem in that it is not rational for them to threaten defection in a game against a minimalist. Suppose the utilitarians had some sort of a commitment device available through which they could make a credible promise not to allow themselves to be exploited. Perhaps they could strap on themselves a kind of game-theoretic bomb that would detonate if they should be the recipient of a sucker's payoff. Could they then escape the difficulties of exploitation?[11]

Such a commitment would be very clever, but it would not solve the problem unless we were to make some rather dubious assumptions. It is implausible to assume that a utilitarian could consistently find such a device. The world is not necessarily full of honest persons who can hold security bonds, and the game-theoretic bomb is (at present, anyway) merely a fantasy. But even if we could find devices, there would be other problems. The expedient of commitments would seem to work only if either (1) only utilitarians could make credible commitments or (2) the world were so structured that utilitarians were always able to make the first commitment, as well as signal the making of that commitment to others before the latter had a chance to make their own commitments.

If we do not assume the truth of (1), then minimalists and even egoists could conceivably make commitments of their own. Suppose that a minimalist comes up with his or her own variety of game-theoretic bomb, one that goes off when, in plays of the Prisoner's Dilemma against utilitarians, the minimalist fails to receive the temptation payoff. If a utilitarian were to meet a minimalist or an egoist who had made such a commitment, what could the utilitarian do? Now, not only would utilitarianism plus the dominance principle compel the utilitarian to take the sucker's payoff, but also, if he or she fails to do so, something even more terrible would occur—the minimalist's bomb would explode—than would have otherwise occurred. Of course, if the utilitarian also had a commitment device, both players would be stuck in an even worse dilemma: there would be no outcome that would prevent either one or the other's or both bombs from exploding.

If the utilitarian could put together his or her commitment first and announce it to other persons in such a way that it could not be suspected that the utilitarian was lying, it would be, of course, quite irrational for the minimalist or the egoist to make a commitment also. But it is just as implausible to imagine that the utilitarian should always be allowed to get to do the clever thing first as to imagine that only utilitarians should be allowed to do the clever thing at all.

A colleague of mine[12] has wondered why anyone, utilitarians or otherwise, would bother to interact with persons who make such monstrous commitments. Could utilitarians not simply avoid minimalists altogether if the latter behave so badly? It seems unlikely; many interactions between persons are not the result of free choice but the outcomes of circumstance: the minimalist may happen to live across a thin wall from the utilitarian or may draw on some common resource, like fish in a stream or clean air, that the utilitarian draws also on. Or the minimalist may have a monopoly on some good or service that the utilitarian might like to trade for. In many cases, not interacting will be quite undesirable, and a utilitarian will have to face a choice between cooperation or exploitation. Utilitarians, then, would seem to need a different reason for not allowing themselves to be exploited.

The Natural Selection of Norms

Every causal force in nature productive of well- and ill-being, no matter how distant, is of concern to utilitarians. They have no more reason for discounting the utility that is to be realized in times other than their own than they do for discounting the utility realized within lives other than their own. For them to do such discounting would surely violate that impartiality that utilitarians count as a selling point of their doctrine.

Unfortunately for many purposes, the far future is inaccessible. Given our ignorance of many of nature's causal forces and the constraints on our capacity for calculation, it would seem that in general there are few means for reasoning about it. But there is at least one means by which we can reason about the far future, or perhaps in some cases the not-so-far future. If we take seriously the concept of natural selection and subscribe to a few reasonably plausible empirical premises, we can make judgments about the probable success of different kinds of norms. As we shall see, utilitarians have a perfectly just concern for the survival of utilitarianism, and natural selection provides a means for reasoning about that survival. What utilitarians need, in short, is a way of making utilitarianism an *evolutionarily stable strategy*.[13]

It is commonly thought that natural selection applies only to the origin of biological species, but this belief is mistaken. The role of evolution in shaping moral norms has been of interest not just to sociobiologists[14] but also to economists,[15] mathematical game theorists,[16] moral theorists,[17] political scientists,[18] anthropologists,[19] sociologists,[20] psychologists,[21] and even philosophers of mind.[22] Consequently, we should feel quite comfortable in using the concept of evolution through natural selection for my own purposes.

Development through selection can take place in any of the following circumstances:[23]

1. There are a set of information-carrying *replicators* and a set of *vehicles* (which includes but need not be limited to biological phenomena) that carry those replicators. In biological evolution, as everyone knows, the information-carrying replicators are genes. The mechanisms of gene replication are the processes of mitosis and meiosis within cells. The vehicles for genes—to use the terminology invented by Richard Dawkins—are organisms. But these replicators do not have to be limited to physical genes. One can treat certain aspects of human psychology—moral norms among them—as replicators as well.[24] People are vehicles for moral norms and other psychological traits, which can be replicated through the various media of cultural transmission.[25] One can both teach moral and nonmoral norms directly or attempt to transmit them through writing or other forms of dissemination. Likewise, individuals can either be taught by others or can teach themselves.

2. There must exist among the replicators *variation*, which makes itself manifest in the structure or behavior of the vehicles. The genes we carry certainly do much to determine our physical forms and capacities, and they may also determine the kinds of behavior in which we engage (although just how they do so and to what extent is quite controversial). Likewise, variation in our psychological traits rather obviously will determine much of how we act in the world.

3. There must be an *environment* on which different vehicles act and in which the differences in structure and behavior translate into differing rates of replication for the replicators. Thus, in biological evolution, we can predict that if there are two possible traits for the same species encoded by their genes, and these traits differently affect the ability of these creatures to survive and leave descendants, the gene that allows the most descendants to be left is the one likely to be selected for. For a species that is actively preyed upon by another and in which the predator species relies largely on its sight to find its prey, we should predict that if there are two different genes—one that gives the preyed-on species a highly visible pelt and another that gives it a well-camouflaged pelt—that over time the gene that leads to a camouflaged pelt will be replicated more often.

Is it possible that moral norms are selected for just as are genes? Many—especially those committed to a belief in metaphysical voluntarism—might find the suggestion offensive. Although it may seem excessive speculation to do so, I can advance at least three mechanisms for the selection of moral norms.

First, there are the effects of *direct interaction between holders of different norms*. Imagine a world in which there are holders of two different kinds of norms. Some persons are egoists or, more accurately, semiegoists; they care only what happens to themselves or to certain other persons in whom they have a personal emotional investment, such as their friends or their children. Other persons are altruists and care impartially about what happens to everyone. Now suppose that this world is a fairly hazardous one and that there are often cases in which a person might have the opportunity to save the lives of a number of other persons while sacrificing his or her own. Egoists, not wishing to sacrifice their own lives, will pass up such opportunities as they arise. But altruists, since they care about others a great deal, will gladly sacrifice their own lives.

Suppose further that the longer one lives, the greater a chance one will have of replicating and transmitting moral norms. There are many submechanisms through which this would occur: one's children are more likely to have one's own moral norms than someone else's, either because one's children inherit whatever genes encourage altruism or simply because one's children are under one's moral tutelage for a given time. What is likely to happen in this world? Egoists, who would never sacrifice their lives for others, actually stand a better chance of surviving a long time than do altruists. For although they might have the advantage of occasionally being rescued by an altruist, they would never have to shoulder the disadvantage of rescuing anyone. They would therefore live longer and be more likely to replicate and transmit their moral norms. Thus, the moral norm of egoists would seem to be selected for in this world. Altruism could be driven to extinction.

Second, there are consequences of the *division of resources and differential replication*. If the evolutionary tale just told seems to be too much of an implausible just-so story, one should consider another set of plausible propositions. Suppose that there is a finite amount of resources in the world and that, again, there is a population consisting of egoists and altruists. When egoists want resources, they attempt to grab as much as they can get; in bargaining situations, they bring to bear all the leverage they can to get as much as possible. Altruists, in contrast, cede as many resources as they can—or at least as many resources as will advance the common good.

Now let us add an additional hypothesis: the ability of one to replicate one's norms is positively related to the amount of resources one gets. The more resources one has, the more children one can rear successfully. One is also more likely to be capable of warding off all those hazards of life—disease, starvation, predation by others, and so forth—that would imperil one's own survival and the success of one's own moral norms. In this world the consequences would be very much the same as in the last world. Egoists would meet with reproductive and personal success; altruists, not having seized adequate resources for themselves, would be exposed to much of the nastiness of life and would again be threatened with extinction.

Third and finally, there are *processes involving the division of utility and psychological determinism*. Psychological determinism holds that there may well be a self-interested core in individuals (probably built in by biological evolution) that compels them to examine—at least subconsciously—their own success in the world and the role that their moral norms play in it. If people are made miserable by the moral norms they hold and realize that the holders of other norms are faring better, they will change their own norms toward those that are more "successful."[26]

Thus, in our world of egoists and altruists, the altruists may begin to realize that because of their few resources; their constant self-sacrifices; and their vulnerability to being ripped off, oppressed, and otherwise exploited by the egoists, they have come to have rotten lives; in utilitarian terms, their levels of personal good are low, and those of the egoists are high. Consciously or unconsciously, they redirect their moral attention selfward. Either they may directly emulate the egoists or they may do so indirectly; perhaps a new philosopher will emerge with a new doctrine that propounds something like egoism to burnt-out altruists and thus mediates the process of transmission and replication of egoistic moral norms. Thus again altruism may become extinct, although perhaps this time with the marginally happier result that the former altruists themselves might still be alive.

It can be objected that the thesis of selection of norms based on psychological determinism defies common sense. After all, we all know people generous with their time and money who would seemingly be better off if they were somewhat more self-centered, and yet they do not burn out and turn into selfish egoists. Against this charge at least three observations can be made in rebuttal.

First, the generous people of our acquaintance live not in a state of nature but in a civilized condition, where social norms and explicit institutions exist to hold in check most of the worst forms of exploitation. No one can kill them, torture them for fun, take away all their property, or enslave them without the risk of running afoul of powerful countervailing institutions. So the worst the generous are exposed to are minor forms of exploitation, against which the selection pressure is bound to be considerably less.

Second, in most social environments norms of tacit reciprocity reward generosity. Being generous earns one a reputation for virtue, which can pay rewards in the long run.

Third, the process of evolution by psychological determinism may be slow (indeed is bound to be slow if circumstances such as norms of civilization and reciprocity lower selection pressures) and stochastic; so just by the operations of the laws of chance, there are bound to be some who, even if exploited over the long term, continue to be generous and do not burn out. The existence of some such persons of our acquaintance should not be surprising. In itself, however, it cannot be enough to falsify the thesis.

Furthermore, some reflection should show that something like this psychological determinist thesis receives support, as well as opposition, from common sense. Just as we all know people who are generous even at apparent continuing cost to themselves, we also know plenty of people who in their lives started as generous and idealistic but after disillusioning experiences became more self-centered. It is sometimes suggested that this pattern is only the unfolding of a typical program of human maturation and development (perhaps, but what about those who *remain* generous— are they immature and underdeveloped?), but this pattern is at least consistent with the thesis of selection of norms in accordance with psychological determinism: try a generous norm, be exploited, and replace it.

The Utilitarian Nonexploitation Rule

If utilitarians are like the altruists in the three illustrative examples just given, things would look very bad for utilitarianism. But utilitarians should not be naive altruists; they should not allow their exploitation generally, and they can disallow it for a reason internal to utilitarianism. If, in general, utilitarians allow themselves to be exploited, then the principle of utility will be selected against as a moral norm. Consequently, there will at least be fewer utilitarians; it is also possible that utilitarianism would die out entirely.

One may make a rejoinder: "So what?" The principle of utility requires utilitarians to maximize aggregate utility in the world, not to maximize the number of utilitarians in the world. Therefore utilitarians might have no business preserving themselves. They could allow their norm to die out and the world would be none the worse in utilitarian terms. Individuals might all adopt norms something like minimalism, cooperation would thus be ensured, and things would be just fine. Utilitarianism might therefore be *self-effacing*.[27]

If the argument I have just sketched were correct, utilitarianism would be doubly condemned: not just somehow self-defeating but also simply unnecessary. This argument, however, rests on what I argue is a false premise: that the world would be just as well off in utilitarian terms if some norms other than utilitarianism came to predominate. We could thus defend a nonexploitation principle through a kind of pragmatic *modus tollens*. If, in general, utilitarians allow themselves to be exploited, they will die out. If they die out, the world will be worse off in utility terms. We see in the following section that there is an important class of games that will come out "wrong" if utilitarian norms or their analogues have no practicing followers. Since the principle of utility requires that utilitarians not allow the world to be worse off in utility terms, they must not allow themselves to die out, and hence they must not allow themselves in general to be exploited.

Gift Optimality

When the Prisoner's Dilemma is explained in most texts on game theory, it is either described in purely ordinal utilities or set out with numbers, but in a manner that makes it appear to be perfectly symmetrical. That game theory texts should make their exposition in such a manner is not surprising since they usually start from the premise that players are uninterested in making each other's lives go better or worse. But, of course, in the real world, we may prefer to think of morally thicker games. If we admit of cardinal, interpersonally comparable utilities, we can imagine two different kinds of Prisoner's Dilemma, which I call gift-optimal and exchange-optimal.

The term *exchange-optimal* is inspired by Russell Hardin's analysis of beneficial, wealth-creating exchanges, like Prisoner's Dilemmas, such as the exchange of a bicycle for money. Of course, in many ordinary, real-world exchanges the difficulties can be gotten over, largely because individuals have norms of honesty, want to interact with trading partners in the future, and can often count on the presence of a third-party enforcer. Difficulties sometimes arise with complicated contracts that require each party to do something in the future. The implicit Prisoner's Dilemma in the bicycle-money exchange (table 3–2) is exchange-optimal. If the utilities in the matrix are interpersonally comparable, utilitarians should favor the outcome in which both players "cooperate," that is, make the cessions necessary for joint exchange.

Since most of the game-theoretic literature is concerned with trying to get Prisoner's Dilemmas to end in mutual cooperation instead of mutual defection, it is seldom noted that the game contains *three*, not *one*, Pareto-dominant outcomes. Let us imagine a different situation. I am a wealthy landowner and number among my vast holdings a small pasture, which, should it be available for grazing your cow, would improve your and your family's health and happiness. The pasture in question is of little concern to me. You are an impoverished peasant who possesses little but who by some accident of fortune happens to own an unusual item—say, an old icon—that I, as a collector of peasant antiquities, would fancy having in my own collection. The icon is something that you take pride in owning but with which you would be willing to part for the sake of ameliorating your family's poverty. Suppose that the values in question stack up something like this: $V(\text{Me,Pasture}) = 1$, $V(\text{Me,Icon}) = 2$, $V(\text{You,Pasture}) = 10$, $V(\text{You, Icon}) = 6$. Again we should assume for simplicity's sake that the values of all nonownership are to be standardized at zero. We then play the game described in table 3–5.

Though it may not be quite so immediately obvious from inspecting the numbers, this game, too, is a Prisoner's Dilemma, and keeping is a dominant strategy for both players. But for utilitarians, this case has a striking difference from the bicycle case. Clearly, a utilitarian would favor a world in which I, the landowner, unilaterally cede my pasture while allowing you to keep your icon: you and I live in circumstances that morally require redistribution. This Prisoner's Dilemma, then, can be called a *gift-optimal* interaction.[28] In this general class of interaction there is a person or persons,

Table 3–5.   A "gift-optimal" Prisoner's Dilemma

	I	
	Cede Pasture	Keep Pasture
You — Cede icon	2 10	3 0
You — Keep icon	0 16	1 6

in this instance you, who can be identified as *optimal defectors*. A utilitarian will, ceteris paribus, approve of your defecting.

The distinction between exchange- and gift-optimal interactions makes possible an argument for having utilitarians in the world. Clearly, in a world in which there are at least some utilitarians, they will from time to time meet in gift-optimal interactions. In these cases, the utilitarians would resolve the game by allowing one player to unilaterally defect. Minimalists, however, will not allow unilateral defections since their principle predicates cooperation upon reciprocity. A minimalist landowner would ask, even when facing a potential exchange with an impoverished tenant, "What's in it for me?"

Thus, in a world in which there are gift-optimal interactions and in which utilitarians can meet and identify one another, there is work to be done through the principle of utility that cannot be done through a simple principle of reciprocity. If utilitarians die, there will be gift-optimal Prisoner's Dilemmas that will be resolved in ways that are inferior in utilitarian terms. Many instances of redistribution, which morally ought to be realized, would not be realized. In such an eventuality, utilitarianism is self-defeating. In such a world, then, utilitarians will have a good reason not to allow themselves to die out. And thus to the extent that allowing themselves to be exploited by nonutilitarians leads to the dying out of utilitarian moral norms, utilitarians have a reason to resist being exploited.

I should note that the utilitarian interpretation of how utilitarians ought to react to one another in a world containing gift-optimal games is a kind of small-scale application of the reasoning that goes into making up a utilitarian moral contract. The requirement of impartiality compels us to imagine that one might be either one of the players in the interaction in the two-player case. Bayesian decision rules, the possibility of interpersonal comparisons, and rational maximization point us toward the gift-optimal cell in the payoff matrix as the outcome to be achieved.

If in life we find ourselves changing places often enough from giver to receiver in different gift-optimal games, utilitarianism or some extensional equivalent might not just be compelled by impartial rationality and the other conditions of a utilitarian contract but might also be a requirement of simple practical rationality. One could thus believe in something like David Gauthier's contractualism and still be a utilitarian of sorts—an intriguing possibility but not one I pursue any further here.

The more important point to be made is that in many interactions, utilitarians will have a reason to establish themselves as being just as tough as minimalists and egoists. They will seek to achieve a reputation as individuals who will punish defections and seek to get their fair share of any utility-producing interaction. A utilitarian emphasis on fairness would have an influence on a number of other important games.

Other Games

The gift-optimal Prisoner's Dilemma is one kind of game in which gift optimality obtains, but it is by no means the only one. There are many others, which present their own distinct problems. Here are a few, given for sake of illustration.

Suppose that two players, a utilitarian and an egoist, must bargain over the division of a prize. There are two possible divisions, A and B. The values of the prize for the two participants, measured in interpersonally comparable, cardinal utility are as follows: in *A*, Egoist gets 30 and Utilitarian gets 5; in *B*, Egoist and Utilitarian both get 20. Should players fail to reach an agreement, each will get nothing. In an ordinary game, played out between two rational, selfish persons, the game could be solved by using the solution concept known as Nash bargaining equilibrium. (There are a number of other possible solutions for bargaining games, but anything that follows in this analysis can be applied mutatis mutandis to them as well.) According to the solution concept, this equilibrium is assumed to exist at the point at which the product of the two utility functions of the bargainers is maximized. In this game, were it played between two rational and selfish persons, it would be clear that 20*20 is greater than 30*5, and that therefore *B* is the Nash equilibrium.

In a game played between an egoist and a utilitarian, however, there is a wrinkle. The egoist is attempting to maximize only his or her own utility function, while the utilitarian is attempting to maximize the sum of two utility functions. Should the utilitarian attempt to do this directly, however, he or she will find that 30*(30 + 5) is greater than 20*(20 + 20) and that the Nash equilibrium would be *A*. This outcome is most unfortunate for the utilitarian without a nonexploitation principle since not only is it "unjust" but it is also worse in overall utility terms than the Nash equilibrium that would be reached between two amoral egoists.

It is clear that in outcome *A* the utilitarian is exploited. If, therefore, the utilitarian has a nonexploitation principle, he or she can credibly resist the worse equilibrium and bring about a better overall outcome at the same time.

Another game worth pondering is the following: three persons have identical utility (U) functions with respect to income (Y): $U_i = \sqrt{Y_i}$. The initial incomes for Utilitarian and Egoist are $10,000; Needy's is $0. Good utilitarians would give at least some of their income to Needy. If Egoist is kept out of the picture, a little mathematics will show that the optimal distribution of income between Utilitarian and Needy is $5,000 each. But if Egoist's income is considered, the optimal distribution of income (as always, it is most important to remember only ceteris paribus),[29] the optimal distribution of income would be $6,666.66 each.

In the outcome in which Egoist keeps $10,000 and Utilitarian and Needy split Utilitarian's $10,000 for $5,000 each, Utilitarian is exploited in that both he or she and the world are worse off here than in some available alternative. Should Utilitarian come across the means to compel Egoist to surrender some share of Egoist's income ($3,333.33), Utilitarian should use them. In general, utilitarians would not be content merely to be charitable. They would want others to take up their fair share of assisting the needy. If others will not, there can be conditions of scarcity under which utilitarians would limit their own redistributive activities if by failing to do so they would impoverish themselves and threaten the survival of utilitarianism.

Remarks on the Rule

As has been noted, utilitarians who follow a nonexploitation principle will not act like pure altruists. There may even be cases in which the behavior of a utilitarian is very much like that of an egoist. Should a utilitarian frequently meet another player in Prisoner's Dilemmas who always defects, the utilitarian may respond by always defecting in turn—exactly the response we would expect in a selfish player but a bit counterintuitive in a utilitarian. For the simple Prisoner's Dilemma game described in table 3–1 iterated 100 times, we might expect the following results. If the utilitarian always cooperates and allows the egoist always to defect, the payoffs will be Utilitarian 0 and Egoist 500, for a total of 500. If both always defect, Utilitarian and Egoist will get 100 each, for a total of 200. Crude utilitarian reasoning would still seem to favor allowing the always-defector to always defect. But an extended game like this would be very bad for utilitarians: they would face a personal opportunity cost of 100 for allowing the egoist to always unilaterally defect. Making such an allowance would be an incitement to egoism and would guarantee the fall of utilitarianism. So utilitarians should respond by always defecting, on the assumption that if they should interact with others not quite so nasty as the egoist, their survival qua utilitarian would be worth it. They will also, in so doing, make future threats against would-be defectors much more credible.

Another question worth addressing is whether there are any limits on this rule of thumb. The desirability of nonexploitation is a subsidiary rule derived from the principle of utility. It obtains only when certain assumptions are made about the evolutionary selection of moral norms, as well as certain assumptions about the kind of games in which moral agents are likely to find themselves. It is not a self-standing principle and as such will not necessarily apply to all conceivable cases. There are at least two principle classes of cases in which the nonexploitation rule will be overridden by the principle of utility.

First, there are cases in which evolutionary considerations do not apply for some reason. In any case in which utilitarians would be prevented from transmitting their moral norms by their own imminent dissolution anyway—if a utilitarian is marooned without hope of rescue on a desert island with an egoist or if the world is about to end—there can be no reason for wanting to keep their norms intact. In that case they might be willing to let the minimalist or the egoist get away with a last unilateral defection.

Second, there might also exist cases in which evolutionary considerations do matter, but any good that could be done by enhancing the evolutionary success of utilitarianism would be strongly outweighed by the benefits that a utilitarian could convey by some important self-sacrificing act. Especially in a world in which serious gift-optimal games occur often—and utilitarians have the chance to interact with one another in such conditions with considerable frequency—utilitarians would not be willing to sacrifice their own lives to save the lives of some *small* number of minimalists, for if that were a utilitarian policy, enough damage would be done to the chances of survival of utilitarianism that it would have consequences that would be, in fact, negative overall. But it would have to be a very bizarre world indeed in which a utilitarian would not sacrifice his or her own life to save a very large number of lives of minimalists. After all, the living of those lives would no doubt contribute greatly to the aggregate well-being.

Moral Mimicry

The applications of the utilitarian nonexploitation principle that I have made have assumed that there is a reliable way for utilitarians to tell who is a utilitarian and who is not. In the real world, however, it is not obvious how to make such judgments. Minimalists do not normally have this problem, at least not in Prisoner's Dilemma games. If their interacting partner consistently cooperates, he or she is most likely to be either a minimalist or something extensionally equivalent. But utilitarians cannot simply read the nature of their partner from that partner's strategy choices.

Consider the interaction in table 3–6.

Suppose that it can be determined that $T > R > P > S$, and thus defection is a dominant strategy for a self-centered player. What is the utilitarian to make of the fact that in a given interaction his or her partner defects? If it is the case that $(T + 0) > (R + 3)$, the partner may be a utilitarian who is taking a gift in a gift-optimal Prisoner's Dilemma. But if it is the case that $(R + 3) > (T + 0)$, then the partner is exploiting the utilitarian and hence is not a utilitarian oneself. There is also the question of whether the utilitarian ought to have cooperated or defected in response to cooperation. Obviously, if $(R + 3) > (S + 5)$, the utilitarian is obliged to cooperate; whereas if $(S + 5) > (R + 3)$, the utilitarian would be required to defect.

The whole matter turns on determining the interpersonally comparable values of T, R, P, and S, a task that is not easy, even though for the sake of analytical simplicity I have ignored it until now. In chapter 2, I suggest that interpersonal comparisons could be made by a variety of means. We can reflect on our own experiences and on the relevant similarities between ourselves and others. We can extend our imaginative sympathies in various directions and try to figure out what it would be like to be another person in a given situation. But the engagement of our sympathies and our capacities of inference is a highly fallible exercise.

Some kinds of experience, especially the primal and the universal, are comparatively easy to render judgments about. Almost all of us have suffered physical insults

Table 3–6. A Prisoner's Dilemma with uncertain utilities

| | | Utilitarian | |
		Cooperate	Defect
Stranger	Cooperate	R 3	S 5
	Defect	T 0	P 1

and know firsthand the badness of pain, illness, hunger, and fear. Furthermore, these events in others are often marked by publicly observable behaviors and signs. So when we see someone burned or battered or wounded or shivering and feverish or starved or wide-eyed with fear in the face of imminent death, we are unlikely to be led too far astray in judging the badness of the suffering and the corresponding goodness of relief. Thus, putting ourselves in the shoes of that unhappy someone is not very difficult. Because we all feel pain and know its marks, we can readily use ourselves as a model for the other person.[30]

In other instances, our inferences are more difficult because the characters and capacities relevant to the circumstances vary considerably. The amount of pain involved in being subjected to a day's manual labor, even for two men of the same strength and health, may vary greatly, depending on the different preferences and expectations of the two men. Here a direct inference of the difference may be quite difficult because preferences and expectations are not the sort of thing that are available for direct public inspection. We can try putting ourselves in the shoes of the two men, but doing so is highly prone to failure because we may lack direct experience with one or the other's outlook.

Finally, for some interpersonal comparisons we have almost nothing except tricky inferences from signaling. The satisfaction one woman gets from going to the opera and that which another gets from a rock concert can at most be inferred very indirectly. My putting myself in the shoes of the latter woman, I fear, would be a futile effort.

People have ways of signaling the extent of their satisfactions and dissatisfactions with states of affairs. But unfortunately any signal that can be made can be faked, or at least made highly misleading. A person may make a verbal expression of disgust with a particular state of affairs but try to lead others to think of a given situation as a disaster, when in fact it is only a minor inconvenience. If the others are even a little concerned with the person's welfare, this person may be able to influence their conduct to his or her advantage. When the utilitarian is trying to decide whether the Prisoner's Dilemma described in table 3–6 is gift- or exchange-optimal, a less-than-scrupulous partner may attempt to indicate that receiving the gift payoff T is of great importance (i.e., that $T > 6$). The partner would do well to praise the value of T to the skies, hop up and down, express utter delight at the prospect of T, and so on, even if in fact the value of T would not justify ($T < 6$) a unilateral defection.

For any self-interested agent in a world where utilitarian norms are followed, there is a rational temptation to engage in such fakery of signals. There is also an evolutionary selection pressure to do so since in an environment in which there are at least a few utilitarians or others concerned with the welfare of potential fakers, those reproducing psychological traits that allow for effective fakery would have a reproductive advantage over those who do not. Hence, if we may borrow another term from evolutionary biology, there is a problem of *mimicry* that utilitarians must deal with.

Mimicry in general involves sending a signal that confuses others in such a way as to give the signaler a selective advantage. The classic example of biological mimicry is that of the viceroy butterfly *Basilarchia archippus*. Viceroys, which are colored a brilliant orange and black, closely resemble another species, the monarch butterfly *Danaus plexippus*, which because it feeds on milkweeds (Asclepiadaceae) is toxic to various species of birds whose diet consists in part of butterflies. The viceroy is perfectly nourishing to these avian predators but, by virtue of its close resemblance to the toxin-laden monarch, manages to confuse its would-be predators into staying away. It signals, falsely, "I am toxic."[31]

Moral mimics want to confuse potential partners into interactions that the latter would otherwise avoid. The mimic tries to resemble the honest person or the person with great needs in order to attract the attention of those who, as the whole or the part of their moral duty, undertake to improve the state of the world and the well-being of its inhabitants. It is important to note that moral mimicry and the ability to falsely signal utility information would be a problem for utilitarians even if my argument for the utilitarian nonexploitation principle turns out not to be correct. Even if utilitarians have no direct concerns about being exploited, they still face various problems that involve the utility opportunity costs of beneficent actions. If, for example, a utilitarian faces the choice of aiding either person A or person B and cannot aid both, he or she must try to make a rational determination of which of these two persons would benefit most from his intervention. If one or both of these potential beneficiaries is even partly self-interested, there will be a rational incentive for them to try to mimic the signals that would indicate to the utilitarian that they are in great need and would benefit from the intervention more than anyone else.

What should the utilitarian, concerned about the survival of utilitarian norms and not wanting to waste energy on less worthy cases, do about the problem of moral mimicry? Utilitarians may well find themselves locked in a form of epistemic arms race with others. They may attempt to improve their signal detection ability, while others try to improve their capacities to deceive.

The very possibility of moral mimicry and successful deception is a huge potential problem for the utilitarian. One may have very little idea about whom to trust. Mimicry and deception raise a nightmarish possibility: a utilitarian-Hobbesian state of nature. It is thought that the war of all against all, which would make life solitary, poor, nasty, brutish, and short, would subsist between all persons in the absence of appropriate institutions if those persons were egoists. It might, but not just if everyone actually *is* an egoist. It is enough merely that everyone *suspects* everyone else of being an egoist. And if signals of utility are sufficiently unreliable and utilitarianism is insufficiently evolutionarily stable, the social world could spiral into chaos. The mere possibility of invasion by egoists—either because they actually exist or because of the possibility that an undetected "mutation" may have taken place—would be enough to sabotage the moral order.[32]

One escapes the state of nature between egoists by building institutions, as Hobbes would have us do. One may do the same for the world of uncertain utilitarians.

FOUR

A Skeletal Theory of Institutions

What Are Institutions?

This chapter has two aims. First, it articulates and defends a conception of institutions as the equilibria that result from the rational choices of individuals. Second, it shows that utilitarians face particular strategic problems in holding such a conception, specifically problems of equilibrium selection in worlds in which not everyone is a utilitarian and in which interpersonal comparisons of well-being are difficult. To open a conceptual space in which thinking about such problems is tractable, a simple analytical apparatus, the κ and ν apparatus, is developed.

This chapter is thus a rational reconstruction of what institutions are and the challenges they have to face, a skeleton of a theory of institutions. The bones of this skeleton are rather dry. Explanations of institutions as equilibria are in a certain sense still in their scientific infancy. Some elementary and highly suggestive models exist, but there are no comprehensive models of society as an equilibrium. There is thus in this theory a split between microlevel and macrolevel explanations, rather like that found in the science of economics. The microlevel models discussed are meant not as comprehensive explanations but as thought experiments to show how institutions *can* work as equilibria, rather than claims about how any given institution *does* work. It is in chapters 5 and 6 that flesh is hung on the skeleton, and this apparatus is deployed to defend different kinds of institutional arrangements for different worlds.

Readers who are amenable to rational choice explanations and familiar with the elementary theory of repeated games will find little of novelty in the first several sections and may wish to skim until the κ and ν apparatus is introduced. Others should read the following sections with more care. The material here is a bit abstract but necessary for making sense of the rest of the book.

Institutions are to be conceived of as a set of rules, which (1) provide information about how agents are expected to act in certain situation, (2) can be recognized by those who are members of a relevant group as the rules to which other agents conform in these situations, and (3) structure the strategic choices of actors in such a way as to produce equilibria.[1] The first two parts of this definition should be unexceptional since they are clearly present in almost anything one would care to call an institution, from the trivial to the grand.

My use of the term *rule* here can be somewhat confusing, so it merits a few additional words of explanation. In the previous chapter I used the term *norm* to describe various substantive moral or quasi-moral positions like utilitarianism, egoism, minimalism, and so forth. Norms are not the same as rules. Norms may describe or justify the actions of agents and can be said to represent central tendencies of the choices the agents make, but norms need not exist as mental representations in those who are carrying them out. That is, norms are principles that stand behind the choices people make but which are seldom, if ever, directly invoked in picking actions out of a set.

By *rule* I mean a fairly specific mental representation shared among some set of agents that picks out the duties that one or more sets of agents have in given circumstances: given circumstances c and agents of a relevant type t, each of type t has an obligation or a permission to do or refrain from doing some kind of act. Often a rule will also have an "enforcement" or an "or else" component: should agents of the relevant type fail in their duties, another set of agents has an obligation or permission to do or refrain from doing some other act.[2] Circumstances c may include both brute facts and symbolic acts. Thus if I happen to find myself in a Prisoner's Dilemma (a brute fact), I can have a rule telling me to cooperate; and if I fail to do so, the same rule may require my partner to retaliate. Or if someone tells me, "You may use my car this afternoon," I have permission to do so.

Rules may also be recursive and iterated. Part of conditions c can be the satisfaction of prior rules or their requirements. Thus your capacity to give me permission to use your car stems in part from your having satisfied rules that enable you to have lawful ownership of the car, which in turn stems from rules that allow agents like judges and legislatures and police to create and enforce lawful ownership, and so on. These are simple examples of how rules may work, but if they are iterated and intermeshed in sufficiently complex ways, very complicated kinds of social structures can be created, as John Searle has shown.[3]

It is worth noting, and indeed important to the analysis that follows, that there is no one-to-one correlation between norms and rules. Different people may share rules without sharing norms, for example, a utilitarian and egoist may both, at least in principle, subscribe to a rule that forbids the use of violence against another person except in retaliation for a specific wrong. The utilitarian may do so because such a rule keeps the peace in a way that may be justly calculated to maximize aggregate well-being in the long term. The egoist may do so because in a world in which everyone else subscribes to this rule, one's use of violence may lead others to act in such a way as to bring about worse consequences for oneself. Moreover, rules may diverge even when norms are the same. Two different utilitarians may disagree on what is to be done in a given situation because they come from different strategic environments and have different experiences.

It is also worth noting that the complexity of different levels of rules may go a long way in explaining why it is that we cannot read morals directly off moral intuitions and why an apparent divergence between intuitions and theory need not refute the theory. If rules are equilibrating devices for agents and if the content of our intuitions agrees with our rules and not our norms, it is quite possible for us to have apparently nonutilitarian rules even if we really do have a utilitarian norm. At the same time, it is also important to see that the possibility of divergent rules that stem from a single background norm presents a rebuttal to claims that the mere divergence of moral intuitions and surface-level disagreement on moral convictions are enough to show that there is no such thing as an underlying morality.

Perhaps the idea of institutions as just things that live in the heads of agents is a bit counterintuitive, in part because we encounter institutions in our daily life as constraints that are apparently external to us, and in part because of the linguistic usages that have grown up around them. Institutions are often referred to as social "structures": certainly the first image that enters my head when I think of the institution of Princeton University is that of the campus and its buildings and not an abstract set of beliefs and practices. But a little reflection would show that institutions really must reside in the heads of those who inhabit them.

Consider the all-important social institution of money. Any individual certainly experiences it as a kind of objective constraint, just like gravity or a stone wall. What one can do is limited by how much of it one has, no matter what one prefers or believes; and the value of money in general is for all intents and purposes not dependent on anything in one's head. But what agents in general believe and prefer has everything to do with the institution of money. If, per impossibile, everyone forgot what money was or simply became indifferent to it, the institution would go out of existence. Little engraved slips of paper, embossed disks, and numbers in computer accounts would continue to exist, but they would no longer be money.[4] Likewise, if everyone forgot what Princeton University was or if everyone simply decided to stop obeying the rules, there would be no more Princeton University, even though Nassau Hall would still stand as stately as ever. And it is the same for every other human institution.

It is part 3 of this definition, in which it is insisted that institutions must be equilibria, that the theory becomes distinctive and perhaps a bit controversial. Since some readers may be either unfamiliar with rational choice theories of institutions or doubtful about their utility, a few words should be said in their defense.

Rules, Equilibria, and Self-enforcement

As is explained in the previous chapter, an *equilibrium* is a state of affairs in which every agent does as well as one can for oneself, given what every other agent is expected do. Thus in a one-shot Prisoner's Dilemma, the outcome defect-defect is an equilibrium because neither player can do better for oneself by unilaterally choosing a different strategy. Cooperate-cooperate is not an equilibrium because when any one agent is cooperating, another agent can do better for oneself by defecting. The reason I require norms that pick out equilibria as part of my definition of institutions is that some rules, being only mental representations, are incapable of enforcing themselves. The distinctions of interests among individuals—of which the most important is no doubt that most individuals are to some degree self-interested and rational—guarantee such an incapacity. A rule that specified, for instance, that one should always co-operate with one's fellows but not retaliate against another who does not cooperate could not enforce itself because some opportunist would almost certainly figure out that one could improve one's own situation considerably by defecting all the time.

To head off a possible misunderstanding, it should be stressed that both self-interest and rationality need to be understood in a fairly broad sense. Self-interested need not for these purposes mean being selfish or self-centered, only that one has interests of one's own *distinct* from those of others and potentially in conflict with them. Rational does not mean narrowly calculative or consciously maximizing. In this context it may mean as little as having habits of choice that typically serve one's own interest. Prisoner's Dilemmas can thus arise in situations that would normally be understood as cases of altruistic and instinctive behavior.

Consider this example: I am altruistically devoted to my four children and you to yours. In a crisis involving our children we unthinkingly rush to the aid of our own children, a habit of decision that normally has the effect of maximizing their well-being. Now suppose that our eight children are playing at the seashore. Your four children are nearest to me, mine nearest to you. Suddenly a huge wave appears that threatens to drown all the children. Because of the times and distances involved, I can save either one of my own children or three of yours. You can save either one of yours or three of mine. We are thus in a Prisoner's Dilemma, and if we follow our instincts we will end up in a situation of mutual defection, saving only one child each when three could have been saved.

The ubiquitous problem of defection suggests that it may be difficult to get many rules to be self-enforcing. Certainly a rule that requires that one should be indifferent between one's own children and others and simply save the greatest number would not be. Or would it? Some strong sociological and anthropological views might hold that any possible set of rules could be followed because individual persons can be so completely socialized into following a given culture's rules that the thought of doing differently becomes unthinkable.[5] Or at least, if the thought of breaking the rule is a thinkable one, this prospect is so attended by internalized feelings of guilt that one who contemplates breaking the rule would never go so far as to actually do it.

In these views, there is no such thing as self-interest distinct from what one has been brought up to believe is in one's interest. All sorts of things are feasible because human beings are tabulae rasae, on which something called "culture" can write what-ever message it likes. Thus, in my hypothetical example of a world of pure pacific cooperators, everyone would have so internalized the rules of cooperation and non-retaliation that the defecting opportunist in my example simply could not come into existence.

This strong sociological view is not entirely implausible, and it does draw on some commonsense facts about moral psychology. Most people do feel guilt when they violate certain rules. Perhaps they would not feel guilt about speeding, but certainly they would about committing murder. Many of us would not commit murder even if it were to our advantage to do so and we were in possession of a Ring of Gyges that would guarantee getting away with it undetected. Furthermore, we do endeavor to instill in our children a moral sense that certain acts are not to be done even if one can escape punishment for them. It is also certainly the case that we feel, and sometimes even act on, sympathy for fellow creatures and that this sympathy reinforce rules of conduct that support social institutions generally.

The strong sociological view would also seem to gain support from the fact that people do generally follow the rules of their society and that these rules (apparently) vary a great deal from time to time and place to place. Since we do not generally see much physical compulsion, it is fairly natural to think that people have simply internalized these rules. And because the rules do vary a great deal, it also appears natural to think that almost anything could be internalized.

But any argument that would attempt to found a strong sociological view on these claims is mistaken about what rational choice explanations of a society-wide equilibrium actually require. In many equilibria, there may be the appearance of straightforward conformity with social norms without compulsion. But of course, this conformity is just what one would expect of rational agents—even the more calculating, narrow, and selfish of rational agents—in some cooperative equilibria. The mere potential for being punished and not its actual incidence is enough to obtain conformity among rational agents. And as shall be shown, in repeated games there are many equilibria, so one cannot infer simply from the existence of a considerable variation in rules that just any set of rules would be self-enforcing.

As a general claim about the foundations of social institutions, the strong sociological view is not plausible. Or if it is at all plausible, it is only so for very small and insular societies. Certainly in every largish modern society, the possibility of breaking with institution-creating rules is thinkable for most individuals, and probably psychologically feasible in the case of many rules for many persons. Most persons can readily distinguish between the behavior that would best serve their own interests if they could get away with it and the behavior that would be best for them given that societies do actually enforce these rules. Just because the rules of social life say that I should not cheat does not mean that I could not be better off by not cheating, nor does it mean that I am not clever enough to figure out that I would be better off by getting away with cheating.

A thought experiment can show just how commonsensical this cheating problem is. Suppose that we were to replace the complicated set of rules that now enforces the payment of income taxes—which include rules that permit agents of the state to determine individuals' tax liability and impose penalties (some of them criminal) on cheaters—simply with a rule that requires everyone to pay one's appropriate share of income tax while forbidding anyone from punishing anyone else for not doing so. It is only a guess, but one would suspect that this latter regime of purely voluntary taxation would not be self-enforcing; anything like full payment of taxes would not be an equilibrium outcome under that kind of simple rule. Some individuals might be spurred by a sense of guilt or fair play into paying their fair share, but many, probably most, would not. They would be better off with the extra income even if social rules imply that they are not entitled to it, and they would be clever enough to figure this out. Moreover, it would be difficult to imagine any scheme of enculturation sufficiently powerful to get everyone to voluntarily shoulder their taxation burdens, especially everyone in a large and diverse society. Any such program would require brainwashing of a science-fictional nature.

More worrisome still, in any large society there are bound to be amoral individuals who do not internalize rules and who can only be restrained by external enforcement. It would doubtless only take a few exploitative individuals to undermine a society of purely pacific cooperators. Even if none existed in a society that somehow managed to establish itself at some time, the possibility of their reemergence through some kind of cultural mutation cannot be discounted. And once such exploiters managed to establish themselves, it would be a quick downward evolutionary spiral into a very different kind of world as the purely pacific cooperators die off and are replaced with more efficient and selfish agents.

It is also worth remembering that we adhere to the rules of moral behavior in a world in which doing so is largely in our self-interests because of the institutions we have. For example, the cost of killing is high because many killings are detected and punished. The cost of not killing is usually low because the restraints on killing that are applied to agents other than ourselves mean that we seldom face a situation in which we must preemptively kill another or face some terrible consequence ourselves. So our commonsense morality and our tender consciences come mercifully cheap, at least most of the time. But would our consciences really be so tender in a Hobbesian state of nature in which we were faced with the choice of killing or perhaps being killed?

When one has beliefs about what would make one better off and a willingness to pursue the end of being better off, one is a rational agent. One need not be a rational agent all of the time; but it would be the soul of folly to deny that there are many times in which people will act as rational agents, and an adequate social theory must take this fact into account. Game theory thus becomes an appropriate tool for modeling one's interactions with others, and it predicts that we can expect only those outcomes that are equilibria. The first challenge to be met is to show that there can be forms of social order that are in equilibrium: that social order can subsist even if socialization and sympathy alone are not enough to support it. To meet this task is to show what it is that we can expect from our social order. Only then can we construct what we ought to do, given our moral theory. If we accept that in ethics *ought* implies *can*, the task for utilitarians is picking out the best of the available equilibria.

Coordination

Some rules effectively enforce themselves because if generally followed, there are no relevant actors who have an incentive to defect even in a one-off interaction. The classic example of such a rule is driving on the right side of the road in North America. When all drivers are following it, no individual driver (at least, no individual driver whose motivations are not suicidal) has any reason to drive anywhere else. Rules of this kind pick out equilibria in games of *coordination*. Much of the social life in any society is made possible by a dense network of such rules, in which everything—the rules of etiquette, the meaning of words, weights and measures, and so forth—depends on individuals successfully coordinating with one another.

Some rules of coordination, like the meaning of words or the habit of driving on the right, arise spontaneously among agents who follow them. But at times problems of coordination arise from the fact that there are many possible equilibria. The habit of always driving on the right is a self-enforcing equilibrium, but of course so is that of driving on the left. When there are multiple equilibria and no one equilibrium emerges among cooperating agents themselves, an equilibrium may arise through a rule of deference to some authority. The values of weights and measures used by scientists, for example, are established by an International Bureau of Standards, and those in common use in the United States are established by Congress through the explicit power granted to it in Article I, section 8, of the Constitution. The words and gestures through which we express due respect for other persons are an intermediate case of coordination. To some degree, they emerge spontaneously from everyday life, but they are also clarified and given shape by certain authorities who graciously make themselves salient for that purpose—Miss Manners, for instance. Thus, institutions for coordination often display some measure of institutional complexity: a division of labor in the management of tasks and information.

Although much of what we would consider property raises institutional questions beyond mere coordination, certain kinds of property rights may also be established by rules coordination. The arrangement of rights to use parts of the electromagnetic spectrum for the transfer of information is a form of coordination. No given broadcaster can benefit from switching frequencies to another part of the spectrum already in use since the result would simply be to make gibberish of one's own signal. Likewise, the right to use certain natural resources that are not scarce can be governed by coordination rights. When apples are abundant, no one can really benefit from taking the apple I have in hand away from me, so a rule that gives me exclusive use of that apple can be self-enforcing. If there ever were such a thing as a state of nature, a rule such as the Lockean proviso, in which one may possess anything taken from nature as long as one leaves as much and as good for others, could have served the purposes of coordination.

The particular strategic problems a utilitarian faces are not difficult in what game theorists call *pure coordination*. Pure coordination exists whenever there is no conflict between the preferences of different agents with respect to equilibria. The question of which side of the road to drive on is usually a case of pure coordination. A payoff matrix for such a game, which involves two drivers named Bravo and Charlie, might look like that described in table 4–1.

Utilitarianism may have some rather commonsensical advice to offer in some cases of pure coordination, in that it would recommend the choice of Pareto-superior equilibria. If both Bravo and Charlie own left-hand-drive cars—which are easier to drive through right-handed traffic—then for both to drive on the right would be such a Pareto-superior equilibrium and would be recommended by utilitarianism.

Not all coordination is pure coordination, however. There are some games with multiple equilibria that may be self-enforcing but in which the preferences of the players involved diverge. If Bravo has a *right*-hand-drive car and Charlie a *left*, we have an example of impure coordination, described in table 4–2. Game theorists sometimes call such an interaction a "Battle of the Sexes." I leave it to the reader to imagine why.

All other things being equal, a utilitarian should prefer that equilibrium in which the aggregate utility is greatest. Of course, not all other things will necessarily be equal:

Table 4–1.   Pure Coordination
Interaction

		Bravo		
		Drive Left		Drive Right
		2		0
Drive Left				
Charlie		2	0	
		0		2
Drive Right				
		0	2	

interpersonal comparisons of utility in a particular interaction may be too vague to make the notion of greatest aggregate meaningful; or, as in the case of pure coordination, some existing equilibrium may be too well established by tradition to be readily changeable.[6] Often agents will find that for whatever reason there exists tacit and common knowledge that allows them to get together and do things to the benefit of all. Such knowledge leads to the creation of what Thomas Schelling calls "salient points,"[7] rules that just seem obvious to the agents in question. In that case, a utilitarian may prefer to be a conservative and let stand any existing equilibrium in preference to some ideally optimal one.

The distance between ideal and feasible equilibria is a central problem for utilitarians, one that becomes even more important when one turns one's attention to problems of cooperation.

Cooperation

Two-Player Interactions

In the previous chapter we saw how a simple game called Prisoner's Dilemma can represent a ubiquitous set of problems in human interactions. A two-player version of the game lurks underneath what appear to be the simplest questions of property, exchange, and one's own bodily integrity, whereas multiplayer versions plausibly represent problems of the use of common resources. Of course, not all interactions that are not coordination are Prisoner's Dilemmas. But because this particular form of interaction provides such perverse incentives to the agents involved, it is useful to show how even here cooperation can emerge under the right circumstances. If we

Table 4–2.   Impure Coordination

	Bravo	
	Drive Left	Drive Right
Charlie Drive Left	2 1	0 0
Drive Right	0 0	1 2

can get cooperation here, we have gone a long way toward showing that there can be equilibria in general even when self-interest and rationality reign.

In the previous chapter, I invoked norms for the purpose of solving cooperation problems. The conception was naive because it assumed that there are persons who would automatically cooperate in any Prisoner's Dilemmas when matched against the right kind of player (minimalists) or who really are straightforward impartial altruists (utilitarians). In that discussion, these norms were treated as if they were the self-enforcing determinants of behavior. But in this chapter I have criticized the idea that just any set of rules can be self-enforcing by assuming that at least part of the time people are self-interested and rational.

Given this rather more disillusioned assumption about what people are too often like, how is cooperation to be sustained among them? It may seem highly counter-intuitive to expect that a society of rational egoists could ever keep itself going if there are incentives not to cooperate. Many people have the intuition that it would simply lapse into an amoral state of nature, in which there is no cooperation and the life of man in general is solitary, poor, nasty, brutish, and short. This section presents the outlines of a rebuttal to this intuition.

The general solution to the problem of cooperation among the rational and self-interested lies in *iteration* and *reciprocity*: given a future in which one might be punished for misconduct in the present, even the most egoistical agent has an incentive to behave better.

Robert Axelrod has shown[8] that under certain specific conditions, self-interested maximizers who play each other repeatedly in Prisoner's Dilemmas can produce a stable regime of cooperation if each uses a tit-for-tat rule. If each player has a memory of what a given player did in the previous round of an iterated game and is willing to punish defection with defection and cooperate otherwise, and, further, if the two interacting players do not discount future outcomes too much, it will be in the interest of both to always cooperate. The threat of future punishment—known to game theorists as the "shadow of the future"—can guarantee good conduct in the present. Axelrod has been able to show, furthermore, that a community of users of the tit-for-tat rule will enjoy greater evolutionary success than users of other rules and that such a community could not be "invaded" by the user of a different rule. Thus, given some not implausible additional rules about how evolution works, one might expect a version of Axelrod's rule to become widespread.

In the real world, however, a number of conditions make the application of the simple tit-for-tat rule highly problematic and serve as serious impediments to the achievement of cooperation through it alone. The salience of these complicating conditions has led to a number of serious criticisms of Axelrod's theory as a general explanation of social cooperation. In many kinds of interactions, players may discount the future too much to make the threat of retaliatory defection too feeble to encourage cooperation. Interaction may simply be too infrequent or too uncertain to make the future very valuable to a rational, self-interested player; the shadow of the future needed to guarantee cooperation may be too short.

Worse, it has been shown by game theorists that if there is a small chance of a player misperceiving the action of another—if one thinks another player has defected when the player has in fact cooperated—tit-for-tat and similar rules may lead to disaster. A rate of misperception as low as 1 percent, combined with adherence to the tit-for-tat rule, will eventually result in at least one player defecting 70 percent of the time.[9] Axelrod's results are sound, but they are not sufficiently general in scope. The aim of what follows is to show how that scope can be broadened.

First, though, it will help the reader to be introduced to a few general properties of repeated interactions in games. There is a fundamental result in game theory called the *folk theorem*,[10] which is a demonstration of the following: in an infinitely iterated game there is a convex set that contains infinitely many sets of payoffs, *every one of which is an equilibrium.* The infinity of equilibria is a central reason why I have proposed rules as the bones and sinew of institutions; trying to find a desirable outcome for a game on purely logical or algorithmic grounds would be just too hard for any players with finite cognitive capacities.[11] Consider, for example, the Prisoner's Dilemma described in table 3–1. The folk theorem shows that in an infinitely iterated game in which every iteration has the payoffs there described, every outcome from that of repeated mutual defection (1,1) and every Pareto improvement over that outcome, including repeated mutual cooperation, is an equilibrium.

Tit-for-tat is a rule. It specifies to each player that when one finds oneself in an iterated Prisoner's Dilemma, one should cooperate, and if one fails to cooperate, one should expect to be punished by the other player. When two players are playing tit-for-tat, they arrive at an equilibrium of (3,3). Other rules will pick out other equilibria. A short-sighted egoistical rule that calls for players to always defect will also pick out an equilibrium, in this case the maximin point (1,1). A more complicated rule can be devised, for example, one that punishes defections like tit-for-tat but which also occasionally defects on its own in randomly selected periods. If both players are playing with this rule, they will arrive at an equilibrium somewhere between the two extremes.

The set of possible outcomes is bounded by a frontier called the *convex hull* of the game. If we graph the payoffs of the game in a Cartesian plane, this frontier is all Pareto improvements over (1,1), lying on two line segments between mutual cooperation (3,3) and the two points that represent the payoffs for unilateral defection.

The utilitarian's problem, sensibly conceived, is to get as close to that point in the feasible set that represents the greatest aggregate well-being. This point will always lie on the Pareto frontier, so I first try to show what ideal rules in different kinds of iterated games will be likely to get us close to that point. I then consider certain practical complications that utilitarians will face when trying to maximize an aggregate under real-world conditions.

The first is *misperception*. As we have seen, tit-for-tat has been criticized as a decision rule in situations in which one player may perceive another as defecting when in fact that other player has cooperated. As little as a 1 percent change of misperception would result in a game in which tit-for-tat punishments would echo throughout and cause at least one player to defect some 70 percent of the time. Such an equilibrium would be fairly undesirable if all the iterations in question were of exchange-optimal Prisoner's Dilemmas. So in games in which there is a possibility of misperception and which satisfy this exchange optimality, there are usually better rules for players to adopt than straight tit-for-tat.

These rules differ by being more forgiving of apparent defections. A simple example of such a rule, suggested by Barry Nalebuff and Avinash Dixit, would be a tit-for-two-tats: a player should defect to punish another player only when the former observes two defections in a row.[12] A player known to be following such a rule could, however, be exploited by a clever opponent who throws in occasional random defections; so a more sophisticated strategy might be to maintain a record of what one's opponent has done over many iterations and to be more prone to punish that player whenever his or her rate of defection exceeds the rate of misperception. Thus it is possible to get closer to an optimal equilibrium and to avoid echoing cycles of punishment.

It is not implausible to think that such more-forgiving rules are present in ordinary social life. Some people have reputations of being reliable and trustworthy, and whenever we observe or think we observe a departure from good behavior on their part that harms us, we may be more inclined to extend to them the benefit of the doubt and refrain from punishing them. If my dear old friend fails to honor his promise, I am more inclined to think that his failure to do so was the result of circumstances beyond his control rather than an opportunistic defection on his part. Others have altogether less fortunate reputations, and we are accordingly more likely to treat them less well.

The second problem is *gift optimality*. Rules for achieving best aggregate equilibria when there are gift-optimal iterations in the game are rather more problematic because here a "defection," even if properly perceived, may in fact be a step in achieving a result that is optimal in the aggregate. In conditions in which interpersonal comparisons of utility are easy, it is not too difficult to come up with self-enforcing rules for sustaining the right mix of exchanges and gifts: each agent can commit to punish another agent by defecting in succeeding iterations whenever that agent fails to pick the right strategy—cooperation or defection—in a given iteration. But when interpersonal comparisons of utility are difficult or impossible, it may be hard to get an optimal equilibrium in this manner. A version of the misperception problem would arise again in the identification (or not) of optimal defectors, and there could be a problem with echoing punishments or a complete breakdown of cooperation.

It should also be noted that to the extent that players in such interactions are self-interested, the best aggregate outcome that is an equilibrium may not be the best of all logically possible outcomes. In a repeated version of the lord-peasant gift-optimal game, the best of the logically possible outcomes would be to have the redistribution (0,10) repeated over and over. But this is not a Pareto improvement over mutual defection (1,1) and hence is not in the feasible set of equilibria.

Gift optimality thus leads to some serious problems in selecting rules. These particular problems are instances of more general strategic problems in normative equilibrium selection, which I characterize in my discussion of κ and ν. But before turning to that discussion, I wish to present some more examples of self-enforcing rules.

Multiple-Player Equilibria

Another limit on the relevance of Axelrod's results is that they deal with achieving cooperation only in two-player games. A model elaborated by Michael Taylor suggests that cooperation may be possible in the N-player Prisoner's Dilemmas that plausibly represent problems in the provision of public goods.[13] Taylor's model is designed to rebut a common contention that because this problem every nonprovision of public goods is a dominant strategy for every person involved, the only way to get anything approaching an adequate level of provision is to invoke a Leviathan—the state—to coerce agents into providing their fair share. Taylor argues that the provision of public goods is not a one-shot game but rather an infinitely iterated interaction.

This argument is quite plausible for many public goods. For a public good like clear air, for example, I have not just a one-off, once-and-for-all choice about whether to burn dirty coal in my stove or not but rather a series of choices about whether to burn dirty coal today, tomorrow, the day after tomorrow, and so on into the future. What Taylor demonstrates is that when such problems have this iterated structure, and given certain constraints about payoffs and the rate at which agents discount payoffs in the future, there exists an equilibrium when agents make their cooperation conditional on the cooperation of other agents. Thus he shows that there is an analogue for the tit-for-tat rule for multiple-player games.

Unfortunately this particular analogue shares a number of shortcomings with Axelrod's original rule, some of which would seem to be even more serious by being in a multiple-player context. Conditional cooperation is just as or more vulnerable to being sent into a spiral of echoing punishments by misperceived defections in a multiplayer case as in a two-player case. Indeed, because there are far more choices to observe on each iteration, the chance of a misperception is ever greater in the former, if all other things are equal.

The problem of possible gift-optimal iterations also grows more complex in the multiplayer case. Not only is there the problem of deciding which defections to punish, but in many cases there will also be a higher probability that some people really should be defecting to bring about an optimal outcome. In the clean-air case just mentioned, it seems rather likely that there are some persons (poor invalids, perhaps) who would (1) benefit greatly by being allowed to burn cheap, dirty coal in their stoves and (2) impose relatively little cost on the rest of us. Unfortunately, the fact that some should be allowed to defect opens the possibility that all sorts might begin to get a free ride while pleading poverty and necessity.

No doubt modifications can be made to rules of conditional cooperation in the multiple-player case that will cut down on the amount of sabotage of the would-be equilibrium. The damage caused by misperception here, as in the two-player case, can be limited by adopting more tolerant or forgiving rules than those of strict conditionality, and some gift-optimality questions may be handled through rules of thumb.

A more serious problem for sustaining desirable equilibria now arises, however. As the number of agents involved in the interaction increases, so does the complexity of monitoring the behavior of each individual agent to determine when breakdowns of cooperation have occurred that merit some kind of punishment. Consequently, the cost of compliance with the rules of conditional cooperation rises for each agent, and this may cause the breakdown of cooperation in equilibrium.

Let us illustrate this last point by continuing with the example of clean-air provision. Suppose there is only this one public good in need of provision, and I, as one agent, am following a rule of conditional cooperation in the hope of sustaining an optimal equilibrium; I refrain from burning dirty coal as long as others do so. Now suppose the world to be complicated by the fact that there are some defections that would be optimal to ignore because of gift optimality. So I resolve to follow a modified rule of conditional cooperation: I will cooperate as long as all others who are not exempted from cooperation because of gift optimality cooperate.

Now there is plausibly some cost for checking on individual agents to determine whether their use of dirty coal is or is not an optimal defection. I would have to determine each agent's poverty and need for heat and make an interpersonal comparison of well-being across the set of relevant agents to know whether this condition of gift optimality is met. If the set of potential optimal defectors is small, these checks are not too costly. But for a large set, the cost becomes too large for me to rationally bear: all the possible gains from having a desirable equilibrium will be eaten up by the costs of following the rules that sustain it. And as mimicry of utility signals becomes easier, so much the worse. Therefore, where there are sufficient information costs, even more sophisticated conditional cooperation rules will not be self-enforcing.

This problem of information costs is a serious one because in the real world there are many interactions that involve many—sometimes millions of—individual agents. To begin to get at a solution we need to introduce a new concept into our mental armory of rules: institutional complexity.

Complexity

By *complexity* I mean the introduction of a division of labor between agents in bringing about an equilibrium. Most of what we ordinarily call institutions exhibit such a division of labor. Courts and corporations and churches and colleges seldom, if ever, lack structure in the way that the models of individual coordination and cooperation

I have discussed have. In most institutions some agents specialize in gathering information, others in making decisions, still others in enforcing those decisions, and there are many who obey.

It is a tricky matter to show how institutions like these can be equilibria in a game, or as the term of art would have it, to *endogenize* them. One pioneering effort—which I explain here to make clear how more complex social institutions can be equilibria—has been made by Randall Calvert,[14] who has elaborated a model of individual cooperation with a division of institutional labor.

Calvert begins with a simple model of cooperation in which individuals are matched at random with other individuals to play in Prisoner's Dilemmas. A simple tit-for-tat rule will not generally work to ensure cooperation here because in a sufficiently large population with enough mixing, the chance of soon meeting another agent again is small and therefore likely to be discounted so much that the shadow of the future is inadequate to ensure cooperation. Another rule is needed. Calvert demonstrates that there is a cooperative equilibrium with the following rule, which can be shown to be self-enforcing: observe what your partner did in previous iterations of the game no matter with whom, and do that.[15]

Calvert then complicates the model by assuming that there is an information cost for monitoring the behavior of each individual. When this assumption is added, the cooperative equilibrium breaks down whenever the cost of monitoring rises too high or the set of individuals to be monitored grows too large. Calvert thus faces the challenge in his model of finding an alternative cooperative equilibrium.

Calvert adds a simple assumption to the model—that players are allowed to communicate with one another—and suggests the following set of rules: one of the agents is designated as a "director." The director alone monitors the play of the other players and communicates to each player at the start of each iteration what an opponent did on the previous iteration. Each player then cooperates with or defects against an opponent in an appropriate tit-for-tat fashion, with one exception: since the director absorbs all costs of monitoring and communication, he or she is "compensated" by being always permitted to unilaterally defect against whatever player the director is matched with in a given iteration. The director is encouraged to do the assigned job by a rule that allows individual players to defect on the director should he or she shirk responsibility by failing to collect or report relevant information.

Calvert is able to show that these rules are self-enforcing, given a set of bounds on group size, costs of monitoring, and rate at which agents discount the future. What is normatively significant about Calvert's result is that he is able to demonstrate the existence of an equilibrium with a director that is Pareto-superior for a larger group with greater monitoring costs with the director than without the director.

The benefits of this kind of hierarchical structure have led Calvert to suggest that more complex structures of rules and conduct could be equilibria among rational and self-interested agents, in effect that any bureaucracy can be modeled on an equilibrium.[16] I do not attempt a demonstration of this as a formal result, but it should not be hard to see how Calvert's results could be so extended. In a sense the next two chapters are an informal example of such an extension, in which we are concerned first, with getting a working regime of cooperation and, second, with identifying optimal defectors from that regime, but a few possibilities deserve at least brief mention here.

For ever larger groups more levels of monitoring could be added. For the provision of public goods, the function of the director could be changed to an investigation of whether or not there has been the kind of defections that should trigger a withdrawal of conditional cooperation; and for problems with gift-optimality complications, the function of the director could be the investigation of individual claims that withdrawal from provision would in fact be welfare maximizing. Hierarchical organization also makes possible more direct and efficient forms of encouragement for agents to participate in the provision of public goods than might be made by simple conditional cooperation: that is, free riders may be sought out and punished directly in two-player interactions between themselves and a director, who here begins to look increasingly like a Leviathan.

As with all models invoking iteration to sustain cooperation, there will have to be modifications in the rules to adequately accommodate problems with misperception. In particular, the best available rules will have to specify just how readily players should punish other players when the information they get is flawed and how ready they should be to punish a director for shirking. Concrete suggestions on how to achieve this end await the next chapter. Before we can begin to study that problem, we must see how certain subproblems exist within the problem of social cooperation.

Rules, Equilibria, and v

Consider a purely abstract, two-player game with a feasible set between a breakdown point of (0,0) and a Pareto frontier described by the potion of an ellipse $(U_x)^2 + 2(U_y)^2 = 40$ in quadrant I of an ordinary Cartesian coordinate plane. The variables U_x and U_y in this equation are taken to represent the utilities of two players X and Y. The ellipse itself is the convex hull of the game and here is curved rather than straight, which is how we might expect it to look if the game that two players live out contains a very large number of possible strategies. In the abstract, the set may be thought of as a representation of the division of the fruits of social cooperation.[17] All these fruits, the products of nerve and muscle and the benefits of life and exchange, are amalgamated into one lump, whic h may be divided in various ways. All the strategies of labor and leisure, bargainir. and conceding, and conquest and defense are amalgamated as well. This representation thus is at the macrolevel; the individual strategies and payoffs have been abstracted away in order to make the example tractable.

The outcomes at the Pareto frontier are the most perfectly efficient divisions of these fruits, while outcomes below it are divisions with waste. The breakdown point (0,0) is the point at which there is no cooperation—a Hobbesian state of nature perhaps.[18] In this representation, the set is asymmetrical: it is assumed that the two agents do not necessarily benefit equally from social cooperation. If they do, so much the better because, as becomes evident, this eliminates a significant problem for utilitarians. The part of the quadrant under the ellipse represents all the equilibria that exist, according to the folk theorem.

Suppose now there is a utilitarian demiurge—a moral deity not powerful enough to change the boundaries of the feasible set but powerful enough to establish institutions between the two players. If interpersonal comparisons of utility are possible and if utility scales are such that player X's utility units are equal to player Y's, our demiurge would find that there is a unique point in the set at which the sum of utilities is maximized, in this case approximately at the point $(5.3, 2.4)$, which is to be preferred to all other points. So the demiurge would want to have X and Y follow whatever rules would allow them to reach that equilibrium outcome. Just what these rules would be would, of course, vary with the nature of the game and its associated strategic problems; in any event these rules would be the best available functional equivalent to utilitarianism for that game.

Now as it happens, no one is in the position of a utilitarian demiurge. The aim of this rational reconstruction is to show what our moral theory would require of us under real-world constraints. The point of utilitarian theory is to show what its followers would be doing when they are doing the best they can, given the world as it is. They cannot construct anew the moral universe. At most they can decide which among salient, alternative, possible institutions to foster, starting from whatever point in which they happen to find themselves and seeking better local maxima in their vicinity. So let our utilitarians descend from moral heaven to moral earth and incarnate themselves as one of the players.

Now they face a different problem because they do not have the ability to pick just any point out of the feasible set that is most desirable. Rather, because the opponent follows whatever rules he or she happens to follow, the utilitarians will have to do the best they can with these. There may still be a range of equilibria to choose among, but the ideally preferred utilitarian point need not be among them. If the other player has some kind of minimalist-cooperative norms rather than those that are a functional equivalent to utilitarianism, that player may decline to extend gifts to another player in gift-optimal interactions. Or the player may extend such gifts but only up to the point where they are reciprocated in other interactions by other players, and only up to the point where these reciprocations can be extended to the player's own maximum benefit. If the player treats the game of life as a bargaining problem in this manner, the best equilibrium available may turn out to be something like the Nash bargaining solution.[19]

As the reader will recall, the Nash solution is the maximum *product* of the utility gains from cooperation of the players rather than the maximum *sum* of these utilities.[20] A little calculation shows the Nash solution to lie near the point $(4.4, 3.2)$. Because Nash or a similar solution is the probable result of bargaining between perfectly foresighted, hard-headed, and self-interested players, we refer to it hereafter as the *exchange-optimal point*. In an asymmetric bargaining set, the Nash and utilitarian solutions will not coincide. As in the simple case of gift-optimal games between utilitarians and minimalists, there will be a less-than-optimal amount of redistribution between the two players.

There are equilibria that, in utilitarian terms are superior to the exchange-optimal point but less than ideal. In this algebraic example these are all the solutions that lie in the feasible set and satisfy the inequality $U_x + U_y > N$, where N is the sum of utilities at the exchange-optimal point, here approximately 7.6. If we sketch this inequality as a line in the same Cartesian plane as the ellipse that represents the abstract game, we will find a small region lying beneath the ellipse and above the line. This area is hereafter referred to as the *potentially optimal set*. It is *in principle* possible that the other player may follow rules that, in combination with the best available rules of our utilitarian, will achieve an equilibrium somewhere in this area.

The phrase "in principle" needs emphasis in the previous sentence because an important caveat attaches to it. Picking an equilibrium in the potentially optimal set contains a risk of exploitation. If a utilitarian should find herself in the position of Y, an opposing player in the role of X may be happy to settle for an equilibrium in the potentially optimal set over something like the exchange-optimal point since, of course, in so doing X would make himself better off. X may be inclined to pick such an equilibrium because he is a utilitarian or something close to it himself and wants an outcome that is as close to the utilitarian's optimal point as possible. If this is so, the exploitation problem is not too serious. But X may settle for such an equilibrium not because he is any kind of utilitarian but because he is just selfish and clever and knows that he will be better off with any point in the potentially optimal set than with a exchange-optimal point equilibrium. If this is so, there is a problem, because Y is now in a position where she has made herself worse off. If my argument about the evolutionary effects of such exploitation is correct, Y will not remain a utilitarian. This could be worse in the long run because in future feasible sets the absence of utilitarians may mean that opportunities for gains in aggregate well-being are not realized.

Thus here we have an example of a case in which short- and medium-term maximizing permit exploitation and are therefore at odds with long-term maximizing. The best available equilibrium could lie outside the potentially optimal set when evolutionary considerations loom large enough.[21] Such a problem may be especially salient if the background norms in a population diverge, so that many people do not share a background norm of utilitarianism and are instead egoists.

In other cases, the best available equilibrium may lie far from either the exchange-optimal point or the utilitarian's optimal point for rather sinister reasons that are harder to illustrate algebraically but are easy to explain. In a multiplayer case, some coalition of players may get together to exploit and oppress another group of players. These exploiters may hold together their coalition by holding norms or rules particular to it: cooperate with one another in the use of violent force, for example, and beat down the rest.[22] They may raise their own utilities quite high while pushing that of others toward something rather awful. For example, if Y is a member of a ruling junta, the best—perhaps only—available equilibrium may lie near the intersection of the Pareto frontier and the y axis of the plane, close to the point $(0, 4.47)$. If such rules should happen to be deeply entrenched in the world in which utilitarians find themselves, there may at best be only the most marginal improvements in equilibria to be found.

It is also often probable that the best available equilibrium may be less than ideal for more innocent reasons. The persistence of the problem of misperception, especially when there are gift-optimal interactions, is a large part of the reason. Even when players want to achieve Pareto-optimal equilibrium, the path to that equilibrium may require punishments of one another for defections from cooperation, but such conditional cooperation can be undermined by the epistemic limitations of the agents involved.

As has already been suggested, there may be ways to tune our rules in a way to make them better able to handle problems of misperception. But it may not be possible, and indeed is probably completely impossible, to tune our rules in such a way that we always agree on what constitutes cooperation and what constitutes defection from optimality; thus people will end up punishing each other fruitlessly, fighting each other either in court or on the battlefield.

Often social life will lack what may be called *transparency*: the ability to discriminate reliably between defections and cooperations. We may both know that we are made better off by honoring our contracts, but even the more sophisticated body of rules—of contract law and custom—will not enable us to always agree on what constitutes performance. Rulers of states may both know that in the long run they are better off respecting the integrity of each other's territory, but even the most finely tuned body of international law may be vulnerable to different perceptions. From a god's-eye point of view, these struggles may seem wasteful and irrational and hence show up in a game-theoretic feasible set as departures from Pareto optimality, but moderately self-interested agents of finite cognitive capacity may end up in them even when they are committed to the best rules available.

In any kind of complex equilibrium, moreover, there can be shortcomings in the desirability of the outcome brought about by the cognitive or moral limitations of the director or hierarchy of directors. Transparency may be lacking up and down the levels of a hierarchy, as well as across society. Directors may be subject to a variety of errors in determining when defections take place, especially when the rules they have to enforce are complicated. And of course, directors may be corrupt, inclined to make side deals with players to look the other way when they defect. The ability of other players to detect this defection on the part of the director may in turn be limited by their own cognitive shortcomings since not all of the referee's doings may be open to inspection. Or players may want to punish the director but may fear falling into an even worse equilibrium because they cannot coordinate in the choice of a different director. Even when the ruling prince is an idiot or the existing constitution dysfunctional, there may be no alternative that is salient enough to agree on. The resulting equilibrium may thus either fall below Pareto optimality or be pushed to an edge of the feasible set, far away from a utilitarian outcome.

Thus nature and history conspire to limit what might be achieved by utilitarians—nature by making various forms of misperception and exploitation ineliminable possibilities, history by providing agents whose rules may compel the selection of less-than-ideal equilibria from the feasible set. Relative to any set of historical and natural circumstances, there is a distance between the *best available equilibrium* and the *ideal equilibrium*. One may give a fairly precise quantitative representation of this distance, which will hereafter be referred to as ν:

$$\nu = \frac{U_b - U_w}{U_i - U_w},$$

where U_b represents the best available equilibrium, U_i the ideal equilibrium for utilitarians, and U_w the worst equilibrium in the feasible set. Thus ν will measure an interval between 0 and 1 inclusive, where those worlds in which circumstances are worst in utilitarian terms tend toward 0 and those that are best tend toward 1. I often call the former low-ν worlds and the latter high-ν worlds.

The concept of v can be made less opaque by a momentary descent to the microlevel and consideration of another example. Suppose that Cain and Abel live on a desert island and are condemned to play in an infinitely iterated Prisoner's Dilemma, with the following twist: every individual iteration of the game is gift-optimal, but in any given iteration Cain and Abel have equal chances of being the optimal defector. Suppose further that the payoffs in any given iterations of the game are the same as those in the field-icon dilemma mapped out in table 3–5. If Cain and Abel share a utilitarian rule, in every iteration the optimal defector will defect and his partner cooperate, and the expected average aggregate payoff in any iteration is 16. Since this is the ideal outcome, $v = 16/16 = 1$.

But it is possible for historical reasons that Cain and Abel share a tit-for-tat rule, and thus both cooperate on every given iteration. Possibly both just evolved that way before arriving on the desert island. This outcome is less than optimal, for it means that the average aggregate payoff on any given iteration is 12; thus $v = 12/16 = 0.75$. Still worse, it is possible that both share a norm of short-sighted egoism and thus follow rules that direct them to always defect: $v = 7/16 = 0.4375$.

Even if Cain and Abel are utilitarians, they may fall short of the ideal arrangement because their existences are not transparent. Perhaps one time in five a misperception leads to mutual defection. Even if their idyllic relationship is promptly restored, the expected average aggregate payoff would fall to around 14.2 (thus $v = 0.8875$). And this assumes that they can promptly restore relations. The best available rule that they can at once hold in their heads and that is self-enforcing may do even worse. However, v is far from the only thing utilitarians have to worry about.

Institutions and Interpersonal Comparisons: κ

We have already seen, in our discussion of moral mimicry and in some of the problems presented in this chapter, that whenever there is uncertainty about how to compare utility across persons, there is a possibility of exploitation.

Let us return to the previous algebraic example. Suppose there are uncertainties about, for example, how to compare X's utilities to Y's. Perhaps each of X's utility units are not obviously equal to Y's but may vary when we compare them, so it may be appropriate to count X's units as being up to a times as important as Y's. This may be the case, to give a crude example, when we suspect that X may get more pleasure from a given quantum of resources than Y does, but we are not quite sure how much more. If such an inequality obtains, the set of equilibria in the feasible set that a utilitarian prefers to the exchange-optimal point will not be just those satisfying an inequality $U_x + U_y > N$ but may be all those satisfying $aU_x + U_y > N^*$ (where $N^* = aU_x + U_y$ at the exchange-optimal point). So there will be an area in the feasible set that contains equilibria that a utilitarian *might* prefer to the exchange-optimal point. This again is the area between the curve of the ellipse and a line, a line that "pivots" around the exchange-optimal point according to the value of a. A salient fact about this new, potentially optimal set is that it may contain many outcomes that were not in the previous exchange-optimal set.

Now suppose that the utilitarian is Y, and one of these questionable equilibria becomes available as an alternative to the exchange-optimal point, given the norms held by X. Should Y cooperate in achieving it? It is hard to say with certainty what the best policy should be, but as a general rule Y should be quite wary of such questionable equilibria. As has already been argued at some length, uncertainty in interpersonal comparisons of utility is a consequence not only of our mere ignorance of other people but also of the fact that they may have an active interest in deceiving us about their utilities when they think they might get something for it. Certainly X would like an equilibrium that lies to the right of the exchange-optimal point, and he might try what he can to get it. And if he is a clever mimic, he may well try to plant in Y's head the idea that he can get more pleasure out of a given quantum of resources than Y can. Whatever means X may have available for signaling that he would get great utility out of an unequal division, he will be sure to use.

Now Y has a double duty to herself not to be fooled by X into making a bad interpersonal comparison that leads to an equilibrium that looks better but is in fact worse. If she brings about such an equilibrium not only is she failing to be a good utilitarian, but also she is allowing herself to be exploited. All the points in the expanded potentially optimal set lie below the exchange-optimal point, which means that she is making herself worse off for an outcome that is also worse in aggregate utility. So if evolutionary forces work on the survival of utilitarianism, it is important not to allow this to occur.

What is a utilitarian to do? The way to avoid deception is to rely on those features of the world that allow us to make interpersonal comparisons but seem the least vulnerable to manipulation. Some kinds of interpersonal comparisons are less easy to subject to mimicry because of enduring features of human biology and psychology— the comparisons involving pain from injury and disease, for example. Other kinds of interpersonal comparison, involving what are often thought to be more idiosyncratic preferences, are much harder to make.

But the degree to which mimicry is possible is not fixed in all times and places. Advances in human knowledge, for one thing, can improve our understanding of what generates the well-being of other people; for example, improved understanding of human health and nutrition may help us to better understand just how well individual persons convert certain kinds of resources into well-being. Great works of art may improve our capacity for sympathy with others. And to some degree, cultural homogeneity may affect our ability to make effective interpersonal comparisons of some kinds. In a community in which everyone values scholarship very highly, for example, it is plausible to think that we can make more effective judgments about the welfare loss to an individual who fails to be a scholar than we can in a society in which tastes for scholarship vary widely.

Thus, like the best available equilibrium, the degree to which we can make interpersonal comparisons varies with the fixtures of the social, technological, and natural world we happen to be inhabiting at the time. And just like the feasible equilibrium, this degree can be represented quantitatively. In a world in which absolutely no interpersonal comparisons are possible, the line above which a utilitarian would prefer a solution to the exchange-optimal point could conceivably be any line with a negative slope running through that point. The angle between the highest such line and the lowest would have a measure of $\pi/2$.

As uncertainties diminish, the measure of the angles between the highest such line and the lowest will also diminish, until at the point at which there is no uncertainty whatsoever the measure of the angle will be zero. We can thus specify an interval, hereafter referred to as κ, that is the overall measure of uncertainty in interpersonal comparisons. It would be formally (again, for a two-person case) defined as follows:

$$\kappa = 1 - \frac{V}{\left(\dfrac{\pi}{2}\right)},$$

where V is the measure of the angle between the highest and lowest lines.

For a multiple-person case, this definition would have to be modified to take account of some measure of central tendency in the measure of the many angles between the lines of many different agents. The κ values that approach 1 indicate worlds in which interpersonal comparisons are easy, readily available, and not much subject to deception and mimicry. The κ values that approach zero indicate worlds in which interpersonal comparisons are difficult, costly, and readily subject to deception and mimicry. Of course, κ is only a general measure, and at times in the discussion it will make sense to use the expression κ in a different kind of shorthand, referring not to worlds as a whole but to specific goods. High-κ goods are those the enjoyment of which for most agents is readily interpersonally comparable, while low-κ goods are those the enjoyment of which is not readily interpersonally comparable.

When looking for solutions in games in which κ values approach zero, the utilitarian may well prefer institutional outcomes that resemble those that would be recommended by someone urging a Nash or other scaling-neutral bargaining solution as a just social outcome. Unlike any solution that requires comparing or aggregating across individuals, Nash-like solutions are invariant with respect to the actual utility scales used. No matter what positive affine transformations you make of the utilities X and Y, the maximum product will come at the same point. Only when κ values are reasonably high can a utilitarian aggregate with confidence, a point that is of considerable importance in institutional design, as we see shortly.

The point can be illustrated further by returning to Cain and Abel on their microlevel desert island. If whatever goods Cain and Abel are passing back and forth in their interactions allow for ready interpersonal comparisons of utility, optimal outcomes may be readily available as long as rules and other conditions so allow. But suppose that interpersonal comparisons are so imprecise that they can only be estimated within a range; thus Cain knows at best that Abel's units of utility might be anywhere from half as valuable as his to twice as valuable, and Abel knows only as much about Cain.[23] In aggregate utility terms, this means that the benefit of a unilateral defection to the optimal defector would range between 8 and 32 units, while the aggregate benefit for cooperations would range between 6 and 24 units. Naturally enough, Abel should be suspicious of Cain's claims to be the optimal defector, and

Cain of Abel's: each could well think that the one would be trying to exploit the other by any given act of defection. Under these conditions, the best that the two may be able to achieve is a general agreement for mutual cooperation, even though there may be losses to both and thus in the aggregate.

But enough of toy examples. Let us see how κ and ν may apply in the world of real institutions.

FIVE

Basic Distributive Institutions

Introduction

The preceding chapter presents a view of institutions in the abstract; this chapter defends some concrete institutional arrangements. Naturally, even this defense of the kinds of institutions that a utilitarian will find desirable is more of a sketch than anything else. The range of institutions to be considered is limited to those that establish the basic structure of a political economy. It leaves out quite a few rather important parts of civil society. I do not devote much attention to secondary associations nor, except as a passing part of my discussion of redistribution in the next chapter, to the family or educational institutions.

There are both negative and positive reasons for this narrowness of focus. The negative reason is my incapacity to know much about the whole social universe. The positive reason concerns the problem of moral overdemandingness, which is one reason for this book's existence. And the state, in the contemporary world, is the principal source of the greatest demands that can be placed on any one person.

Because it wields the most effective means of coercion, it is the state that has the greatest power to take away one's life or property. It is also the state that has the greatest power to prevent others from taking away those things most important to us. Thus, in my counterutilitarian example of the forcible redistribution of body organs, the state would probably be the central coercer, one that would have the power either to compel or to prevent such a redistribution. The state is thus the most powerful arbiter of horrible acts and of imposing costs. In other eras, such tasks may have been undertaken by the clan or family, by religious institutions, or by some other means. But since the state is what we have now, it is the central object of my concern.

Not surprisingly, it is also the state that is the main concern in satisfying the publicity criterion for a proper theory of justice. Not for nothing did Bernard Williams dub a utilitarianism in which decisions are made for our own good without our understanding or consent a "Government House utilitarianism." That private persons might be conspiring for one's own good may be either gratifying or obnoxious, depending on one's point of view. That people who are backed up by an effectively incontestable armed force are conspiring to run our lives, however, is more than a little terrifying. Thus I attempt to show why utilitarians should, under at least many plausible prevailing conditions, support an open society and the rule of law. Of course, no state is likely to be engaged as a direct arbiter of the fates of all citizens under its control. Much of its work is done indirectly, through various economic distributions. I thus make this chapter a discussion of political economy.

My method in so doing is to make some speculative comparisons. I deploy the analytical κ and ν apparatus to describe some different possible political worlds. Joining that apparatus with the proposition that utilitarians will seek to avoid being exploited by other agents, I try to describe what institutions might be appropriate to each world in order to serve the principle of utility. I also use a number of quasi-empirical generalizations at various stages of the argument. I confess that many of my conclusions are only as strong as the empirical premises on which I base them, and at times these premises may not be as strong as they ought to be. I cannot avoid this weakness, but at least I can try to make my arguments for these premises as explicit and as vigorous as possible.

This discussion breaks down into three parts. First, I discuss what I call "utilitarian utopias," in which no real problems of rule enforcement or exploitation exist. Second, I discuss a proposed institutional structure for a world in which there is some problem with rule following and exploitation but in which these problems are relatively tractable. Finally, I discuss briefly certain kinds of "utilitarian dystopias," in which the exploiters have gotten the upper hand more or less completely.

The point of discussing utilitarian utopias is to show that, although there are factual circumstances under which utilitarianism really does recommend some of the horrible and alienating things we saw in the parade of horribles, the worlds in which these factual circumstances subsist are very much unlike our world. They are so radically different from that with which we are familiar that we simply cannot expect to have intuitions tuned to them, and thus we cannot really expect to have valid intuitions about what goes on in them. The imperfect world, in contrast, is meant to be a much more realistic discussion of what utilitarianism would in fact recommend for us. I argue that the institutions that utilitarians would try to bring into existence would bring about outcomes largely congruent with our intuitions.

The point of discussing utilitarian dystopias is to serve two rather different functions. The first is to show that the practical source for some of our worries about horrible policies comes from our experience of worlds in which exploitation runs rampant. The existence of certain practices in these worlds—inquisitions, Roman arenas, slavery, torture, and so on—colors our intuitive interpretation of them and no doubt leads us to intuit that wherever these practices exist, an exploitation that we have learned to reject must be going on. The second function of this discussion is to illustrate a point, which becomes clearer in chapter 7, about why utilitarianism might be prepared to allow individuals to pursue their own private lives even in the face of the considerable needs of others—and thus to avoid alienation.

Utilitarian Utopias

Utilitarian utopias are those worlds in which all or almost all agents are practicing utilitarians. In my technical language, v values for these worlds are very high. Our world is not a utilitarian utopia, to be sure, but it is instructive to look at them for comparative purposes. Needless to say, these utopias have a straightforward advantage over our world in that meeting the publicity criterion is not much of a problem. Everyone knows that utilitarianism is the theory of justice on which these societies are founded, everyone or almost everyone acts like a good utilitarian, and that's that.

Utilitarian Communism

A high-v world is one in which the absence of much noise and error in enforcing rules means that near-ideal solutions to the problem of equilibrium selection are possible and, further, that actual agents happen to have norms that make it easy for them to coordinate on rules that bring them very close to a utilitarian solution. A high-κ world is one in which interpersonal comparisons of utility are easy enough to allow trade-offs between individuals without substantial risk of exploitation. In a high-κ world, the distribution of virtually everything that might fall within human power to distribute could be made more or less directly; the maximizing of well-being could be accomplished as a straightforward matter of solving a set of simultaneous equations in which every person's utility function and every good's production function were represented. The problem of human motivations would not exist as we know it; the high-v character of the social equilibrium would mean that every agent would make his or her choices in accordance with the principle of utility. The guiding principle of such a society, a Communia, would not be the rather conservative "a fair day's wages for a fair days work" but the radical "from each according to his abilities; to each according to his needs."[1]

The life and practices of Communia's inhabitants will offer little comfort for those who have qualms about utilitarianism. Since everything can be available for redistribution, it is quite possible that in such a society even one's body parts might be considered public property—to be removed and transplanted should the need arise. The cost that such a world might impose on some individual agents, therefore, could be quite large. Of course, it might be open to question whether taking body organs from one committed utilitarian to save the life of other committed utilitarians is really a morally horrible act in spite of its cost to the donor agent. After all, a truly committed utilitarian would volunteer his or her own organs if the principle of utility were best served thereby.

A communist utilitarian society might contain a few dissenters from utilitarianism, and thus horrible acts would be possible in such a society. It may turn out that the tissue types of one of the few dissenters (and of no one else) happen to exactly match those of the best classical violinist, who is about to die of heart failure. That dissenter might well be abducted and butchered without consent for his or her still-healthy heart—a set of acts that to most intuitional moralists or Kantians would be quite horrible indeed. It is also conceivable (albeit remotely) that Communia might have a kind of Roman arena if the enjoyment of cruelty is somehow ineradicable among the Communians.

No doubt many opponents of utilitarianism have something like a vision of Communia somewhere in their minds: a totalitarian society in which individuals are blithely sacrificed for an abstractly defined common good, determined by mechanistic calculations of utility and production functions. Such a universe does seem a bit awful, even to convinced utilitarians. Nonetheless, I do not attempt to defend a communist-utilitarian society against these hostile intuitions; if my thesis of congruence between intuitions and different factual universes is correct, I am simply not required to do so.

Clearly, our factual universe is not one in which almost all agents follow strictly utilitarian rules, nor is it one in which interpersonally comparable utility information is readily or easily available for many goods. We thus should not expect our moral intuitions to be tuned to such a universe. Nor should we expect that if somehow we were to meet people from such a moral universe that they should share our intuitions. No doubt they would find our social world as intuitively obnoxious as we find theirs. It would be an act of becoming (but atypical) theoretical modesty for present-day moral intuitionists not to try to impose their considered judgments on other worlds. Utilitarianism does not imply communism in this factual world, for precisely the reason that the absence of the right kind of agents and the right kind of utility information would make communism a futile and self-destructive social venture. Thus, the charge that some morally counterintuitive acts would take place in Communia has no evidentiary weight against utilitarianism.

The communist-utilitarian universe is an extreme case. I now try to move closer to our own universe along one dimension: that of κ values.

Libertaria

In a world in which interpersonally comparable utility information is scarce or non-existent, a truly communistic society is impracticable. It might be possible to make decisions about how to produce goods efficiently, but one could not get a purchase on what to produce, on whom to impose the costs of production, and on how to distribute what is produced. Even if everyone is willing to contribute according to one's abilities, none can receive according to one's needs because the utility information necessary for weighing different needs is unavailable *ex hypothesi*.

Does this unhappy fact mean utilitarianism gives no advice when interpersonally comparable utility information is unavailable? By no means. A certain moral order would be recommended by utilitarianism even if, as a matter of fact, no such information were available.[2] For all games that have a structure like Prisoner's Dilemma, *mutual cooperation between fully-rational agents is utility-superior to mutual defection.*[3] I call this the *quasi-Pareto principle,*[4] and it further extends to coordination interactions. Some outcomes can be identified as superior to others simply because they contain more personal good for at least one person while making no other person worse off.

Thus, if there is a set of coordinating conventions that attach things in the world to specific agents, so that each may cede or keep them, a society of agents could achieve a maximally desirable set of utility improvements by (1) always seeking those exchanges with other agents that would make them best off and (2) never unilaterally defecting. The first rule is justified by the quasi-Pareto principle. The second is a coordinating convention in its own right: any different convention would lead to the danger of some unintentional mutual defections without producing a corresponding benefit since there is no way of comparing a unilateral defection with mutual cooperation in utility terms. In following these rules, we should expect agents to be guided by the well-known invisible hand to the best of possible destinies. Slightly more complicated exchanges would be worked out in N-player interactions, for example, provision of public goods. Every agent could contribute just as much effort to, say, pollution control as the value to that agent of a clean environment.[5]

Such a society merits the name Libertaria because it would leave all individuals free to seek their own best interests. A world in which rules very close to utilitarian rules are scrupulously followed would have a greatly reduced role for the state. Indeed, in a world with sufficient transparency and a long enough shadow of the future, there may be no state at all. Cooperation may rest entirely on reciprocity among individuals, as Michael Taylor argues.[6] Given a set of ownership rights in this world, no utilitarian would seek to disturb them since doing so could only lead to a world that is not demonstrably utility-superior and may be utility-inferior. In game-theoretic terms, respecting ownership rights would weakly dominate not respecting them for utilitarians. The aim of the state could be limited to enforcing property rights and contracts.

Because of the impossibility of interpersonal comparisons, Libertarians might thus be prepared to countenance certain horribles that we would not. It is possible that under a regime of nothing but trucking and bartering, some persons will be unlucky and fall into penury and worse. We might find toleration of such poverty morally offensive: after all, those who are sufficiently badly off may be living terrible lives, selling themselves into something like slavery, and so on. But Libertarians would have nothing to say about it since, *ex hypothesi*, they have no way of comparing the well-being of those who have fallen into poverty with that of those who have risen to riches. They would have no redistribution in situations in which we might think it morally mandatory.

Our world is clearly not a Libertaria. The conditions for a high-v world do not fully obtain, as a fair amount of noise and error is involved in enforcing the rules of society. Moreover, some interpersonally comparable utility information *is* available. Utilitarianism in this world does not lead us simply to libertarianism.

The Imperfect World

A world in which κ and v values tend toward middling is one in which noise, error, and history make it impossible to select truly optimal equilibria. The best self-enforcing rules fall short of a utilitarian solution, and difficulties in interpersonal comparisons of utility make exploitation a problem in many cases. This world is not Libertaria in two ways: (1) the existence of some κ values greater than zero means that utilitarianism sometimes gives us standards by which to evaluate the distribution of goods; (2) the possibility of agents getting away with exploitative behavior makes necessary rather more complicated institutional solutions to get as close to optimality as possible. Let us call this world, then, Imperfectia.

Some of what applied in Libertaria, however, would still apply in this imperfect world. It would remain the case that in Prisoner's Dilemmas, mutual cooperation would always be utility-superior to mutual defection; thus, the quasi-Pareto principle would still apply. We can thus start from an initial distribution that utilitarians would endorse and then count on the voluntary exchanges of individuals to improve the world still further. Of course, some means would have to be found to ensure that force and fraud would not prevail over voluntary exchange. In many cases these means would be the institutions of coercive power, that is, the state.

This discussion thus proceeds in two sections: in the first, I show what kind of distribution utilitarians would endorse and, in the second, I show—in the broadest outlines—what kind of institutions would be necessary to uphold a regime of voluntary exchanges based on that distribution.

Social welfarists—but not libertarians—will object that a regime of voluntary exchanges will not provide a morally desirable pattern of distribution even if those exchanges start from an initially justifiable distribution. I am in partial agreement with the welfarists, but here I offer them only a promissory note: I discuss redistribution in the next chapter.

Ownership

SELF-OWNERSHIP

The set of (ownable) things that can be called the self includes a physical body and a brain and the powers and capacities that can be exercised by each. An agent can be said to be *self-owning* whenever there is some moral requirement on other agents to acquire the owning agent's permission before using or disposing of any part of the ownable self.

A simple-minded act-utilitarian would recognize the general obligation to seek permission to dispose of ownable selves only if it were generally the case that, barring a revelation of utility information to the contrary, the value to an owning agent of parts of his or her ownable self were greater than the value of said parts to any other agent. Less abstractly, I should be self-owning if and only if my time and energy and body parts are worth more to me than they would be to anyone else. Now, even to a simplistic utilitarian, a rule that requires agents to respect each other's self-ownership would be a fairly robust one. Detecting violations is relatively easy, and retaliations for violations are generally to be expected; thus in cases in which there is noise and misperception, such a rule can often select a desirable equilibrium.

This simply formulated rule may cover quite a few practical cases. Anyone who has been in the uncompensated and involuntary service of another person no doubt appreciates how deeply unpleasant an experience it can be; the expropriation of one's own time and energy is a terrible event. Surely, one might think, the utility gains that stem from the relief of toil on the part of a master do not outweigh the utility losses suffered by the indignity of a slave. There probably are not many involuntary organ donors walking around to explain to us how awful their experiences have been, although the exercise of our imaginations should show that the uncompensated loss of one's organs would also be terrible. But we are certainly not limited to our speculative imaginations alone in discovering the truth of this last point. To be the victim of a sadistic battery, kidnapping, or rape is, in a manner of speaking, to have suffered a loss of part of the ownable self. Certainly, the losses in these cases are quite terrible, and the enjoyments of the assailants seem to pale when weighed against the sufferings of the victims. It might thus seem that as a general principle, even simple-minded act-utilitarians could endorse self-ownership.

But the moment they do, an antiutilitarian parade of horribles will be sent marching in their direction. "In the case of slavery," an antiutilitarian interlocutor would remark, "while it may be true that even *in most cases* the time and energy are worth more to that person in whose body they originate than to any other person, it is not necessarily so in every case. It seems possible that one person may find another person's slavery intensely gratifying, so much so that the disutility of the indignity of one's person's being enslaved is outweighed by the utility of the gratification of one's master. The same might be true of certain cases of assault or rape undertaken to gratify sadistic passions. While in practice there may be few cases in which the balance of utilities favors the assailant, such cases can exist. Utilitarianism cannot rule out in principle some cases in which the optimal thing would be to allow the assault or the violation to occur. It is not the case, therefore, that utilitarianism contains within itself adequate resources to found any principle of self-ownership."

Some utilitarians will concede the point of this argument and introduce restrictions on maximizing, thus becoming distribution-sensitive consequentialists. But we have already determined that such a solution should be avoided if possible, on the grounds that it may be either completely unacceptable at worse and arbitrary at best. The antiutilitarian's argument that utilitarianism cannot rule out certain horrible practices in principle is correct, but its inference that utilitarianism cannot provide any basis for a principle of self-ownership is not.

In the cases cited in the antiutilitarian argument, an argumentative slight of hand is comparing two rather different kinds of utility information. The utility information we have about physical suffering and the deprivation of liberty is high-κ information. The sufferings of the violated and the enslaved both have a certain terribleness and a terrible certitude. We have a rich store of both individual and collective experience to back up such a proposition. Most of us have experienced at least some pain and fear and indignity and are well set to appreciate their horribleness, especially if we have sufficiently active imaginations to extrapolate from our own experiences to those worse experiences of others. We also have a deep and complex historical record that testifies to the awfulness of physical suffering and bondage.

In contrast, the utility information about the joys of inflicting suffering and bondage, we may be confident, is low-κ information. Within the population of humanity there seems to be a great deal of variation concerning the attractions of lordship and cruelty. Some persons no doubt would become ill at the spectacle of intentionally inflicted suffering, while others might find some sly but minor pleasure in it, a pleasure perhaps akin to what one might experience at a boxing match (indeed, no doubt that is part of the pleasure for some followers of boxing). And for a few sorry examples of humanity, sadism might so enter into the constitution of their psyches that the only project that could possibly make their lives worth living would be the infliction of suffering on others.

The problem here is that because the contribution of lordship or sadism to a person's well-being is locked away in one's brain and does not leave obvious marks, it is really rather difficult to determine *ex ante* whether the claim of a utilitarian reason to use or dispose of another self is actually deeply connected with one's well-being or whether it is simply an opportunistic attempt to cadge a minor benefit from other agents by exploiting their benevolence or their weakness. Especially if a minor sadist is an egoist, there will be a strong selective pressure for that person to attempt just such an exploitation.

A given population may contain a fair number of minor sadists and a small number of major ones; only the latter class could even conceivably have such a utilitarian claim on other persons. But the whole distribution of major and minor sadistic egoists would be likely to attempt to signal their claims if they think they have a reasonable chance of getting them recognized. Signaling is usually pretty cheap, so one might as well cast one's line even if one is likely to reel in only a small fish.

Claims of utilitarian reasons for other-than-self ownership ought therefore to be viewed with the profoundest suspicion in these cases. The question of how well-being is divided up among agents is here an eminently practical question. If the distribution is made in such a way as to reward nonutilitarians, as an evolutionary matter it is quite likely that the nonutilitarians will invade the moral universe and take over. Thus, when confronted with low-value utility information that vies with high-value information, the utilitarian recommendation must be to take the side of the more reliable information. The antiutilitarian's objection that utilitarianism cannot guarantee self-ownership in principle in all cases thus misses the point. Utilitarianism stakes its claims on empirical plausibility rather than on logical possibilities.[7]

Of course, not all cases to which an antiutilitarian would object involve high-κ goods vying with low-κ goods. Forcible organ donation, for example, represents high-κ goods vying with other high-κ goods. The forcible donation may impose suffering or even death on the donor, but it would spare suffering or even death for the recipient. In my contrived case in which the death of one prevents the death of five, the balance of utilities seems clearly to favor an involuntary sacrifice, to which my utility-information argument provides no obstacles.

There might well be other cases in which the high-κ disutility of involuntary servitude might be comparable with equally high-κ utility gains on the part of another moral agent. Four hours a day of uncompensated menial work may be a major loss to me, but if those four hours are a source of support to a paraplegic who would otherwise perish nastily, the utilitarian's case that I (or someone) would owe the paraplegic that service, seems fairly clear.

If we are considering whether it might be a good policy to render aid to those demonstrably in desperate need of it, we might want to consider the strategic consequences of doing so. A number of significant cases in which people find themselves in desperate circumstances might be avoided in less costly ways than by forcible redistributions. For instance, suppose that I have two younger brothers whose tissue types are compatible with my organs. One younger brother is inclined to smoke too much, and so is likely to need a new heart in a matter of decades. The other is inclined to drink too much, and so will need a new liver. Both brothers are selfish egoists. I have the vicious inclinations of neither of my two brothers; I am a good utilitarian with healthy habits.

I strongly suspect that the aggregate cost of my younger brothers' restraint of their vices will be less than the cost of my surrender of my own heart and liver some years down the line. At the very least, I would strongly suspect that the κ of brother number 1's desire to smoke too much and the κ of brother number 2's desire to drink too much is rather low. Perhaps they really do crave their vices; or perhaps they simply find their vices mildly pleasant but would like me to believe that their vices are terribly important, in hopes of exploiting me. Should I be willing to give up my organs?

A simple application of the utilitarian nonexploitation principle indicates that I should not do so. To subsidize the misbehavior of selfish agents would introduce the problem commonly known as *moral hazard* and provide a perverse incentive for conduct. Moral hazard is a generic problem that emerges whenever one considers whether or not to underwrite risk. If one party reaps the benefits from taking risks while another has to pay the costs of risk taking when things turn out badly, the first party has a clear incentive to do the risky thing and pass the costs on to someone else. It would in this instance clearly be more cost-effective to demand the prevention of problems rather than the cure.[8] Furthermore, if utilitarians provide perverse incentives to egoists, they will jeopardize the evolutionary stability of utilitarianism. Utilitarians thus have a double incentive to demand that body organs not be given away in a number of cases.

An appeal to moral hazard knocks a number of marchers out of the antiutilitarian parade of horribles, but it still leaves some of them standing. Certainly people get into desperate circumstances through no fault of their own,[9] including a number of "appeal to cost" cases. Throughout the world millions of people suffer hunger, disease, and mistreatment that they can in no reasonable sense be said to have brought upon themselves.

No doubt, in even a crude utilitarian calculation, if I were to sacrifice substantial parts of my own time and energy I could relieve their suffering and generate an outcome that would almost certainly be utility-superior to the status quo, but doing so would almost certainly involve a surrender of my control of my own time and energy, in short, a loss of self-ownership. But were I to become a slave to the suffering of others, the world might well be a better place.

With this case of slavery, however, as with all others, it makes sense to ask R. M. Hare's question: "What on earth are the slaves doing that could not be done more efficiently by paid labor?"[10] To see the meaning of this objection, we must understand that it is often not possible for utilitarians to disentangle neatly the question of self-ownership from that of world ownership, which I discuss in greater detail in the next section. For now, however, I should make it clear that the kinds of demands other people need to make on utilitarian agents would often be conditional on the resources available to these people.

In many cases in which claims on our own time and energy might be made legitimately—that is, unobscured by worries about moral hazard—the claims may arise from the fact that the claimants are subject to a distribution of worldly resources that in itself is morally illegitimate. For example, those who suffer hunger or sickness may do so not because of their lack of control over someone who will take care of them but because of their lack of access to resources that can be converted into food or traded for medical assistance; had they arable land or marketable skills they would be able to take care of themselves. Those who are poor and incapable of taking care of themselves—because of disability or age—may fall into one of two classes: (1) they may have lacked the necessary resources to insure themselves against misfortune and would have then suffered a misfortune for which they were not to blame, in which case their problem is not one of self-ownership but of world ownership; or (2) they did have the resources with which to insure themselves but neglected to do so, in which case helping them raises issues of moral hazard.

It is important to see that in the cases of people who might have claims on our time and energy, the problem should usually be one not of self-ownership but of world ownership. That is, under a more just distribution, they would never need to make direct claims on our time and energy. Of course, if the distribution of things in the world is not justifiable in utilitarian terms, some redistribution may be called for. Would such a redistribution necessarily require the enslavement of anyone, including utilitarians? I discuss the issue at some length in chapter 6, but let me note now that considerations about evolutionary stability in redistribution games, already discussed in chapter 3, will militate against voluntary self-sacrifice by utilitarians in favor of rather different policies.[11]

Of course, there would now still be a few stragglers in the parade of horribles. Some of these are not so horrible: it is not morally controversial to say that there are some cases in which utilitarian considerations override self-ownership, plain and simple. If I am the only person who can call an ambulance for someone who has been badly injured in an accident on a lonely road, I have a strong moral obligation to do so, even if it means an uncompensated disposal of some of my time and energy. Even if there might be a small degree of moral hazard involved in this case (perhaps the injured person should have been more prudent), the large utility benefits that would accrue to his or her deliverance from suffering would probably override the minor utility cost to me.

There are some remaining hard cases in which the κ values of utility that might result from sacrifices of self-ownership are very high, while the corresponding risk of moral hazard is low. Consider an example: some central agency has begun keeping records of organ tissue types of all citizens to facilitate a system of postmortem organ donation. Two patients—who are strangers to me—require organs, one a heart and another a liver. It so happens that I am the only living citizen whose tissue types are an exact enough match to the two strangers to make a transplant successful (perhaps I and they are identical triplets, possessing several rare alleles, who were separated at birth and reared by different sets of parents). I am assured that the strangers have come to their medical conditions through no fault of their own; hence, moral hazard is not a problem in this case. Furthermore, I am assured that the strangers hold norms that pick out rules that are at least as good as mine in selecting a high-v equilibrium, and therefore my dying and their continued existence will not pose any problems for the evolutionary stability of utilitarianism. The question would then become this: is this case one in which utilitarianism requires overriding any claims I might have to my own body?

The reason for my answer, a probable no, becomes clearer as my discussion of institutions proceeds, but I can give an outline of the response here. The slippery part of the problem comes in the formulation "I am assured that. . . ." "Assured by whom?" one may ask. Obviously not by my own experience since, *ex hypothesi*, these two persons are strangers to me. In any case, making a determination that people have a medical condition "through no fault of their own" is a nearly intractable matter for even the most expert judgment. Even a doctor with detailed knowledge of the medical history of a patient and a full (indeed fuller than is perhaps realistic) understanding of the etiology of the particular medical condition in question cannot make that judgment with much confidence.

It is logically possible that externally identical behaviors with identical causal contributions to diseases may or may not be indicative of moral hazard. What counts as taking due care of oneself varies a great deal with one's cognitive capacities or one's particular needs. But even if some kind of super-physician could make that judgment in his or her own head, what I am to make of the assurance that a lack of responsibility applies in this case? Might this doctor be corrupt? Perhaps one of the strangers has bribed the physician to make that pronouncement. Or perhaps the doctor is secretly harboring some enmity for me. The transaction here proposed, after all, takes place in an only middling v world, in which the use of exploitative strategies is not transparent.

The assurance that the strangers' norms are at least as good as mine is equally, and probably more, problematic than the quasi-medical judgment about moral responsibility for disease. I suppose that one could imagine a magistrate or a committee somewhere that is in charge of evaluating the conduct of persons and of ascertaining the degree to which they lead honest, sober, and prudent lives. But that person or body would be subject to all the failings of the super-doctor, and perhaps more. After all, since that person or body would be charged not just with factual but also with normative evaluations, it would be possible for it to be subject not just to corruption (and who, after all, would ascertain the honesty of the ascertainers of honesty?) but to systematic bias and ideological blindness as well.[12]

Barring a solution to these problems, then, I think that the claim that utilitarianism lacks a concept of self-ownership robust enough to deal with real-world intuitive objections is vastly overrated. We should conclude that there are good reasons for utilitarians to support self-ownership in all but a few unusual cases.

WORLD OWNERSHIP

I have already begun to address the question of how the world might be divided up among people to achieve, through the medium of many exchanges, an optimal outcome. My suggestion is that world ownership might be capable of compensating for some of the shortcomings of self-ownership. I now try to fill in my conception, though one should be aware that because of the (often) lower κ values associated with appropriation of material things, the matter is trickier than with self-ownership.

What is an ideal distribution of wealth? In the theories of justice advanced by Nozick[13] and Gauthier,[14] some initial state of distribution that arises out of a state of nature is justified; any subsequent distribution that arises out of the initial distribution through morally legitimate exchanges is assumed to be just. Nozick argues that the rules of just exchange are justice preserving, just as the rules of inference are truth preserving. To the extent that those rules have been violated, one has a morally legitimate reason to change a distribution on the grounds of rectificatory justice, but no redistribution would otherwise be allowed.

The role of an ideal distribution in this theory is not quite the same. Rather, it is what Nozick would call a "patterned" theory in that it uses a criterion of continuing validity to assess the pattern of distribution. In theory, the distribution I propose would be ideal to bring about through a redistribution at some time. Such a redistribution would not necessarily need to be justified as a rectification of past wrongs.

Of course, the various imperfections of the world make redistribution from any given distribution rather problematic, as we shall see. But since I have already discussed the role that world ownership may have when played off against self-ownership, and since the institutions discussed in the next main section are largely concerned with preserving both self-ownership and world ownership, it is important to address the question of just what such institutions would, ideally, be acting in defense of.

One possibility would be to distribute worldly wealth in accordance with what are sometimes called *Lockean provisos*. Simple and straightforward rules for the just distribution of parts of the world go back to John Locke.[15] They have a general form as follows: one must justly claim as one's own any material object in the world as long as by that appropriation one leaves no other person worse off. Initial ownership thus attaches to the right of first possession. Subsequent title to material objects is achieved by obtaining the consent of the owners, often through gift, inheritance, or trade of labor or other objects.

This principle is more popular among antiutilitarian writers[16] than among utilitarians, probably because there are alternative schemes of distribution that, if interpersonal comparisons of utility are permitted, seem to be more plausibly utility maximizing than a simple rule of right of first possession. Those who arrive late in the scramble for appropriations can find themselves with far smaller shares than would be optimal: they may become poor and propertyless proletarians working for a handful of barons, which on the face of it seems unlikely to be the best situation for aggregate well-being.

At least one self-identified utilitarian, however, has defended the right of first possession as a utilitarian rule for distribution of material objects. Richard Epstein has argued that while alternative schemes of distribution and redistribution may look better in theory than does any kind of Lockean proviso, in practice something like this rule is likely to be superior to its competitors because the costs of alternative schemes are too great to make them worthwhile.[17]

Whether Epstein is right in this contention turns on an empirical matter that cannot be definitively resolved here. If κ turns out to be quite low in any situation of initial distribution, he is most likely right because when interpersonal comparisons of well-being are difficult or impossible, it is hard to know how in any straightforward matter to sort out competing claims about who could make the best use of material objects. If I claim more land than you on a newly discovered island because I think I would get well-being out of eating more food or just enjoying the view of unimproved wilderness, and you claim likewise, it would be difficult to know how to settle our dispute. A simple rule that enables us to coordinate on a solution would be most desirable. But if interpersonal comparisons are not so difficult, better solutions are available for a utilitarian.

An alternative to Lockean provisos is an *equal* distribution. Some utilitarians, conjoining the principle of utility with a general thesis that the marginal utility of material wealth declines for most persons, seem to suggest that an ideal distribution is an equal one. In a world in which both exchange and self-ownership are common or universal practices, however, it does not seem clear that even if the marginal utility of material goods declines at a roughly equal rate for most people that an equal distribution would lead to anything like a utility-optimal outcome.

If we assume that people marshall both their own talents and their share of the world for the sake of exchange, the likely consequence would be a most *unequal* distribution of material property. The natural endowments of different persons differ. Some are robust and healthy, others weak and sick. Some have a profusion of valuable talents, others few or none. If all started out with equal shares of the world, the likely consequence would be a world in which some would be wealthy and others impoverished. Even granting the thesis of the declining marginal utility of wealth, this outcome could hardly be called optimal.

But egalitarian utilitarians may well be on the right track. It is possible in theory to rate each individual in terms of his or her productive capacity, that is, in terms of his or her potential aggregate output per unit time. This aggregate output could conceivably be measured according to either a money value or a *value numeraire*. If each individual has a production function in which labor and capital are fully substitutable, it is possible to equalize this output per individual by making appropriate allotments of material wealth to each.[18] Should such a distribution obtain, every individual would be capable of producing for oneself a roughly equal amount of wealth; thus an *egalitarian baseline* of sorts would be an ideal distribution from a utilitarian perspective.

Not everyone would necessarily work. Some persons might be so severely handicapped as to be largely incapable of making a productive contribution; their shares of wealth should be large enough to permit them to survive as socially honorable rentiers. To the extent that the marginal utility of wealth declines equally for all individuals, then, such a distribution should lead to a utility-optimal outcome. Of course, under a regime of free exchange, not all individuals would necessarily produce the same amount of wealth if they do not have identical preferences for consumption and leisure. Some persons may choose to produce only enough to live on and devote the rest of their lives to leisurely pursuits, while others with more expensive tastes may work much longer—sacrificing leisure—to be capable of purchasing what they desire.

Of course, one may wonder to what extent the marginal utility of wealth does decline for each individual. Those critics of utilitarianism who do not think it sufficiently egalitarian have often raised the possibility that, at least in principle, the marginal utility of wealth does not so decline. There are, of course, cases in which it does not, one of which I discuss shortly. In general, however, the principle is a fairly sound normative generalization, which provides a good reason for a fair amount of egalitarianism in distribution. But even to the extent that this generalization is not sound, it is possible to construct a subsidiary argument for utilitarian egalitarianism based on the problem of evolutionary stability. To see how, let us apply some more analysis that stems from interpersonal comparisons of well-being.

For practical purposes, what seems to be declining may not necessarily be marginal utility per se but rather the quality of information of utility effects as the wealth of an individual increases. For a first number of marginal units of wealth, those that make the difference for an individual between slow death and biological subsistence, the κ values are quite high. Everyone knows and understands what a terrible fate starvation is. For the next several units, those units that to an individual might make the difference between possessing the rudiments of culture and leisure and a life of nothing but drudgery and boredom, κ is also quite high. Indeed, the value of κ for these units of wealth may be even higher than those that provide for mere biological subsistence since for at least some of us, nonexistence would be preferable to a life that consists of nothing but the meanest kind of toil.

After some rudiments of culture have been secured, κ probably declines a bit: the contribution to one's well-being of basic literacy is quite clear, but the contribution of being able to read Attic Greek is less clear. It is logically (and perhaps in some cases psychologically) possible that the latter is a centrally constitutive component of one's well-being. But this psychological propensity resides deep in the psyche: if someone claims that he should be given some useful resource because he really needs to learn to read Attic Greek, our skepticism about his claim seems much more readily justifiable than another's claim that she really needs to learn how to read her own language.

As we advance into the realm of more and more resource-costly goods, the κ values decline ever deeper. Perhaps a rich man's toys really do make more of a measurable contribution to some aggregate measure of welfare than a poor woman's meal. But in the rich man's case especially, we might reasonably infer self-servingness in the claim that his toys are a better use of resources than another person's dinner.

From an understanding that the quality of utility information for wealth declines with marginal increases in wealth, we can construct an argument for a distribution of things in the world that ensures a rough equality in the productive capacity of persons. Even to the extent that marginal utility itself does not decline, an initial distribution that fails to take into account the fact of declining marginal κ values would reward those who engage in perverse behaviors at the point of distribution.

If we were to take at face value all claims about what parts of the world would be worth to agents, we would incite the selfish to make outrageous claims to the effect that they would be greatly benefitted by having disproportionate shares of the world's wealth. In such claims, disproportionality would be (allegedly) justified by the claim that those who were most shrewd in pursuing their self-interest had utility functions such that they would be able to singlehandedly boost aggregate well-being by doing no work at all and consuming vast quantities of goods produced by others. Allowing that kind of lopsided distribution would surely drive utilitarianism into extinction in very short order.

Hostile critics would claim that even to the extent that my generalization is correct, it is still only a quasi-empirical generalization, which cannot rule out lopsided distributions in principle, and that (some of) our moral convictions seem to invoke egalitarian principles. Quite true, but as always, there is no reason to believe that our moral convictions are tuned to all factual worlds. I consider here one exception to my generalization. If my critics believe that—as a factual matter—there are other weaknesses in my generalization, I invite them to point them out with specificity rather than merely gesturing toward a logical possibility.

An important exception is to be made in my generalization as follows: even in a world in which the productive capacities of persons are roughly equal, certain persons may be ill served by such a distribution. Some people may not only be so severely handicapped as to be eligible to fill the roll of honorable rentiers but also may suffer from medical conditions so costly to control that the amount of wealth they would produce if their productive capacities were roughly equal to those of other persons would be insufficient to give them lives worth living. It may not be possible to insure against some of these conditions: they may be so rare that it would be unreasonable to expect people to exercise rational foresight in insuring against them, or they may occur in such a way that these people might not otherwise be able to be held rationally accountable for them. Being born with a severe condition is the most obvious case, although there could certainly be others.

These people might very well be able to claim a share of the world's wealth that would give them greater productive capacity than the norm. But this disproportionality would not be deeply problematic, and it is important to see why. (1) Ex hypothesi, there is no problem with moral hazard: risks that cannot be insured against cannot raise this problem. (2) The κ values for the consumption of additional wealth in this case are high rather than low because the use of wealth is to prevent some conditions (physical pain and suffering) and facilitate others (minimal human flourishing), the utility value of which is not controversial. For this case, then, and for others that are structurally similar (if they exist) any utilitarian principle of equality might be overridden.

There is an additional problem to be considered, that of *inequality and cultural growth*. By "cultural growth" I mean the accumulation and improvement of knowledge, technological capacities, and artistic achievement over time. Determining its preconditions is a complex scientific matter, and much of what I have to say about it in this short discussion is largely speculation. There is at least some cause for believing that some kind of inequality in an initial distribution of wealth may be a precondition of cultural growth. The removal of certain persons from the cares of earning a living may be necessary, for example, to promote pure research that over the long run makes possible technological change. The existence of a well-off class also might, in the right factual circumstances, be a spur to artistic achievement by providing leisure to people who may choose to pursue artistic careers, by providing the resources for artistic patronage, or both. Also, the accumulation of unusual amounts of economic capital in a few hands may also be a precondition to certain kinds of change; if there are sufficiently marked economies of scale in technological investment, a few large capitalists might well establish industrial research laboratories, whereas numerous small producers may not.

If these facts hold, what of them? Some very difficult questions of intergenerational justice are to be faced here. If a distribution that equalizes productive capacities is ceteris paribus a utility-superior one but a more inegalitarian distribution might allow technical development, we might ask whether we may legitimately impose utility sacrifices on earlier generations for the sake of later ones. Theories of justice that are distribution-sensitive would tend to be opposed to the imposition of sacrifices on earlier generations for the sake of later ones.[19] But utilitarianism of my variety is not directly distribution-sensitive. In principle it may endorse serious sacrifices for certain early generations.

The history of the industrial West has had its share of inegalitarian moral horrors, as any reader of Dickens's novels or Marx's section of *Capital* on primitive accumulation knows.[20] The history of the industrial East—Stalin's Soviet Union in particular—contains horrors far greater. But the awful path tread by progress has also achieved some remarkable effects. I think it is hard for an inhabitant of the late twentieth century to imagine vividly the scale of human suffering eliminated by the technological progress of the last two centuries. And if there is no technological regress, the particular kinds of suffering eliminated will not plague humankind again.

Over the course of centuries, the aggregate amount of suffering might well make us think that the history was worth it. Exactly whether it was worth it is too large an issue to be addressed here, although my intuition leans strongly toward an affirmative answer. For any sufficiently distant period in history, there is a large mass of human achievements the elimination of which would create an almost certain regress in well-being. Consider even the comparatively advanced and comfortable century of John Stuart Mill. Suppose that in the name of distributive justice, certain policies had caused cultural growth to stop or stagnate. Imagine all the things that humanity would lack. Elementary medical achievements such as antibiotics or the public health measures that eliminated tuberculosis, for example, would not exist. The absence of efficient contraceptives would have imposed on women (or on both sexes, had more gender-egalitarian social arrangements somehow been brought into existence) the unhappy trade-off of long periods of celibacy for professional and cultural achievement. Without the new technologies of information recording and transmission, many of the highest cultural achievements of our age would be inaccessible to the vast majority of the population. The edifying and uplifting revelation of the workings of the universe and the origins of humanity would never have been achieved. The list of hypothetically lost accomplishments goes on and on and on, and placed next to them mere egalitarianism seems to be a rather dubious achievement.[21]

The question of just what technological progress would achieve remains an empirical one. There is no reason in principle why the parade of human achievement should not continue. Certainly plenty of tasks remain to be done. There is an additional consideration, however, with respect to inequality. Given that we must always start from some distribution and some level of cultural achievement, the argument from inequality to greater achievement is always open to abuse; it may be correct, but it may also simply serve as a rationalization by those who wish to keep or acquire amounts of wealth that would otherwise be thought morally illegitimate. Permitting too much inequality for the reason of cultural advancement may have the same pernicious effect that other forms of inequality have: it may reward those who are powerful and egoistical in a competition with the more altruistic, and thus undermine the evolutionary stability of the latter.

I conclude, therefore, that the argument for cultural advancement to justify inequality in distribution is rather limited. Exactly how limited requires another book-length study to determine, but the possibility of corruption is one to remember. The fact that it is remembered by most prudent minds may do much to explain why people have egalitarian, "counterutilitarian" intuitions.

Adequacy

Are self-ownership and world ownership enough? Some will object that my idea of what people ought to own leaves out too much. Communitarians in particular may charge that it focuses too narrowly on mere wealth and personal liberties of the exclusion to the goods of human community and mutual recognition. Even a Rawlsian may wonder where in my conception one might find the primary good of the social bases of self-respect. These charges are partly correct and partly misinterpretations, albeit misinterpretations made easily understandable by the rather abstract manner in which this argument has been proceeding.

No doubt some measure of confusion stems purely from abstraction, so that an incautious reader might think that I imagine the world to consist of socially atomic individuals who find themselves linked from time to time in binary units through the cash nexus. Certainly the use of the language of ownership and exchange would contribute to such a view. But such an inference is incorrect. A closer look at specific requirements of distribution would show, in many cases, complex forms of collective and public provision of goods, if for no other reason than that the structure of the world requires that some goods—like environmental protection—be provided publicly. Furthermore, cultural and economic development often require both public lives—through, for example, the exchange of information—and public provision of goods, such as education.

One should suspect, however, that communitarian objectors have more in mind. They might deplore the absence of the public provision of various symbolic goods or the public protection of ways of life. A regime of ownership and contracts does not provide for these goods directly, but such institutions do not derogate the goods of recognition, community, or self-respect. Nothing in the conception of utility that is defended here necessarily rules out the weighing of these goods. But to a large extent, one should doubt that to the degree that self-ownership and some measure of world ownership are protected, any further political intervention would be needed to achieve these other goods. Persons who are free to dispose of themselves, who have adequate means to provide themselves with some goods and some leisure, should be perfectly competent to provide goods of recognition and community for themselves. If they wish the goods of a community, they may pool their resources to raise temples to their gods or meeting halls for their cultural associations. They may coordinate their leisure for religious worship or the joint pursuit of intellectual, athletic, or aesthetic avocations.[22]

As for the good of self-respect, it is normally the case that when one has a means for making oneself a living and knows that one is protected in one's person by rules of justice, self-respect will follow. One may be the victim of slurs and insults, but slurs and insults have their greatest effect when they are the markers and the signs of a dangerous and physically hostile world. To address a crude epithet to a member of a persecuted minority is an attack on that person's self-respect because it is a reminder of real violence in the past and potential violence in the future. But to address an analogous epithet to a person secure in oneself and possessions is likely to elicit nothing, under normal circumstances, but a cold stare.

Of course, to some extent, there are certain goods of community that my conception of ownership does not protect. The communitarian utility of knowing myself to be a member of the right church; or of seeing my symbols and markers of uprightness and decency enforced by gendarmes and prisons—these things would all be denied to me. One can cheerfully admit that the institutions of ownership provide no room for the protection of "sacred" traditions of any particular community—and what of it?

In the most plausible analysis, the utility of symbols and traditions—while it may be perfectly real—is of dreadfully low-κ value. *Pace* Hegel and his late communitarian progeny, it is simply not the case that all persons crave the goods of community to the same extent that all persons crave food or the absence of pain. There is, in fact, considerable human variability concerning the recognition of any possible set of communitarian goods.[23] Common sense and experience teach us that some find solace in religious communities but that others strike out in atheist or radically Protestant directions. Some stir to the flag and the sounds of martial music; others revel in rootless cosmopolitanism. Some crave the good opinion of the world, while others march resolutely to their own drummer.

Because communitarian goods have low-κ values, there is the same problem of extending political recognition to them as there is for extending political recognition to the desire for lordship or harm, which would interfere with self-ownership, or the desire for special goodies, which would interfere with roughly egalitarian world ownership. A political economy that made such an extension would touch off a run of conflicting claims that would be a disaster for impartial utilitarians. Of course, the case of communitarian goods is somewhat different: instead of utilitarians being threatened with exploitation by those who are partial to themselves, the threat may well be the exploitation of the impartial by those who are partial to a favored community or tradition.

However, there is no reason why a moral world cannot be invaded by selfish groups, as well as by selfish individuals. Any group—be it composed of religious believers, patriots, or devotees of some collectivist vision of the good life—might be able to represent its utility from the use of social resources for the protection of its traditions, which are of greater value than those that could be used for other purposes. For example, what I might use as my own property might—if we accepted certain communitarian arguments—be taxed away from me to pay for the expenses of fighting a "war on drugs" (or liquor or dirty books or what have you), the motivation for which is that some group wishes to have a world in which its particularistic precepts are especially protected from challenge. It is, as always, logically and psychologically possible that such a protection could be utility-optimal. But, as is also always the case with low-κ goods, it could be that the partisans of the war on drugs are simply misrepresenting the utilities that can be found nowhere, except deep in their skulls, in the hope of cadging resources from the impartial and the benevolent. If the impartial and the benevolent accede to this pressure from the partial and (collectively, perhaps) self-interested, so much for the worse for the evolutionary success of the former.

Political Institutions for Imperfectia

In Imperfectia, unlike in Communia or Libertaria, getting a set of self-enforcing rules can be a tricky matter. Some, one would hope much, cooperation will emerge spontaneously. But in a lower-v world, there are more opportunities for defecting from cooperation, and therefore a more complex solution will be necessary to get a social equilibrium with desirable properties. In Imperfectia, therefore, we are much more likely to find institutions like the state playing a more complex role in maintaining social order.

The abstract form of an organized institution is one in which there is a social division of labor between agents who monitor the behavior of other agents, and punish certain kinds of behavior, and those who do not. Under the regime of property rights just described, monitoring agents would have to detect invasions of properties and contracts that their holders could not deter on their own, as well as administer penalties—deprivations of utility sufficient to deter agents from these invasions.[24] As was demonstrated by Calvert's models, the practical utility for a special group of agents who monitor the conduct of all other agents stems from the prohibitive cost of having every agent monitor every other agent. But the principals may be corruptible: they may attempt to extort utility from others by threatening to find violations where there are none, or they may attempt to share in the misbehavior of other agents by failing to find violations where violations in fact exist. If opportunists find a way into the ranks of the watchers, they and their norms will have found an extraordinarily efficient way to invade a moral world. *Quo custodiet ipsos custodes?*

One may set up a group of meta-watchers for the watchers. There are special police officers for the police, usually in departments of internal affairs; trial judges are watched over by appellate judges; and so on. But of course, a "meta" group will itself be subject to corruption by those over whom it is supposed to watch. Indeed, as many levels of review as can be set up can be corrupted. So long as there is not an infinite number of levels of review, there will always be an incentive for an egoist or some other villain to try to find a way into the topmost level of oversight.

One possible solution for Imperfectia would be to try to identify incorruptible individuals and to install them at the top level or levels of oversight. From their lofty positions, these incorruptible persons would detect and deter failures to detect and deter failures, and so on, down to the lowest level of review, thus keeping the entire system running well. There is nothing impossible about such a solution in theory. In practice, however, it creates two insoluble problems.

First, the members of this moral elite are unlikely to be infallibly marked in any way, shape, or form. Persons do not walk about with "Incorruptible" stamped on their foreheads. But because they are not infallibly marked, someone must be responsible for choosing them. But if the someones who are to do the choosing are just as inclined to self-interest as the rest of humanity, it is more than a little likely that various forms of corruption can be brought to bear on the choosers to choose the corruptible as members of the moral elite.[25] Who chooses the watchers to watch the watchers? It does no good to refer to any other group since then, who chooses the choosers?

Second, the existence of a moral elite to which persons may be from time to time elected creates a perverse incentive to an exploiter—because of the potentially great benefits that could be reaped from being a corrupted member of that elite—to mimic whatever criteria might be used to select the members. I might find it foolish to spend twenty years of my life leading outwardly the most upright and virtuous existence imaginable, harboring my essential badness deep in my heart simply so that I can swindle my neighbor out of a bicycle. But it may not be at all foolish to spend those same twenty years putting up a false front if it will get me elected to a position from which I can rake in untold amounts of graft and gratify lust upon lust.

A pyramidal structure of political control thus creates a perverse moral incentive, which in turn exacerbates the selection problem for any possible moral elite. The vicious infinite regress of institutional structure cannot be escaped that easily.

One possible step away from the model of the pyramid would be not to have a single top principal but rather multiple principals with overlapping jurisdictions. Thus, for example, police officers are monitored not just by departments of internal affairs and internal conduct review boards but also by civilian review boards, by public prosecutors, by elected officials such as mayors and governors, and even to some extent by private citizens through courts of civil law. In a world in which we are uncertain about the ethical soundness of individuals but know that some individuals are more sound than others, we might maximize the chances of detecting and deterring violations by lower-level agents by having a number of different principals who are capable of detecting violations.

In this theory, the more branches of review in existence, the greater the likelihood that there will be at least one branch on which there are honorable persons who will do the right thing. It may be that the mayor, the chief of police, and the internal review board turn a blind eye to the extortion by the police of private citizens; these worthies may even be on the take themselves. But perhaps there is also a young district attorney, a paragon of rectitude, whose criminal prosecution of the malefactors will put an end to corrupt practices.

This vision is an attractive one. Unfortunately, while the division of powers into multiple branches of review may allow more opportunities for do-righters to put a stop to do-wrongers, it will also allow do-wrongers more opportunities to do wrong. Certain kinds of misdeeds may be foreclosed, but opportunities for new ones will be opened. Any kind of review that can impose sanctions provides a road to corruption. The mayor, the chief of police, and the police internal review board may all be upright and honorable, but if there is somewhere a villainous young district attorney who can threaten to harass police officers with prosecution if they do not pay graft, either (1) the other branches of review will fail to do their jobs and there will be corruption anew, or (2) the other branches will do their jobs, the police will be caught in a double bind, and they may well collapse as a consequence.

One might try to defend the "multiple branches of review" model by arguing that the conflict between the good mayor and the bad prosecutor could be resolved by giving the mayor authority over the prosecutor. But to do so is not an answer since this would simply restore the pyramid in place of the multiple branches of review. The potential existence of the conflict, however, is important and feeds into a better model.

A chain of monitors can be corrupted as long as the top monitor is corrupt or incompetent. But a *circle* of monitors has no top and thus can weed out corrupt monitors. Consider this: Mephistopheles is charged with detecting and deterring wrongdoing by Beelzebub, Beelzebub is charged with detecting and deterring wrongdoing by Asmodeus, and Asmodeus is charged with detecting and deterring wrongdoing by Mephistopheles. In this little universe, what goes around really does come around. If Beelzebub attempts to use his position over Asmodeus to extort goodies from the latter and Mephistopheles refuses to stop this wrongdoing, Asmodeus can punish—and has an incentive to punish—Mephistopheles. An attempt at wrongdoing anywhere else in the circle will provoke a similar response, with different names attached to different roles.

Such an institutional arrangement would exploit *negative feedback*; that is, any perturbation in the system can generate a counteraction, which will push the system back into equilibrium.[26] Negative feedback of exactly this kind is built into Calvert's simple model: the director delegates punishments and is in turn punished should he or she fail to punish.

To keep equilibrium up, it is necessary to have a link in the chain of feedback that is not too corrupt. In Imperfectia, the population as a whole may serve in that capacity. The reason that the whole population may be the unit best suited to the task of some oversight is that no official is likely to have enough wealth on hand to make a side payment to the whole population, or even to a substantial part of it. Even if the official did, the substantial costs of so doing would take much of the fun out of corruption. *Democracy* is thus the safeguard of the constitution of the society.

The detection and deterrence of wrongdoing by political officials can be thought of as a kind of public goods provision. One person may bear the costs of doing so, but the benefits—in the form of a corruption-free administration of justice—may be spread very thinly over a large number of people. In this theory, political institutions may work as follows: agents of the state watch over individual citizens; there is a variety of punishment mechanisms available to deter wrongdoing by citizens. There is also a pyramid of superagents over the agents of the state whose job is to make sure that lower-level agents do their jobs. In turn, individual citizens monitor the performance of the state and have a mechanism for punishing actors in the form of a standing threat of removal from office, usually through some kind of voting mechanism. The incentive for individual citizens to monitor and vote stems from some form of mutual interest.

The mutual interest is crucial here because without it or some other normative proxy, it is hard to see what might motivate individuals to keep themselves informed about public affairs and to vote. There are at least two possible explanations, either one of which is adequate to explain political participation.

The first explanation suggests that some degree of mutual sympathy plays a part in political life. In an election in a large political system, the chances of any individual's vote actually making a difference is vanishingly small: perhaps a hundred million to one against.[27] But the aggregate effects of corruption in a large political system are quite large. Even if a single corrupt president cost every citizen only a single unit of utility, the aggregate loss in a nation of a quarter billion persons would be staggeringly large. The expected utility for an impartial altruist of voting to throw the crook out (assuming the replacement is not so corrupt) would actually be measurably large: 2.5 utils. While persons are not impartial altruists for the most part, it is unrealistic to deny that they have some sympathy for one another, even for strangers, and this may be enough to motivate the sympathetic and rational to vote.[28]

The second explanation for political participation appeals to self-interest more narrowly understood. Even if persons are not sympathetic to one another, there may still be an equilibrium in which individuals participate in politics. If a rule that requires political participation is sufficiently widespread and political participation is a public good, iteration and reciprocity alone may be enough to explain it. It is unlikely that in a large society an explanation like that of Michael Taylor based on pure conditional cooperation, will succeed because it is too difficult to properly perceive defections. But a general rule of political participation combined with mild social sanctions— shaming those who do not participate and those who do not shame those who do not participate, say—against nonparticipators could be self-enforcing, especially if the costs of participation are not high.

One clear problem of institutional design is lowering the cost of intelligent political participation; if participation is simply too costly, even fairly altruistic agents may fail to participate, even under rules that penalize nonparticipation. There are a number of ways in which these costs might be lowered.

First, there is the *splitting of institutions*. The simplest form of representative government imaginable might be that in which a single executive is subject to election. This elected prince has sole oversight responsibility. Unfortunately, the costs of oversight of this elected prince in any large polity will be very high. His ability to conceal information would be potentially very large. Since much of his activity will necessarily be undertaken by subordinates without his knowledge or control—one man can, after all, only do so much—he may be able to plausibly deny any particular instance of wrongdoing. Also, if all agents of the state are answerable directly to him and to him alone, he may be able to punish—slyly—other persons who inquire too closely into his activities. Finally, since his activities will necessarily be spread over a whole sovereignty, it may be quite hard to scrutinize the whole of his activities and those of his underlings to find a pattern of activities from which an inference of corruption could be made.

Any given agent may well be aware of a number of personal grievances. But acts of the state that lead merely to individual grievances may be indicative either of the moral unfitness for office of those who run the state or of plain bad luck. An innocent man may be wrongly convicted of a crime because of the malfeasance of prosecutors or judges. But he may also be convicted even when prosecutors and judges were following proper procedures simply through an unfortunate conjunction of circumstances. It may often be the case that only by looking at a whole system can one infer malfeasance. But looking at that whole system may be prohibitively costly if the whole system is too large.

There are different ways to reduce the costs of participation. One may divide participation by dividing responsibilities, and one may opt for government by representation. By so dividing participation, one may take advantage of economies of smaller scale. Rather than overseeing a single elected prince, one may prefer to monitor a president, a governor, and a mayor. So doing may actually be less costly than overseeing a single official because the individual realms of activity of each official will be easier to survey, and thus patterns of wrongdoing can become easier to infer. One may also choose to send representatives, who will devote all of their time to monitoring other officials.

This is not the place to begin a long technical discussion on the different possible patterns of organizing democratic control; it should be sufficient to note that any number of different organizational arrangements might be given different schedules of the costs of political participation. There are certain devices, however, whose role in potentially reducing costs of political monitoring is often sufficiently salient that they merit additional notice.

A second way of lowering political costs is to ensure the *free flow of information*. That political actors must actually be able to determine what rulers are doing in order to assess their fitness seems almost too obvious to be worth mentioning. There are, however, different interpretations of just what ought to be freely expressible. Certain legal interpreters believe that institutional guarantees of information flow—such as the free speech and press provisions of the First Amendment of the U.S. Constitution—protect only political speech, that is, speech about legislative proposals or executive action.[29] Defenders of such propositions often invoke what they think are utilitarian arguments—arguments that an amalgamation of majority preferences about nonpolitical expressions ought to triumph on simply utilitarian grounds. Such an interpretation is not obviously mistaken, but it seems unlikely that this utilitarian analysis of political institutions will uphold it. Why not?

Careful readers will note that certain distributive questions have been left open. Though I argue that the κ of certain goods is low, it is far from clear that this condition always obtains. Perhaps through some arts of persuasion or exposure to new information, we may actually raise the κ. Through different kinds of scientific or artistic expression, for instance, we may come to believe that the existence of public art—which might be thought of as a somewhat low-κ good—is actually a fairly high-κ good; through exposure to it, we may come to have an ever better appreciation of its value, and we may thus be capable of having for it more equitable distributive institutions. We may, through a process of edification, come to believe it is a good thing to provide art as a public good rather than to rely only on private provision.

Of course, scientific or artistic expression may also show that what we thought to be high-κ goods are really low-κ goods. Our contact with a wider range of persons—something that might be made possible through literature—may convince us that what we thought was universally valued is in fact only valued parochially, and hence something we thought ought to have been distributed publicly should have been distributed only through private provision.

Artistic and scientific speech may also help us to make judgments about the character of specific persons, classes of person, or persons in general. We might find that

people we thought normatively untrustworthy are trustworthy or (more pessimisti-
cally) vice versa. Such information as may be communicated by such expressions may
turn out—for reasons discussed at greater length in chapter 7—to be morally and
politically relevant.

Third, to find the most important means of all for reducing the costs of running
a polity, we must consider carefully *the role of procedures*. Established rules of conduct, in addition to providing coordinating functions (e.g., determining just when to
hold elections), also play a role in reducing the cost of evaluating the fitness of rulers
by reducing the complexity of figuring out their conduct. One may often use the
adherence of officials to rules as a measure of whether they are doing their jobs properly or whether they are attempting to expropriate the powers of the state for their
own interests.

Consider, for a simple example, a rule of legal procedure such as that requiring
law officers to acquire a warrant for the search and seizure of private property by
showing the probable existence of criminal activity to a magistrate. Officials may be
punished for violating the rule directly, through jailings, fines, or dismissal, or indirectly, by exclusion of improperly garnered evidence from future legal proceedings.
Such a rule potentially impairs the efficiency of the police, which in turn impairs their
ability to detect and deter criminal activity. Why, then, should it be tolerated?

In a world in which all law officers were known to be incorruptible, it would be
hard to justify the existence of such a procedure; evidence garnered by them in whatever manner might be considered legal. Unhappily, if law officers are corrupt in any
number of ways, the threat of search could be used in any number of ways to further
corrupt ends. Searches and seizures are disruptive to the lives of those subject to them;
in the case of body searches, they can be violations of the most intimate kind of personal dignity. Law officers subject to merely venal corruption might attempt to extort
payoffs from citizens for the privilege of merely being let alone. Bigoted law officers
may use searches and seizures as forms of harassment against whatever class of persons is the object of their hatred.

One could, of course, imagine a regime in which politically active persons tried
to monitor searches on a case-by-case basis. They might well ask of any given search,
"Was it really necessary? Was the aim of such a search the detection of criminal activity, or was it to harass or intimidate the victim of either extortion or hatred?" Elec-
toral or other procedures could be used to punish the police or their supervisors for
an excess of unreasonable searches and seizures. But the information costs of such an
inquiry are likely to be prohibitive, given (1) the large number of such activities that
the police would be expected to conduct and (2) the fact that corrupt officers would
have a rational incentive to lie about or at least rationalize the motives that underlie
their activities.

A simple universal rule that triggers punishment whenever it is violated might
well be more cost-effective. The proper set of rules for any given imperfect state might
vary; the determination of the right set would, again, be rather difficult *ex ante*, for it
would depend on determining the modi operandi of potentially corrupt officials. Again,
I do not want to explore the exact details of all possible factual universes—that, too,
would be a book in itself. I merely want to point out why institutions that utilitarians
would want to foster could have apparently antiutilitarian designs. Legal procedure

may appear to be a set of deontological constraints for officials, but it is not shown to be counterutilitarian thereby.

Of course, with this, as with so many other cases, the question arises of when to break the rules and when to remake them. These are matters for discussion in chapter 7.

Utilitarian Dystopias

In a normatively abysmal world, there are two possibilities: the first is a form of Hobbesian chaos; the second, rule by a self-serving faction. I have little to say about Hobbesian chaos, except that any utilitarians who might happen to find themselves in the midst of it would be unlikely to be much better behaved than the rest of humanity. Any acts of considerable charity by the carriers of utilitarian norms would probably only result in the extinction of those norms in relatively short order, as their carriers would surely be exploited to as great a degree as possible by other frightened, nasty, brutal persons. Utilitarians would probably be best advised simply to cling to survival, pass on their norms as best they can, and hope for the coming of brighter days.

In worlds governed by factions, however, there might still be things for utilitarians to prefer. I distinguish between two kinds of worlds governed by factions: venal oligarchies and moral tyrannies. Both kinds of rule by faction are characterized by classes of persons who share norms of mutual concern, but these are norms of partiality. Members of the ruling classes can thus coordinate with one another on the project of maintaining rule and come to the aid of one another, but they may be rather deeply unconcerned with the well-being of those outside the ruling class. These norms can be instantiated in self-enforcing rules: one cooperates with one's ruling class in oppressing others and sanctions those who fail to cooperate in the project. A group can thus squeeze the social equilibrium toward a part of the feasible set of equilibria, grabbing as much as it can of the gains from social cooperation while leaving others only slightly better off than they might have been under a state-of-nature status quo.

A *venal oligarchy* is ruled by a faction that establishes what Margaret Levi has identified as a predatory state, that is, a state whose function is to extract wealth from other persons and transfer it to its rulers.[30] The preferences of the rulers are simply for the consumption of wealth and what it brings—pleasure and leisure, for the greatest part. Historically, many different kinds of state might be venal oligarchies; extractive feudal and slave societies are the classic examples but certainly not the only ones. Capitalist societies, at least in Marxist views, might also be venal oligarchies in which the bourgeoisie acts as the ruling class, with a state apparatus that works on its behalf. Different kinds of such societies might be held together by different systems of rules, which sociologists would identify as ideologies and rational choice theorists as systems of equilibrium-selecting coordination: Aristotelian natural rulership combined with patriotic duty in slaveholding societies or (more controversially) ideologies of possessive individualism and natural law in capitalist societies.

While a venal oligarchy is primarily concerned with extracting wealth, it should not be imagined that it might serve its ends only by brute pillage and plunder. If the ruling class is so constituted that it is interested in returns of wealth in the far future—returns, often, that might accrue to the descendants of the individuals who actually make up that class—it may actually find that simple plunder or brute force serves its interests rather badly. Other kinds of institutional organization might serve its interests better by promoting economic growth and technological progress; hence, a wide range of economic and property rights might be protected under a venal oligarchy. Only if selfish economic actors can be assured of protection of at least some of the wealth that they create could they have an incentive to accumulate greater wealth over time from which greater amounts of wealth might be extracted in the future. A venal oligarchy in which such rights are protected might be called *progressive*.

Tactics for ruling a population might also be quite varied. While compliance might often be extorted at the point of a sword, managing a large population over the long term might be better served by gentler devices. Rules of legal procedure and guarantees of various civil and social rights, even to the point of some redistribution, may serve to convince a subject population that a given social order is at least somewhat humane and fair and thus encourage at least quasi-voluntary compliance. There are many situations in which provision of a certain level of material comfort and personal liberty is a more effective tactic of rule than out-and-out oppression. A man who has little to lose can swiftly become a menace to himself and others in any number of ways: drugs, crime, terrorism. But he who has some material comfort and the freedom to pursue some diversion that suits his nature (the church of his choice, interesting consumer goods, television, the latest fad in literary criticism) might well be a docile subject, especially for the eight hours a day that may be required of him to heap up extortable wealth. Thus, the provision of public goods—security, civil rights, even limited forms of political participation (though liable to be suspended should things get out of hand for the ruling classes)—might be found in states that are in fact venal oligarchies.[31]

A venal oligarchy need in no way be progressive, however. Often it tolerates slavery and exploitation, as well as oppression in pursuit of its political ends. Certainly the best historical examples of institutions like slavery existed under venal oligarchies.[32] Not surprisingly, whenever we hear of institutions like slavery, a grossly lopsided distribution of wealth, or a Roman arena that is pacifying the masses, we are inclined to think that there is exploitation going on, and our intuition that something morally horrible is happening is triggered.

Our intuitions are no doubt correct: the exploiters had taken over. But we might be led into a kind of cognitive confusion by this historical experience. That the exploiters do take over may be a sufficient condition for the emergence of certain kinds of practices, but it need not be a necessary one. A very particular kind of Communia, in which there are no exploiters, might still have forms of personal servitude or a Roman arena. But because of a constant conjunction between exploitation and the bad practices, we may come to have the intuition that the badness inheres in the practices themselves rather than in the conditions under which they emerge. Hence there is another reason for having intuitions about the importance of deontological constraints.

A *moral tyranny* is a rather different kind of dystopia. It, too, is ruled by an elite but not an elite interested in promoting a hedonistic good life for itself. A ruling class of moral tyrants can be composed of self-sacrificing ascetics. Their project is to impose some form of moral purity and conformity on a whole population by indoctrination and force, and perhaps drive that population toward some project as well. A moral tyranny is thus established when a moral idée fixe, generative of bad consequences captures the rulers of a state and allows them to coordinate on some awful project.[33] Moral tyrants may be religious, seeking to found a heavenly kingdom on earth through the imposition of divinely ordained rules of conduct and the extirpation of heretics and nonbelievers. History is littered with examples of religious moral tyrannies. Or they may be possessed by other mystical notions, such as extreme nationalism; of this latter type the German National Socialists, Nazis, are perhaps the paradigm.

Of course, a moral tyranny need not be otherworldly. Its rulers may line their pockets as they hunt out sin and filth. Various forms of cross-fertilization are possible between moral tyrannies and venal oligarchies. Moral tyrants may simply be content to grow rich by extorting wealth while coercing virtue. Or moral tyranny may be a certain kind of venal oligarchy's false front; a religion or a mystical nationalism may be the ideological justification for the existence of what is, in fact, a collective scam. Or both the moral tyrants and the venal oligarchs may be fully sincere, and rulership may be a more or less stable coalition between them. German capitalists might have found the Nazis boorish and crude but a useful ally in the suppression of socialism and the promotion of rearmament; the Nazis, in turn, may have found the capitalists soft and unenthusiastic but a decent source of financial assistance nonetheless.

So far we have an exercise in taxonomy, which may be well and good in itself, but we must ask the question of what use it is in a book on the institutions that utilitarianism might endorse. It is a difficult matter since here we are considering the low-v basement of possible social orders. Often the difference among them in utility optimality is a tricky empirical matter, one that cannot be properly addressed in a theoretical discussion. A case may be made, however, for some standards of evaluation: some kinds of low-v orders may compare favorably to others. To the extent that they do, there may be some small policy payoff for utilitarianism since it might guide what few utilitarian actors there are in making political judgments (to be discussed later).

Does a utilitarian have anything useful to say about the distinction between venal oligarchies and moral tyrannies? The more progressive kinds of venal oligarchy might be preferable to moral tyrannies because the former would be inclined to leave individual agents with the opportunity to make a living—possibly an ever improving living since they may have reasons to encourage technological progress—and to dispose of some of their wealth as they see fit in their private lives. To be sure, they may be exploitative and even harsh, but in a progressive venal oligarchy the welfare of at least many individual persons may be given weight—both through respect for property rights and through a tactic of rule that seeks to prevent desperation in the ruled.

But different kinds of moral tyrannies will be committed to interfering in the private lives of persons—to the extent of not allowing them the churches of their choice, tenure in literature departments, or even anything decent on television. A worldly moral tyranny may compound the exploitation of a venal oligarchy with these latter outrages. An unworldly moral tyranny may be even worse in some respects: since it has no long-term interest in economic development—except, perhaps, insofar as such economic development is instrumental in prosecuting military adventures against heretics or other enemies abroad—it may let helpful institutions of political economy collapse through neglect. Worse, it might actively promote perverse institutions for ideological reasons, thus interfering even with the process of material melioration by private means.

Might it be possible that a moral tyranny approximates the effects of utilitarian institutions in Imperfectia or Libertaria or, if utility information is sufficiently readily available, of Communia? One could at least imagine a governing elite of Fabian socialists, for example. One cannot rule out *ex ante* such a possibility, although in practice it might be quite problematic. A ruling elite that was neither intent on extracting large amounts of wealth—and thus having large resources available for rule—nor motivated by fanaticism, with its attendant harshness, may find itself having trouble controlling a population that consisted largely of amoral and self-seeking individuals, which is one version of what a low-v factual world is. Nonetheless, if such a mild moral tyranny is somehow practicable, it might be preferable in a low-v world to any other elite-governance options.

Comparative Dynamics

The central tendencies of v and κ for any social universe need not be fixed, and consequently the institutional endorsements of utilitarianism may change over time. From this observation, utilitarianism (and sometimes utilitarians) may have things to learn about policy.

As I have already suggested a number of times, there are many ways in which would-be egoists could use the institutions of political economy to exploit others. They may seek to have low-κ utilities recognized as high-κ utilities and thus extort wealth from others—a form of behavior known to political economists as *rent seeking*. They may also attempt to use the institutions of coercion to extort wealth through corruption.

Much of the institutional structure of Imperfectia cannot be explained by its direct utilitarian effects. Legal and political procedures are often costly, difficult, and frustrating. Rules that permit freedom of expression may permit expressions that are either directly or indirectly hurtful to hearers and readers out of proportion to the benefits that accrue to speakers or other listeners. Just as the explanation for why utilitarians might punish noncooperators in Prisoner's Dilemma does not directly refer to the equilibrium of that game, but rather to more indirect consequences of how it is played, the explanation for the structure of political institutions is instead an indirect and evolutionary one. When crime pays, there is a selection pressure toward criminality. When the virtuous are exploited, virtue tends toward extinction. Rewarding exploitation will drive out rules and norms that might otherwise be good, and with them the possibility of institutions that are preferable on utility grounds to those available in a low-v world. Utilitarianism would thus often endorse actions for the sake of maintaining institutions.

An issue that would require more energy and time to discuss than we have room for here may be raised by communitarians: whether the habit of thinking in a moral universe of property and rights makes persons short-sighted and undermines the moral tenor necessary for Imperfectia. I am not convinced that it would be but if the communitarians have a genuine scientific case to be made for such a proposition, I invite them to make it.

If the institutions of an imperfect world do, in fact, fail, the best that utilitarians might be able to hope for is an influence on the choice between venal oligarchy and moral tyranny (and its hybrids). Unless there is somewhere a coterie of powerful and mutually recognitive utilitarians capable of taking over, the task of utilitarians might be largely ideological. The promotion of secularism and rationalism in a religious moral tyranny or of individualism and spirituality in a secular one (or at least values of toleration and diversity), as antidotes to the fanaticism that can serve as the intellectual foundations of a moral tyranny would be one key strategy.[34]

Utilitarians should struggle against a moral tyranny through the promotion of heresy, unless clearly the only alternative to a moral tyranny is Hobbesian chaos. The emergence of a venal oligarchy under these circumstances might actually be an end to be promoted. Why? There are a number of ways in which a venal oligarchy might grow up to become a liberal democracy. In a world in which property rights are sufficiently stabilized, in which there are security and some measure of due process, it may be possible for the selection pressures against virtue to abate somewhat and eventually reverse. Persons involved in business and trade may find it advantageous—because of the effects of reputation, for example—to be honest rather than crooked dealers.

Furthermore, to the extent that persons have private lives that are stabilized by the suppression of violence and cheating by the state, effects of reputation can reward cooperation and, eventually, generosity. When, or if, v reaches a certain critical threshold, the venal oligarchy may wither away and be replaced with a liberal democracy. To the extent that a venal oligarchy is supported by an ideology of constitutionalism and possesses some participatory institutions, it may be that the old institutional forms—which were once only masks—take on genuine political functions.

Moral Conclusions from Institutions

If institutions are the solution to strategic problems of morality, we might begin to see how the institutions that utilitarianism might endorse indicate that utilitarianism is not so counterintuitive as it may seem.

In chapter 1, the argument is made against utilitarianism that it requires horrible acts and imposes excessive costs on agents. But in our examination here, we have found that the kinds of factual worlds in which utilitarianism would be most likely to actually recommend "horrible" or "alienating" acts are the utilitarian utopias, worlds that are very much unlike our own and hence worlds in which our intuitions are unlikely to be reliable judgments. Not for nothing do I call them "utopias," for as we all know, *utopia* means "no place." The worlds in which horrible acts and alienation are most likely to take place are those worlds that utilitarianism tells us to condemn and avoid—utilitarian dystopias. It is natural to react with intuitive revulsion against those practices that emerge in these worlds, in which the exploiters are in charge, since exploitation is something that utilitarians must avoid if utilitarianism is not to be self-defeating.

In worlds that are closer to our own, many of those kinds of horrible and alienating states, which we learned to fear by watching the parade of horribles, are actually forbidden by utilitarian institutions. The network of substantive and procedural rights that establishes self-ownership and world ownership appears to rule out Roman arenas or forcible organ donations, and it may do much to combat alienation as well. Much of how these rights do their work should be easy to infer, but I make a more explicit case about how they make utilitarianism more congruent with our intuitions in the concluding chapter.

My case for utilitarianism is far from complete, however. The institutional world of property and contracts that I have outlined for Imperfectia is only recommended by utilitarianism against an egalitarian baseline for the distribution of wealth. Now I must try to see what utilitarianism recommends if this egalitarian baseline erodes and redistribution becomes necessary.

SIX

The Problem of Redistribution

What the Problem Is

Redistribution is a topic much discussed among theorists of justice but is not terribly prominent among utilitarians. Most of the debates on the subject over the last few decades have taken place between moral egalitarians of one kind or another, who believe in patterned principles of distribution and are willing to use the authority of the state to maintain them,[1] and defenders of property rights as side constraints, who believe in historical principles of distribution.[2] Utilitarians, perhaps because they are not committed in principle to either egalitarian patterns or historical entitlement, are thus not centrally involved in this dispute.

In the previous chapter, I argue that in at least some factual universes, utilitarians would support the institutions of property rights and contracts as being utility optimizing. It might thus appear that in Libertaria, Imperfectia, and some venal oligarchies, utilitarians would be closer to the Nozickian position than that of Ronald Dworkin and other moral egalitarians. But at least in Imperfectia, they cannot rely exclusively on such free-market institutions. There are implicit pressures toward the patterning of distribution in a number of factual universes, and as Nozick himself reminds us, liberty upsets patterns.

It is important to remember that in large part the moral logic of Imperfectia's institutions is undergirded by the existence of some initial distribution that can be justified on utilitarian grounds; I suggested that a distribution that equalized productive capacity with some exceptions for recognizable special needs would be one such. But it is doubtful that any such distribution ever existed in real-world history. As far back as historical knowledge takes us, we find considerable deviations from this kind of distribution. The distribution of property rights in the past gave individuals vastly differing productive capacities. Furthermore, any distribution extant today is almost certainly the product of institutional arrangements that were not those of Imperfectia.

Undoubtedly considerable force and fraud in the past have been used to bring into existence the current distribution of property rights.[3]

Even if such a justifiable initial distribution ever had existed, and even if there had never been any force or fraud, it is still likely that a justifiable distribution could degrade into one in which there are considerable differences between the capacities of individuals to produce and trade. One generation may pass on its capacities unequally to the next. Even if there is no inheritance of wealth, parents of unusual talent and wealth may pass on greater capacities to their children through genetics, superior socialization, and more expensive educations. Consequently, the children of the fortunate will outperform other children of their generation. The cumulation of resources over time will result in great differences. If there is a tendency for individuals to marry others of similar talent and wealth, this cumulative process may work even faster and produce even greater extremes.[4]

Another kind of accident of fate may be the occurrence of contingencies that could not have been rationally anticipated by agents or groups of agents.[5] Some contingencies can be largely exogenous; natural disasters or wars may destroy wealth. Others may be endogenous. Rapid technological change brought about by economic development can plunge individuals into poverty by making obsolete their physical capital or their talents and skills. At the same time, others may enjoy windfalls as talents that before had little or no value become in demand. A distribution that a utilitarian might wish to condemn can occur, especially when some individuals are struggling and suffering because of a lack of resources while others have a superfluity. Surely a utilitarian would wish to take some resources from those who have too much and give them to those who have too little.

Redistribution is not as simple as all that, unfortunately. There may be losses in the process of redistribution itself, as any institutions that may be set up to do the redistributing are inefficient. Furthermore, redistribution may lead to inefficiencies in allocation and opportunities for exploitation, which in turn lead to utility losses. The point of this chapter is to explore the kinds of redistributive institutions that a utilitarian could in fact endorse, and thereby round out the account of utilitarian justice in the sphere of political economy.

The account I give here is made against an assumed background of the institutions of Imperfectia rather than against any other factual universe. The reason for such a truncated account is not due merely to my lack of energy or space. As it happens, it is primarily in Imperfectia that redistribution becomes a tricky matter.

Redistribution in Communia is, in principle at least, simple. Everyone's honestly reported needs and capacities go into the central-planning hopper and an appropriate allocation of burdens and benefits comes out for every planning cycle. Everyone then does what he or she is told to do, serene in the knowledge that all are really working for the greatest good.

In Libertaria there is simply no redistribution. The inhabitants may be good utilitarians, but they have no means for comparing one distribution with another. Libertarians simply forge ahead, trucking and bartering, gathering quasi-Pareto improvements wherever they can, and knowing that that is the best they can do. The venal oligarchs may engage in redistribution, but if they do so their motives are dictated not by utilitarian morality but by prudence: providing bread and circuses for the otherwise impoverished masses is done to stave off social chaos rather than to maximize well-being. The moral tyrants may also engage in redistribution, but in accordance with ideology (or theology) and not utilitarian morality. Finally, in a Hobbesian chaos, the clever and the strong redistribute from all others to themselves.

Imperfectia is the tricky case because it is here that any patterned principles of redistribution run up against the historical outcomes that are arrived at through private property and contracting. Hence I need a discussion, however sketchy, to show how this might be done. In addition, I assume that the factual universe of Imperfectia most closely resembles our own and that in the inferential theory of moral intuitions, our intuitions about justice will be most closely tuned to the facts of Imperfectia. It is against Imperfectia's institutions, therefore, that we must test our own moral intuitions to see how well utilitarianism measures up in reflective equilibrium as a theory of justice.

I should also note that a number of institutions normally thought to be part of the welfare state will not be considered here on the grounds that while they may at times achieve redistributive effects, their purpose is not, strictly speaking, redistribution but the overcoming of market failures. A regulatory agency whose job is to keep the air clean might de facto redistribute some utility from those who use products that dirty the air to those who merely breathe as a side effect of its regulation. But that kind of agency is really in the business of enforcing a kind of property right individuals implicitly have in the commons of the air.

Likewise, a single-payer national health insurance scheme might de facto redistribute the good of health care. But this redistribution may be something of a side effect from a system put in place not primarily to redistribute the good but to overcome a form of market failure. National health insurance in some cases can be justified without appeal to redistributive considerations on the grounds that, because of asymmetries of information between insurers and insurees, the private market for health insurance is a "market for lemons"[6] that will not function effectively. Socialized medicine is a de facto forcing of everyone to buy insurance in an attempt to overcome adverse selection effects that would otherwise cause the insurance market to collapse.[7] There may, therefore, be some de facto redistribution from those who prefer to have less insurance than that provided by the national health scheme to those who prefer more, but redistribution per se need not be the point of the program.

In making recommendations of utilitarian institutions for Imperfectia, I have to make a fair number of broad empirical generalizations: about the relationship between welfare and income, about the nature of political processes, about the relationship between income and education, and so on. That these empirical generalizations may be mistaken I cheerfully allow. But the factual claims on which the argument is built do not wander very far from common sense. And it is this closeness to common sense, rather than closeness to the truth, that is really important to the argument. After all, if the inferential theory of moral intuitions is correct, our moral beliefs involve the tacit application of that knowledge that we *actually* have, not that which we would *ideally* have, together with moral principles to produce moral intuitions. Commonsense morality is tied to commonsense beliefs, so a test of the adequacy of principles should test them against the background of those beliefs and not necessarily against the purest scientific truth.

The Rule of Political Semirigidity

States do many things that may redistribute property rights and wealth among persons. No utilitarians will object to such redistributions in their primary principle; in the world of Imperfectia, however, they may well object to making it politically too easy to allow redistribution to occur.

One of the facts that defines Imperfectia as Imperfectia is that v is only moderately high. The rules that maintain social equilibrium do so under imperfect conditions in which attempts at exploitation are not always easy to detect and punish. This unfortunate fact is of considerable concern in any political order in which citizens are to have a say in making their own policies and in which policies that have redistributive effects are permitted. It is possible that factions within a society can set in motion a chain of political events that can unravel the whole moral order of Imperfectia. How?

It has been a commonplace of political science ever since the publication of Mancur Olson's *Logic of Collective Action*[8] that self-interested individuals can cooperate in political projects for the collective benefit of all cooperators if there are organizations that provide selective incentives to their members for their participation. Alternatively, it may be possible for a coalition of self-interested individuals to be welded together through the effects of a political ideology.

Whatever the relevant causal story, a group can get together to fight for some collective distributive advantage for itself. This behavior—seeking wealth or welfare through the manipulation of policy rather than through productive activity—is known to economists as *rent seeking*.[9] A profession, through its professional association—say, lawyers through the Imperfectia Bar Association—may engage in rent seeking by trying to get a legislature to establish legal barriers to entry into the legal profession. These barriers, which limit the rights of economic agents to contract with one another, redistribute wealth from clients to attorneys. Rent seeking can also take place when a cultural or ethnic minority seeks collectively to obtain for itself public provision of a privately producible good through the levy of a general tax. Lovers of opera might, for instance, improve their lot by taxing the whole population for the provision of free public performances.

There can be both ideological and utilitarian justifications for such redistributive policies. The former are false claims that these policies are not redistributive at all—that barriers to entry into the legal profession exist not to enrich lawyers but to protect the public; that the use of public revenues to support minority cultural tastes provides cultural uplift from which everyone benefits in the long run. The utilitarian claims are admissions of redistribution, with the stipulation that the outcome that results from the policies in question is utility-superior to that which would be created in the absence of those policies.

The serious problem that can result from these claims is as follows: a very large number of potential coalitions could jump into the redistribution game. And if there are enough self-interested and rational persons in the world, quite a few such coalitions will appear. The result can be called a political-redistributive *free-for-all*. And this appearance is a bad outcome in utilitarian terms, for at least four reasons.

First, fights for redistribution through the political process by many coalitions raise the cost of political participation for all citizens of good conscience. Citizens motivated bt a spirit of civic cooperation will participate in the political process for a number of reasons, not the least of which is to prevent invasion of the social world by potential exploiters. But each political group that makes a demand for redistributive policies may or may not be a coalition of exploiters. For all anyone knows *ex ante*, it may in fact be the case that barriers to entry into the legal profession will protect the public from serious problems of legal chicanery and thereby be justifiable on consequentialist grounds. I personally would like to believe that the cultural uplift provided by public opera would be in everyone's real interest in the long run. And it seems likely that some frankly redistributive policies would produce utility-optimal outcomes: a tax on yachts that provides vaccinations and infant nutrition to impoverished children would be such a policy if any would. But as the number of demands proliferate, the costs to good citizens of scrutinizing them all will rise and rise. Some citizens may cease to effectively participate in the process. Other citizens may become more careless in their scrutiny. Should such public negligence be effected, the ability of the political order to immunize itself against corruption will erode.

Second, as the number of demands for policies increases and as citizen attention begins to waver under the strain, the number of errors that a political process will produce will also increase. Policies that may appear to have a utilitarian justification, but which cause more losses in utility than gains in the transfer of rights from one group to another (or from all society to a subset), will begin to slip through the political process. Not only may there be short-term utility losses through "leaky buckets,"[10] but there may also be long-term evolutionary consequences for the stability of the moral order that undergirds the political order. If those egoists who seek rents prosper while utilitarians find life harder and harder, utilitarianism will be selected against, causing the world to become even nastier.

Third, if rent seeking is profitable, groups will expend resources on fighting in the political process rather than on activities that are productive of wealth.[11] Considerable losses of welfare will follow as resources are burned up in actions that generate no utility in themselves.

Fourth, as individuals become more uncertain about how much of their property they hold securely, they will allocate consumption less efficiently over time. To give a toy example: if I have $100 on Monday, I may adjudge it best to parcel it out in equal amounts in order to eat moderately well every day for a week rather than eating very well at the beginning of the week and poorly at the end. The former allocation is utility-superior to the latter, and that superiority should be reflected in any aggregate utility calculus. But if I think that I may not be able to keep all my money all week long because the state may raise taxes on Wednesday, I may find it rational to take the latter, utility-inferior course of action. Multiply these effects of allocative uncertainty across a whole society, and we again find that the losses of welfare will be considerable.

Given all the bad things that can occur as consequences of a redistributive free-for-all, it should be clear that intelligently designed institutions should have some characteristic that serves as a brake on, if not to prevent, such an outcome. I suggest that it would be wise to instantiate a principle of *semirigidity*, which might be outlined thus: the standards that determine which sorts of redistributive policies are permissible and which are impermissible should be (1) *clearly intelligible to the public* and (2) *relatively hard to change*. There should be clear standards by which members of the body politic can determine whether a policy passes institutional muster or not; when there are such standards, the first bad consequence of excessive struggles over redistribution can be ameliorated. And if the standards are hard to change, the incentives of organizationally or ideologically motivated redistributive coalitions to enter the political game will be reduced.

American constitutional history provides an example of sorts of the principle of semirigidity. The original U.S. Constitution contains provisions that forbid ex post facto laws and bills of attainder—policies that could radically destabilize any distribution of legal rights if permitted. The federal Bill of Rights[12] contains a takings clause ("nor shall private property be taken for public use without just compensation"),[13] and Article IV also contains provisions that forbid the frustration by legislatures of contracts. After the Civil War, federal courts interpreted the Fourteenth Amendment as extending these distribution-stabilizing constitutional provisions not just to the actions of the federal government but to state governments as well. An economic-libertarian line of jurisprudential doctrine grew up that was hostile to any attempt to redistribute property.[14] These standards were, however, only semirigid. The process of constitutional amendment was available to make certain kinds of redistributive policies possible; that process was used, for example, to legalize the existence of a federal income tax.[15] Legal doctrine also gradually changed to become more permissive of policies with redistributive consequences.

A return to a type of nineteenth-century judicial review of economic regulation, in which courts routinely struck down all kinds of economic and social policies on the grounds that they constituted denials of due process of law, is probably not an optimal policy. The needs of a modern society are too complex to be served by the minimalist state such a legal regime envisions. A more substantive reading of the takings and contract clauses than the rational basis standard now in use in the United States might be appropriate; but exactly what the appropriate standard would be is too complicated to determine in a chapter or a book or several books. It might be appropriate, for instance, to prevent redistributive effects not in every instance in which they occur but only in those cases in which there is evidence that redistribution was the reasonably foreseeable consequence of or intent behind the policies. Or if intent is too exacting a standard, some less strict but still rigorous standard of liability could be imposed.[16] What I am more interested in exploring is the question of when redistribution really should take place—the question of when property holders who loose their holdings through state action would have no real claim to compensation.

Comprehensive Redistribution

None but the most radical egalitarians believe that every person should enjoy an equal portion of all social goods. Most egalitarians would rather distinguish between relevant and irrelevant reasons for material inequalities. The endowments that individuals have that they did nothing to create—natural talents, abilities acquired by their rearing as children, good looks, and so on—which in a simple regime of property and contract would lead to inequalities of wealth, are held to be morally irrelevant reasons for inequalities. One person has no moral claim to greater wealth than another simply because one is luckier in life's lottery. One has at least a prima facie egalitarian moral warrant to redistribute wealth from the merely lucky to the merely unlucky.

But toleration of inequalities that result from the choices individuals make is held to be morally permissible, perhaps even morally required. If one man is richer than another because he has worked harder or chosen to take wealth-maximizing risks or chosen to endure a period of sacrifice early in life to become educated for a lucrative profession later, it would seem most inequitable to equalize the outcome between them. Indeed, to redistribute from the hard-working to the not-so-hard-working person would seem to be a violation of the egalitarian's purposes since to do so would create a serious inequality in well-being between them.

A position that I call (by an ugly name) *comprehensive egalitarian redistributivism* maintains that there is a moral warrant for the state to conduct all the redistribution necessary to level the inequalities in the distribution of social goods that are generated by differing endowments while leaving intact those inequalities generated by differential effort, planning, and risk taking. A parallel utilitarian position—comprehensive utilitarian redistributivism—is that social goods generated by differing endowments of individuals will be subject to redistribution when aggregate utility gains are to be had, but those social goods generated by choices made by individuals due to differential effort, planning, and risk taking will not be subject to redistribution.

The moral underpinnings of a program of comprehensive egalitarian redistribution rely on a perceived moral difference between modes of acquiring property. To oversimplify greatly, we cannot deserve that which stems merely from our taking the trouble to be born. But we do deserve that for which we work or for which we undergo pains and hazards. Furthermore, to respect choices while equalizing the effects of endowments is in keeping with plausible corollary principles of moral egalitarianism: nonexploitation and reciprocity.

The moral underpinnings of a program of comprehensive utilitarian redistribution are somewhat more complex. Such a program is an attempt to square the possibility of utility gains from redistribution with the utilitarian rationale for the property-and-contract regime of Imperfectia. If we take away wealth that individuals gain by virtue of their endowments, we are simply redistributing a windfall of sorts. But if we redistribute the wealth that results from their hard work or their risk taking, we are frustrating the workings of institutions that exist to allow individuals to find for themselves a utility-optimizing mix of work and leisure and of risk and security. Economic agents who find the gains from hard work taxed away will choose to consume more leisure and less income; we will thus lose income to redistribute while they will opt for a life they would find to be second best. Furthermore, to redistribute from risk takers and hard workers to others would violate the utilitarian rule of non-exploitation in a world with potential exploiters and threaten the long-term stability of utilitarianism.

The business of sorting out how much of a distribution of social goods results from differential endowments and how much from different choices is a rather tricky one. Some egalitarians have proposed standards of equality to create a distribution that reflects only morally relevant differences: Ronald Dworkin suggests "equality of resources,"[17] Amartya Sen "equality of capacities to function,"[18] Richard Arneson "equality of opportunity for welfare,"[19] and Gerald Cohen "equal access to advantage."[20]

One could easily imagine various utilitarian analogues to these proposals in which the appropriate objects are aggregate maximands rather than equalisands, that is, maximization of opportunities for welfare, resources, capacities to function, or access to advantages. But since it is difficult as a practical matter to see how we are to start again in midstream with equal resources, it is not clear how useful these standards are for the design of policy. A recent intriguing proposal by John Roemer,[21] however, may provide some guidance.

Roemer's egalitarian planning proposal would work as follows: the entire population would be divided into types of persons based on their attributes deemed to lie beyond their control. Thus, for determination of a person's wealth, that person's parents' wealth, parents' education, ethnicity, and gender would constitute his or her type: these determinations of type are all independent variables that have a large amount of causal-explanatory power in the distribution of wealth. But while variation *across* types in the distribution of wealth will be assumed to be outside the control of individual persons—and therefore morally irrelevant—the distribution *within* types will be taken to be a function of that individual's greater effort or acceptance of different risks—and therefore morally relevant.

The goal of Roemer's policy is to redistribute wealth (or more likely, income) in such a way as to equalize welfare across types but not within types, at least to the extent that such welfare is dependent on income. Thus, suppose that there exist a white man of middle-class, college-educated parents and a black woman of working-class parents who never finished high school. If both persons are at the fiftieth percentile of their type distributions, the former person will be wealthier than the latter. To the extent that welfare is a marginally declining function of utility, the latter's welfare is less than the former's. Since both are in the middle of their distributions, Roemer would adjudge them to have exercised an equal degree of responsibility over their situations, and he would recommend a redistribution of income from the former to the latter to equalize their welfares. But between two white men of middle-class, college-educated parents, one of whom has an income at the fiftieth percentile of his distribution and another at the ninety-ninth percentile of that same type distribution, Roemer would recommend no redistribution, even though, in the same assumption of the relation of welfare and income, such a redistribution would also have an equalizing effect on their welfares.

Of course, Roemer is too sophisticated to postulate any simple-minded relationship between income and welfare. It is possible that equalizing the welfares of two different persons will require two different incomes; one person may have greater needs than another or may simply have more expensive tastes. Roemer suggests that the way to handle different tastes is to subject them to the same test of individual control or noncontrol as income itself. Thus, an ordinary person whose type is "child of the middle bourgeoisie," who only gets pleasure from a drink if it is a prephylloxera claret,[22] may be judged to have been irresponsible in the development of his tastes; he would not be eligible for additional income to equalize his welfare with another person of his type. But perhaps if another person's type is "child of impoverished aristocrats," whose tastes are beyond her control, she may be eligible for additional income.

There is a simple utilitarian analogue for Roemer's theory of comprehensive redistribution. In this analogous theory, welfare is, of course, not an equalisand but a maximand. Control over property can be transferred from a person of one type to a person of another type in any case in which that redistribution would produce gains in aggregate utility, subject to the constraint that no such transfers are to take place from a person who has exercised a greater degree of responsibility to one who has exercised a lesser degree.

Thus (keeping for the moment the first assumption of a marginally declining relationship between utility and income) a transfer of some wealth from the white man of middle-class parentage to the black woman of working-class parentage, both of whom have exercised the same degree of responsibility, would produce gains in aggregate utility and would be required. But a transfer between two men within the same type, one of whom is at the far end of the income distribution and the other in the middle, would be forbidden. This latter transfer would violate the basic moral logic of Imperfectia. A moral logic that establishes property rights and contracts to prevent persons from exploiting one another is not going to be hospitable to allowing the middle of a distribution of responsibility to live off the wealth generated at the top.

Of course, a utilitarian scheme of redistribution could conceivably allow different amounts of wealth based on varying needs or tastes, although in a world like Imperfectia—where the utility κ for many goods is likely to be low to middling—the tastes that would allow transfers between persons of equal wealth, much less from those of lesser to those of greater wealth, might be rather hard to find. But even in a world in which κ tends to be low, there are likely to be goods for which it is high or, at least, high enough to create a plausible warrant for redistribution. The good of decent health care certainly is such a high good, and many goods associated with personal cultivation also seem to have a fairly high κ. The widespread availability of public education and public cultural facilities like libraries, which are available to all without regard to one's ability to pay, would at least seem to reflect such a conviction.

But unfortunately, some goods that have a high κ are such that the degree to which they generate utility for people is in part under the control of those same people. Having medical care available provides some utility to most people through peace of mind, that is, knowing that one will be cared for if one is hurt or sick. But medical care is of greatest value to those who are in fact hurt or sick, and whether one becomes hurt or sick is partly under one's control. We are more likely to be hurt if we engage in physically risky enterprises, sick if we fail to take adequate care of ourselves. In the case of activities of cultivation as well, we might have control over our own demands: our tastes for cultural goods often become more expansive the more we expose ourselves to them.[23]

Yet for any redistributive scheme to be welfare equalizing or welfare maximizing, it must take into account that which will actually make the lives of real, living persons go better. For it to take account of relevant and irrelevant reasons, it must have some account of personal responsibility. The components of a person's type should not be under his or her control, for if they are, the redistributive scheme would be open to exploitation by those who would behave strategically. For example, if we were to include in the definition of a person's type whether or not one was a lover of opera, and if it were possible to cultivate in oneself a love for such music (it should not be hard, I think), one would have an avenue for gaining the benefits of redistribution to satisfy one's new—and expensive—taste.

But it is far from clear, unfortunately, that there is any obvious way to determine what is and what is not under the control of an individual person. It seems intuitively correct to say that some aspects of a person—such as the state of one's health—is partly the consequence of choices one makes and partly that of a genetic and environmental endowment over which one has no control. It is rather murky to what extent our tastes are under our control; some seem elemental and beyond our choice, while others are the outcomes of consciously chosen programs of cultivation. Other aspects, such as religious beliefs, also seem hard to evaluate as choices or not. On the one hand, it seems absurd to say that one could choose a new religion as one chooses a new suit. On the other hand, one's religion is hardly an endowment as unalterable as one's genotype; conversions happen all the time. Even one's race or one's sex would not withstand—in this era of advanced techniques of plastic and reconstructive surgery—the most determined attempts at change.

Some aspects of personal type are unalterable. In the case of one's genetic makeup, this immutability may simply be due to the inadequacy of present-day medical technology. In other cases, changing one's personal type may be impossible for metaphysical reasons. The class status of my parents during my childhood is fixed by the passing of time. Unless time travel is a possibility, there is no way for me or anyone else to change these facts. But even in cases of clear immutability, it is far from clear that the *causal influence* of these parts of my type are inalterable. What my genotype is may be fixed by the limits of biotechnology, but how that genotype influences my opportunities for the good life is the function of countless intervening causes, many of which may be said to be under my control. The same goes for the class status of my parents, fixed in the past though it may be.

Here the ugly metaphysical issue of determinism versus free will seems to have arisen. I do not believe in free will; but even among those who do, few would be so philosophically stubborn as to imagine that everything relevant in determining the fate of an individual and permitted by the physical limits of muscle and nerve and sinew is under one's autonomous control. It seems more rational in many cases to make attribution of responsibility not on grounds of metaphysics but on grounds of efficiency.[24] Rather than making an all-or-nothing attribution of responsibility or not, based on an exercise or not of a mysterious capacity called free will, we should attribute responsibility according to the utility costs to different individuals in a situation. We punish a man who steals for simple gain because the social cost of allowing such practices as stealing for gain will almost surely outweigh the benefit in the long run. But we do not punish a woman who participates in stealing under severe duress—a clerk who opens a safe under threat of death from an armed robber—because the cost of noncompliance is so great that any punishment that could deter the clerk would be so inequitable as to defeat the utilitarian purpose of the rule of law. In the second instance no less than the first—possibly more so—the acts of the agent are under conscious "free" control, but in the second instance we attribute little or no responsibility; in the first, full responsibility.

Roemer certainly seems to understand that attributions of responsibility involve social judgment and not metaphysical revelation. He offers no metaphysical theory about how to decide to divide society into types. That decision is made by someone else, someone referred to as "the pragmatic egalitarian planner," or more generally, as "society."[25] The pragmatic utilitarian redistributer, or just society, would also have to make such a decision to make a utilitarian scheme of comprehensive redistribution workable.

But in making such a decision there is a serious problem. The decision of how to divide a society into types under any program of comprehensive redistribution—whether egalitarian or utilitarian, it matters not—provides innumerable opportunities for opportunism and rent seeking. If we delegate such decisions to social planners, we invite that bureaucratic corruption that a well-run polity must try to avoid. If we attempt to make such decisions democratically, we might return to the redistributive political free-for-all discussed in the previous section.

To return to my toy example of classical music: we could reason that classical music lovers might attempt to divide the social world into types in such a way that their expensive taste for classical music becomes something for which they are not responsible; thus they make themselves eligible for additional income, either to equalize their opportunities for welfare with others under an egalitarian regime or to make themselves the objects of maximizing redistribution under a utilitarian regime. They might attempt to do so directly by getting "opera lover" or "opera hater" recognized as part of a person's type, but they need not be so blatant and unsubtle as that. They might simply note that people with a taste for classical music tend to come from certain social backgrounds, backgrounds that seem to be beyond the control of agents—the social class and education of parents—and get these backgrounds represented as personal types.

To take a more serious example: persons who engage in smoking or other health-risking behaviors, and who therefore have generally reduced opportunities for welfare, might try to manipulate the designation of social classes so that they might become eligible for redistributed income. Such people might insist that one should attribute nonresponsibility to their behaviors even if they are under conscious control because their genetic makeup makes them highly prone to addictions, and abstinence or the overcoming of addictions are so costly that attributions of responsibility are inappropriate.

It is also likely that the politically powerful may try to manipulate the system of assigning types in ways that favor the powerful—preventing redistribution to those to whom it might well be justified on egalitarian or utilitarian grounds. In a society like our own, with significant differences in the distribution of advantages between races, whites might fight to exclude race from consideration as part of a person's type—perhaps on the grounds that race is a cultural construction rather than a natural state and therefore not an "immutable" part of a person's type—to prevent the redistribution of income or other social advantages from relatively wealthier whites to relatively poorer blacks, Hispanics, Native Americans, and so forth. Those educated in the Ivy League may fight division into types according to parental education to prevent redistribution to *hoi polloi*.

In principle it would be possible to demand almost any redistribution by manipulating the grid of types with sufficient fineness. There are no divine metaphysical revelations about what we are and are not responsible for; and in the absence of perfect utility information about other individuals, there would seem to be no pragmatic solutions to the problem either.

I think that whatever criticisms I have made of the Roemerian proposal could be applied to any other proposal for comprehensive redistribution as well. Take Dworkin's requirement for "equality of resources" as an example: the question of what is to count as a resource, and therefore of how much redistribution is necessary to establish equalization, is not given from heaven. Is a person's race or gender a resource? Certainly in present-day society, whites and men seem to do better ceteris paribus than nonwhites and women. What about capacity for work? Could it be a resource if a person finds what other persons find onerous a light duty? Perhaps great powers of concentration and strength are part of one's genetic endowment. If that is so, one would certainly find it easy to do better than others. Should there be redistribution away from this person to others more prone to fatigue? The possibility for political struggles and renewed free-for-alls over such questions seems to loom very large, both for egalitarian and utilitarian versions of the doctrine.

We may then be forgiven for having doubts about comprehensive redistribution. I regret that I must have such doubts since programs of comprehensive redistribution—especially ones similar to those built by Roemer—seem very elegant and, at least prima facie, morally persuasive. Are there any alternatives that a utilitarian could recommend? There is one, albeit a much less elegant proposal, consisting of two principal parts: insurance of social minima and boost of personal endowments.

Social Minima

Of course, κ is not equal for all goods. For such fundamentals of human well-being as relief of hunger, exposure, pain, and sickness, the κ is very high, while for "luxuries" or items of symbolic value like the public funding of opera, the κ is comparatively low. Consequently, mimicry of the need for items such as food or shelter or basic health care is highly unlikely because claims of high utility values for them are plausible. But mimicry of the need for such items as opera is, unfortunately, quite likely. It is not necessarily false that putting on an opera is a better utilitarian use of resources than feeding some hungry persons, but it is pragmatically quite difficult to verify such a claim. Hence such a claim may be quite likely to be put forth in the spirit of opportunism, should someone think it possible that we should honor it.

The high κ of certain goods makes it less likely that demands for them can be made for opportunistic reasons. A program of redistribution that was restricted to just those goods, then, is likely to be able to avoid a political free-for-all; since only claims that can be evaluated with some ease in the first place are likely to be honored, the incentive to make such claims is reduced. And the relatively high utilities of certain goods makes them good utilitarian targets for redistributive efforts. The utility gains of redistributing goods with small utilities even if those goods have a high-utility κ are more than a little doubtful, given the leaky bucket of real administrative costs likely to be attached to a redistributive program. But the value of feeding the hungry or healing the sick makes welfare gains likely even if administrative costs are high.

It is possible, then, to have a program of redistribution that guarantees that certain persons will have certain important goods without regard for their ability to pay. Exactly what these goods are and the level of their provision will vary with different social circumstances and different levels of aggregate wealth in different societies, but it is likely that in any society inhabited by human beings these goods will include the basics of nutrition, shelter, and health care.[26] Because these goods have such a high κ, they are unlikely to provoke exploitative mimicry or a redistributive free-for-all; and because their utilities are so high, their redistribution to those who lack them is likely to be easy to justify on utilitarian grounds, even in a society that generally respects world ownership.[27]

Readers will note that this proposal bears certain similarities to those that have long been defended by Phillipe van Parijs for a basic minimum income for all.[28] The different proposals are indeed in many ways congruent, although neither necessarily nor entirely so. They differ in justification and perhaps in application as well. Van Parijs's proposal is based on a conception of social justice that maximizes real freedom for all members of society, which he interprets as raising the greatest possible opportunity for the person with the least opportunities. This end is to be achieved by raising the minimum level of real income. Utilitarianism is concerned not with opportunities per se but with well-being. To the extent that maximizing opportunities does not coincide with maximizing well-being—an extent that may not be all that broad in the real world—there will be a divergence between the justification for van Parijs's proposal and mine. Furthermore, a utilitarian might favor raising the well-being of the average person even at some expense to the worst off, a possibility that van Parijs "takes for granted" is inferior to his maximin proposal.[29] Finally, van Parijs, in part motivated by his desire to maximize opportunity, specifically defends a social minimum that consists of a cash grant rather than goods in kind, like food or housing. This proposal, by way of contrast, is agnostic about whether or to what extent the social minimum should be in cash or in kind.[30]

Of course, there are at least three objections to any such program. First, it might open up opportunities for exploitation of those who work to generate wealth by those who do not. Second, the nature of the goods that have a high κ may not be adequately clear. Third, the level of provision is not completely clear either and may raise problems.

The first and the third problems are closely linked because the extent of the first problem is linked to the level of whatever social minimum there is. If that level is too high, the incentive for exploitation may be too great. Selfish persons who know that they will be taken care of no matter what will be encouraged to take undue risks with the health or their fortunes. And selfish persons who value leisure relatively highly with respect to consumption will have an incentive not to work at all if the social minimum is too high. Thus, too high a social minimum can defeat the logic of exploitation-overcoming institutions like property rights.

The solution concerning the level of social minimum is empirical. Theorists cannot answer the question from their studies, although they can give a rough formula for it. The minimum is to be as high as possible, given the availability of high-κ goods, the transfer of which can be reasonably certain of producing utility gains and the certainty of the loss of some resources in the administration of any transfers. But the social minimum has an upper limit, set not just by the availability of utility information but also by the tendency of a social minimum to make exploitation possible. The social minimum must go no higher than that point at which long-term losses due to expected exploitation begin to outrun short-term gains due to utility transfers.

The level of this upper limit can be expected to vary from imperfect world to imperfect world. In a good version of Imperfectia, one that falls just short of Communia, the upper limit may not apply at all. Because potential exploiters are few and weak, those charged with establishing policies of redistribution can simply redistribute as many goods as high-κ and high-utility information allow. If a few exploiters do slip in and enjoy high social benefits, that is not a severe problem. But in a version of Imperfectia that may be just short of declining into something worse, a world in which would-be exploiters are abundant, the administrators of a social minimum may wish to set that level just above utter privation for the sake of warding off these exploiters. It would be deeply regrettable and tragic if some or even many decent people are caught in a squeeze because of low levels of social provision that could otherwise be higher, but the social instability and economic malaise that would result from too many persons going on a higher dole may not permit anything else.

In addition, there may be effects on economic efficiency on the side of those taxed, which a utilitarian should take into account. People may work less hard if they see part of their income go into redistribution, and they thus opt for more leisure and less income than they would ideally prefer. Van Parijs has argued, however, that to some extent this inefficiency will be blunted by the fact that part of an employed worker's income is not a factor income in the standard microeconomic sense—an amount of income needed to keep the factor in production—but a rent attached to having a job in an economy in which employed workers are generally paid an above-market-clearing wage.[31] To the extent that such rents exist, they can be redistributed without causing static inefficiencies. Beyond that point, of course, the trouble of figuring how much to redistribute becomes much harder.

But in deferring to empirical considerations concerning the level of any social minimum, might I not be in danger of touching off a free-for-all of another kind? After all, who is to decide which goods are high κ and high utility and which are not? Would it not be possible to legislate that opera is not, as I have alleged, a medium to low-κ good but a high-κ good? And who is to decide how much moral integrity a society has, so that the upper bound on the level of provision can be set accordingly? Why should the winners in society not try to legislate into fact policies predicated on the assumption that there are many would-be exploiters in the world, thus screwing down the level of the social minimum and limiting the amount of taxation for redistribution? Conversely, why should the losers in society not try the opposite tactic?

I can offer no absolute answers to such questions, but I must point out that I am here suggesting that the institutions being recommended are for Imperfectia and not for any other factual world. I assume that there is at least some moral integrity in the world for which they are recommended and that citizens can be counted on to deliberate on such matters, *up to a point*, in good faith.[32] In suggesting a social minimum rather than comprehensive redistribution as an appropriate utilitarian approach to redistribution, however, I have tried to outline a policy that may be less vulnerable to opportunistic political manipulation. How might this be so?

The number of decisions that would have to be made in any policy of comprehensive redistribution would be very large; in the quasi-Roemerian proposal just considered, individual citizens might have to make judgments about any number of different candidate traits as causal influences of success beyond the control of agents. Because so many decisions would be necessary, evaluating all the proposals that might be made by opportunistic groups would be very costly. For every possible costly preference, there is a claim that its formation is beyond the control of those who hold it. For every identifiable group of losers, there is a claim that membership in that group is an effectively immutable trait that causally affects success. And the preferences and the groups are many. Political participation might then collapse under its own weight.

In a program of guaranteeing social minima, in contrast, the number of decisions would be small and easy to outline. Conscientious citizens would have to decide on what is probably a fairly short list of goods—including some income, some subsidy for food and housing, and some level of health care (education is a separate matter to be considered in the next section)—and on a level of provision. If I have outlined the problem correctly, then, the amount of room for manipulation would be small, and the costs of political scrutiny would be more easily bearable.

How does the institution of the social minimum relate to our intuitions about distributive justice? There is some empirical evidence that a social minimum may be more in accord with ordinary convictions about justice than other possible distributive schemes. In a recent study conducted by Norman Frohlich and Joe Oppenheimer,[33] subjects in a variety of experiments were given a chance to choose principles of justice under conditions similar to those that might prevail under a Rawlsian veil of ignorance. Participants were given real money payoffs based on the principles they chose and randomization of their "positions" in the hypothetical societies they constructed. Among various candidate principles were rules permitting the maximization of the average income; a principle like Rawls's difference principle in which the worst-off income was maximized; a principle in which the average income was maximized but subject to a range constraint, that is, a form of egalitarianism; and something like a social minimum principle, in which incomes were maximized subject to a constraint that no income was to fall below a certain level. It was the final principle and not any of the other three that groups tended to settle on. Interestingly, when Frohlich and Oppenheimer attempted to replicate their principle cross-culturally in Poland and Asia, they achieved a similar result: choosers preferred maximization with a social floor minimum to maximization of the average or maximization of the minimum.

If Frohlich and Oppenheimer's work adequately reflects commonly considered moral convictions, and if my utilitarian argument for a social minimum is sound, we have a convergence of utilitarian conclusions and commonsense convictions about distributive justice. I consider this important outcome at greater length in the conclusion.

Are social minima enough to satisfy the redistributive requirements of utilitarian justice? However high the social floor may be set, it may not be set high enough to overcome transmission of poor endowments across generations; even a generous welfare state might coexist with a permanent underclass. A child whose parents are well fed and healthy but lacking in social and intellectual skills for whatever reason is also likely, ceteris paribus, to be lacking in social and intellectual skills. Utility gains can be had by giving that child a better life, however, and that is the subject of the next section.

Boosting Endowments

Redistributive policy can be used to help individuals get a better life by boosting their endowments in a number of ways. Education is a principal, though certainly not the only, one.[34] In this section, I briefly discuss education and a few other possible strategies.

This book is not a treatise on education, and with the important exception of arguing for the public provision of some liberal rather than only technical education—as is seen in the following discussion—I do not mean to argue for any very specific educational policies. The burning questions of public provision through public schools or through publicly funded vouchers, the details of specific educational methods, or even the question of how and to what extent public education should play a role in shaping the moral character of future citizens turn on empirical matters far beyond my competence. I do not know how much causal influence formal education has on moral character, and I do not know if I could convince a skeptic that it has any such influence. The question of methods and mode of public provision invokes moral questions concerning the content of education and the relative efficiency of its delivery, which are also matters about which I know little.

It is not controversial, however, that there is a real causal process called education, which can affect to some degree the ability of people to make their way in the world successfully. We are not born with the skills with which we reach our ends; they are imparted to us, and they can be imparted in better or worse ways, so that they will be more or less efficacious. Ceteris paribus, the more successful a person is at pursuing one's chosen ends, the better one's life will go and the more utility it will contain. Ceteris paribus, a better education can be had for the expenditure of more resources than for an expenditure of less resources. It follows from these premises that some gains in aggregate utility can be made by a redistribution that claims resources and converts them into expenditures for teaching skills.

There is another reason for singling out educative redistribution as a special topic. It stems from a difference between the claims of children and those of adults. Of course, even when redistribution takes the form of education and endowment building, there might still be a problem of exploitation. The acquisition of skills, after all, can be financed by private persons as well as by the distributive powers of the state. Why should the investment of resources for the acquisition of skills not be undertaken privately? As we have seen in so many other contexts, making a scarce resource available to all without taking into account the willingness to pay creates problems of free riding and moral hazard: selfish persons may decide to ride on state provision even when it would be more utility efficient if they spent their own resources to acquire those skills. Also, as some skills are both quite expensive and quite lucrative to acquire, an excess of public provision may touch off a redistributive free-for-all. The reader should try to imagine the political consequences if the state decided to offer a free legal or medical education either to (1) all comers or (2) to some subset of society, on the grounds of previously existing disadvantage.

Children, however, present less of a moral hazard problem. Children are not moral innocents; they have the same capacity for moral manipulation and the same tendency to selfishness that the rest of us have. But because as individuals they have sufficiently less foresight and experience than adults, their capacity for the kind of strategic behavior necessary to successfully exploit a system of provision rules is limited. Children may manipulate their parents and bully their peers from time to time, but their ability to sucker the administrators of policy seems rather limited.[35] And because they are politically disenfranchised, there is no danger that they themselves can enter into a political free-for-all for the redistribution of resources. In any case, it would be absurd to expect children to invest in their own educations since (with a few exceptions, such as child movie stars and the early inheritors of substantial wealth) children have no direct control over any resources that they could be expected to trade for education. Furthermore, children's lack of foresight and worldly savvy would make them unlikely to be able to look out for their own interests in an educational market.

A state may then wish to provide some level of education as a means of redistribution. There is a question about what level and about what kind of education it ought to provide.[36]

One possible answer is that it should provide enough education so that each generation of children starts life in the position of those in the ideal distribution for Imperfectia; that is, that other things being equal, each child has the same productive capacity at the start of adulthood as any other child. Education might be a great equalizer, at least to the extent that endowment equalization is utility maximization. Unfortunately, such a suggestion may not be practical. The marginal returns to investment in education in future income may decline so steeply that it would be impossible to invest enough resources in the least fortunate children to enable them to have lives even remotely as productive as the more fortunate children. Or even if it is possible to invest adequate resources, the amount necessary may be so great that the burden of taxation on the present generation of adults would be impossible to justify on utilitarian grounds.

Education is, among other things, a form of investment. For an investment to be utility-optimal, it must cover its opportunity costs at the margin. Thus overeducating or undereducating people is a waste of resources. I would propose a different scheme for figuring out the appropriate level of expenditure on education. For the sake of exposition, let me begin with the case of a single individual.

Suppose that one is asked to act as a trustee on behalf of a single child and make a judgment about how much to spend on her education. The child has no resources of her own, but there are appropriate forms of credit and a wise trustee can borrow to pay for the child's expenses. The amount borrowed will then be paid back as part of that child's earnings over the course of her life. Given enough information about the effect of education on earnings and actuarial information about the child's life expectancy, a lender could make an informed estimate of how much could be borrowed on behalf of the child. Given adequate information about the costs of education and the child's expected utility from different future incomes (and perhaps the effect of education on the child's utility function), a trustee could make an estimate of how much ought to be borrowed to provide the child with an education that will enable her life to go as well as possible.[37] Thus one could make a utility-maximizing decision on behalf of a single child.[38]

A utilitarian, however, would probably not want to simply act as the trustee to individual children one by one. Some children may start out with very large endowments, others with very small ones, and this may affect the amount they would be able to borrow. A child of privilege may be able to borrow much more than a child of the ghetto, on the grounds that given the rest of his endowment, the marginal returns to investment in the former will be greater than those to the latter. Acting as trustee to children one by one could thus actually magnify the effects of initial endowments. To the extent that a more equal distribution of endowments would be utility-superior, this individualism could not be endorsed by a utilitarian.

There seems no reason, however, why we could not calculate how much could be borrowed by an *entire cohort* of children. One could distribute expenditures of resources so that children who start with lesser endowments may have more resources devoted to their educations than would be available to them if they had to borrow as individuals. The greater earning capacity of a child of privilege may contribute to his cohort's greater borrowing power, but the child of poverty may be entitled to a greater amount of resources than the child of privilege. If the marginal gain in productive capacity exceeds the marginal loss for transferring a unit of resources within the pool of resources available, then ceteris paribus, a utilitarian would recommend that transfer. And assuming that the marginal gains to resources invested in education diminish for any given child, most of those transfers of resources will be equalizing.[39]

Why assume that equalizing transfers in educational investment are utility-optimal? It is certainly not true a priori that this should be the case. Perhaps it would be optimal to build up those children who are well endowed even further. The logic behind the argument that equalization is generally the best policy is similar to that behind the egalitarian baseline of distribution for an ideal Imperfectia. The κ for consumption of goods generally declines with income, and we can therefore have more confidence in the utility-optimizing effects of equal productive capacities than we can in unequal ones. The effect of equalizing through education can be analogized to the restoration of the dike of equality, which is constantly being eroded over the course of time by fate and differential transmission of capacity across generations.

Of course, education as an equalizer of equality of capacity is only a rough rule by utilitarian standards. There are bound to be some identifiable exceptions: some individuals with very special endowments may legitimately claim abnormally large shares of resources if that will lead to developing valuable rare talents that would otherwise fail to develop. And there may have to be limits on the amount of resources put into the education of severely handicapped children since the cost of educating them up to an equal level may be great enough to drag down the aggregate benefit in a way that would be counterutilitarian. To the extent that there are well-known causal principles that contradict it—such as increasing marginal returns to productivity for the education of certain classes of children—the equal education principle will have to be modified. Also, it may have to be modified if education affects the utility functions of children in peculiar ways—if it can be established, for instance, that it causes some to realize great utility from great income.

In general, however, the rough equality rule can serve another function in addition to that of a utilitarian rule of thumb: it can serve as a semirigid principle of distribution of educational resources to head off distributive politics concerned with education funding. In the United States, at least, upper-middle-class parents who act for their own children have a considerable interest in manipulating the political process to ensure that their own children receive unduly large shares of resources. Even though most children are educated in ostensibly public schools, school funding is based on local districts, which are carefully segregated by social class in order to transmit advantages unequally. Schools in East St. Louis and schools in Lake Forest are both public institutions within my home state of Illinois, but the difference in resource expenditures in the different schools is quite astonishing.[40]

To build some equality rule into the process—or perhaps a more complex principle, if the causal principles and utilities in education are durable and well established—could help cut off this disgraceful political free-for-all of politicking and gerrymandering. Any principle that is too complex, any principle that represents children as being too liable to special exceptions or expensive tastes, will leave the process open to a rather unfortunate degree of manipulation.

Does utilitarianism give any advice on the form education ought to take? There is a commonsense distinction between liberal and technical education. *Liberal* education is concerned with tutelage in a broad range of knowledge, scientific principles, and cognitive skills that apply not just to specific domains of human activity but also to many domains at the same time. *Technical* education is concerned with tutelage in specific competencies in areas of human activity, in skills that may or may not be marketable. Under a utilitarian regime, a substantial component of the education that is part of endowment building must be of the liberal variety. But why should we be interested in providing this kind of education as a means of building up people's endowments? Why not simply teach them relatively lucrative trades? Or why not simply build up their endowments directly, perhaps by giving every otherwise disadvantaged child a lump of money when he or she turns eighteen?[41] I wish to argue briefly that education of a certain kind is at least a necessary part, although it may not be a sufficient part, of endowment building.

The utilitarian moral logic that I have used to justify a regime of property and contracts in Imperfectia has hitherto relied on two premises, which have been only implicit: (1) individual agents know in what their personal good consists, and (2) individual agents know how to intelligently pursue that good: they can evaluate evidence and estimate probable consequences of courses of action. In short, agents must be rational. If they are not, they cannot be expected to realize utility gains through trades because they will trade stupidly.

Hitherto I have assumed *sub silentio* that rationality is simply an inborn trait of human beings. I suspect that it is partly that, but a fair amount of knowing what is good for oneself and what the consequences of actions are likely to be involves the use of cognitive skills, which must be learned. The good for a person may not simply appear on its face; sometimes it must be searched for and discovered. Opera is part of my personal good, but I was not born knowing that fact: only through exposure to it did I learn about it. Moreover, the evaluation of evidence is often a very difficult task:

it requires substantial background knowledge, as well as many cognitive skills like literacy and numeracy.

Because of the complexity of our personal goods and the world in which we might realize them, we need a broad background of knowledge and cognitive skills that are applicable over many domains if we are to trade intelligently. Those who lack that knowledge will not be able to do so. Thus it would not necessarily be a good idea to try to overcome small endowments simply by handing the disadvantaged a lump of money, and it would do relatively little good even to teach them a lucrative trade: they could at best parlay that trade back into money, which would leave them no better off than if they had received money as a gift. Furthermore, we may have a hard time predicting what would be a good trade to teach, given that technological change is likely to be occurring around them; whatever skills they may receive might become obsolete, leaving them even worse off.

One key function of an education should thus be to make individuals rational enough to benefit from the political economy of a property and contract regime. But this rationality-making function of an education is surely not enough alone since no matter how clearly one realizes one's own interests or how clever one might be in achieving them, one will not be likely to achieve much if one has nothing to trade. It is a fortunate coincidence, however, that teaching cognitive skills and factual information that apply across a broad range of human endeavors will make those who learn them not just more rational but also more capable of acquiring cognitive skills with more specialized uses later. Students who have been made literate, numerate, and savvy about the uses of evidence are going to be good candidates for training in some remunerative occupation. And not just a single remunerative occupation; their more general cognitive skills will make them good candidates for retraining as technological changes make older skills obsolete.

Exactly where the resources are to come from for this more specific training is another empirical question, but there are a number of possible solutions. A state may publicly finance a vocational addition to the liberal education it would guarantee to all people; or it may not offer such an education directly but give all people who lack endowment with a lump sum of money when they are old enough and wise enough— thanks to their prior education—to make good use of it. They may wish to be trained in specific skills or use the capital to go into some small business for themselves. Of course, it is seems unlikely that one could provide enough resources to every person for advanced training in very remunerative occupations—law or medicine, for example—even in a very wealthy society. Those individuals who do wish to take such training, however, should have reasonably good opportunities to borrow the required funds, given their expected greater earnings and the existence of a well-functioning educational credit market.

Most important, liberal education also helps individuals to be good citizens in the political institutions of Imperfectia.[42] It seems clear that only people who are literate, numerate, and capable of evaluating scientific and historical evidence are likely to be much good at setting up and running systems of rights and redistribution. I mention this point only briefly not because it is trivial but because I take it to be largely obvious. I should also note that if my argument about liberal education is correct, the redistributive and citizen-making functions of education are capable of being realized jointly.

The existence of state-provided education and para-educational goods provides a second kind of social floor consistent with a property and contract regime. It redistributes some goods from those who would otherwise be quite well off to those who would not be so well off for the sake of allowing the latter to realize greater utility gains in the property and contract world.

The Private World and Redistribution

In addition to the redistributive efforts by the state, some important redistribution may take place privately in Imperfectia. It may be inappropriate for the state to make judgments in favor of funding low-κ goods or making too generous a level of provision for a social minimum. But private persons may be able to form more accurate estimates of the character of persons with whom they associate or more accurate interpersonal comparisons of utility than could the state as a whole. I can often form a fairly good estimate of what it is that will make the lives of close friends go comparatively well.

We should not be surprised, therefore, if in at least some situations where exchanges might occur between strangers, gifts take place instead. Wealth may be passed from richer to poorer family members with no expectation of reciprocity. Philanthropic donations may be set up to benefit whole classes of people based on a well-justified belief that these will be for the public good. Nonrelatives may provide assistance and comfort to "deserving" persons—those who are judged not just to be in need but also not to be potential exploiters.

Private associations allow individuals to get to know each other better and thus provide for the redistribution of low-κ goods. This is good because many of the things that do in fact make life go well are low-κ goods, for example, opera. The state probably has no business redistributing to provide opera (unless the liberal-educative functions of the state would thus be served), but a private association of individuals might organize to do so and thereby realize great welfare gains. Any number of other good things may be privately provided in a redistributive fashion.

A private world with private associations could also be an important part of Imperfectia. That being so, the state could have good reasons to allow and encourage its existence by permitting freedom of association and expression to its citizens, among other means.

The existence of such private benevolence is why I come to no conclusion here about the institution of inheritance. It has been proposed to me at various times that an ideal mechanism of redistribution would be confiscation of the wealth of persons who have died and redistribution according to whatever criteria seem morally appropriate. This proposal seems quite impartial and also quite utilitarian. The dead no longer need their wealth, and if they are allowed to transmit it through testamentary disposition, they are more likely than not to leave it to their heirs. And inherited wealth is the ultimate in unearned endowment advantages. Even the best genetic endowment for musicianship or basketball does not generate income for its possessor unbidden, but inherited wealth does.

I am willing to consider the possibility, however, that enough redistribution will take place in the private sphere, using private information about interpersonal comparisons and moral reliability of individuals, to make institutions like the testamentary disposition of wealth morally justifiable. It seems to be a hard empirical question, one that I am unwilling to venture any opinions on here.

SEVEN

The Acceptability of Utilitarianism

Intuitions, Institutions, and Evidence

My sketch of what institutions utilitarianism require should now be, if not complete, at least full enough for its outlines to be discernable. It is now time to begin a summary assessment of the adequacy of utilitarianism as a theory of justice.

The reader will recall that the most telling objections to utilitarianism are based on intuitions against it. In chapter 1 we saw how these intuitions are evoked by thought experiments and how they form a parade of horribles. Chapter 2 introduces a theory of moral intuitions—the inferential theory—which explains their production as a process of unconscious inferences of rightness or wrongness, using both implicit moral principles and tacit background knowledge. In this theory, it is necessary to reconstruct the background knowledge and the inferences that might follow it in order to test the closeness of the implicit principles to a proposed moral theory.

In the discussion of utilitarian institutions I did just this; it is now time to test the closeness of the institutional solutions for moral problems to our moral intuitions. As I suggest in my first exposition of the inferential theory, there could be evidence against utilitarianism if there were no plausible reconstruction of our intuitions as utilitarian under prevailing factual circumstances. Of course, it may still be possible to find cases in which there are isolated counterintuitive *acts* that would be recommended by utilitarianism; but if the inferential theory is correct, it is possible for our moral sensibilities to be "fooled" by unusual conjunctions of circumstances. The logical possibility of such counterintuitive recommendations even under prevailing general conditions should therefore be considered as evidence of little or no weight.

At the same time, the possibility of such strange utilitarian acts is a somewhat disturbing one since it suggests that there can be cases in which utilitarian moral theory recommends to agents one act, while the institutional arrangements of their social universe require another. This theory in these instances is open to the objections of rule worship and the commonsense effacement of utilitarianism. In a later section of this concluding chapter I consider what work might be left for utilitarianism once institutions are up and running.

Utilitarianism as a Horrible Doctrine

This discussion of utilitarianism's parade of horribles proceeds in two parts. The first discusses the interpersonal cases that are of interest to intuitionist moral philosophers; the second discusses political cases. Readers who find the thought experiments of intuitionists irritating may wish to skip ahead to the section on society-wide cases.

Interpersonal cases

One of the first marchers in the parade of horribles is the case in which a doctor must decide whether or not to sacrifice one healthy patient to save the lives of five sick ones. In chapter 5 a subsidiary principle of self-ownership is derived, which if applied to this case, would clearly rule out any such sacrifice. Even in cases in which it is apparent that the sacrifice was utility-optimal, moral hazards would be created by allowing potentially exploitative agents to think that they need not take care of their own organs because other organs might be available to them. The threat of such moral hazards gives us good utilitarian reasons to stick to the rules that protect self-ownership even in these cases. There are thus good utilitarian arguments for not allowing the sacrifice as a general practice, which is fortunate for utilitarianism because that is what our intuitions also require.

It is useful to contrast the organ-sacrifice case with another very popular thought experiment, which also involves the sacrifice of one to save five: the notorious trolley example.[1] In this case, our moral agent is sitting at a switch on a railroad line. A runaway trolley is careening down the track toward five workers, who have their backs turned to it. The switchman cannot do anything to warn these five workers, so if he does nothing they will be run over and killed. He can, however, throw the switch and divert the trolley onto another track. If he takes this latter course of action, only a single worker on the other track will be killed. Should he throw the switch? Most people think he should. At least, they think that it is permissible, if not obligatory, that he do so. The utilitarian judgment about this case seems fairly clear: the switchman should throw the switch.

Thus it would seem that commonsense morality has an internal conflict: in the organ-donation case it is impermissible to sacrifice one to save five, whereas in the trolley case it does seem permissible. How might a suitable utilitarian theory shed any light on these two cases?

We should begin by noting that the utilitarian rationale for a principle of self-ownership and the thicket of procedural and substantive rules that enforce it is the prevention of exploitation. By protecting individuals' control over their own bodies, we aim to prevent persons from being exploited by others and thus protect the evolutionary stability of utilitarianism. Forcible organ donation raises a serious problem of exploitation; would-be exploiters can exercise foresight in hopes of doing better for themselves than equitable arrangements would otherwise allow. But cases of quick decision in unusual accidents like the trolley case raise fewer—virtually no—worries about such exploitation.

There is a certain plausibility about rational exploiters who decide not to take care of their organs if they think there is a good chance of getting new ones at little or no cost to themselves. Furthermore, we can easily imagine corrupt arrangements being made between exploitative patients and amoral doctors to provide such organs if this provision were formally prohibited. It would, after all, be quite pleasant to smoke and drink and eat too much grease with impunity, as well as quite rational to act in such a way to realize the benefit of doing so. But it seems unlikely that even the most selfish and calculating individual would base a decision about working on a particular track on the possibility of an unforeseen accident, the statistical likelihood of which is very small; the expected benefit would simply not be worth the cost of an accurate calculation. So a utilitarian could endorse the throw of the switch without creating much room for would-be exploiters to succeed in their aims.

A utilitarian would approach the commonsense conclusion by a formal argument about exploitation and self-ownership. The intuitive conclusion probably results from an *exploitation detector* built into our processes of moral inference: in cases in which conditions that allow for exploitation are created, a little red flag is raised in our minds. It seems highly probable that such an exploitation-detection cognitive mechanism would be the product of either biological natural selection or cultural evolution; any agent or any group without such a detector would probably have been driven into extinction.[2]

What is to be said about the so-called utility monsters? In chapter 5 we saw that many of the classical cases raise severe questions about exploitation—so severe that a derivative principle of self-ownership should be enough to take care of them. It is not worth the bother to respond to the most explicit kind of utility-monster case, one in which there is a mythical creature that somehow automatically turns disutility of others into greater utility for itself. That is a magical beast like a chimera or a unicorn; it is not of this universe, and it is simply bizarre to imagine that our moral intuitions could have developed to deal with it.

There are some approximations to such a creature in the form of sadists, and these do seem to exist. But the value of utility information attached to the enjoyment of sadistic pleasures is very low; most people have only minor sadistic desires and cannot enter in any comprehensive way into the minds of full-blown sadists. Consequently, there is very good reason to expect that we are faced with a case of exploitation when sadists claim that the joys they experience in torturing a victim are great enough to outweigh the victim's obvious agony. It is not impossible that the sadists' claims are true, but more than likely they want to fool us into allowing them something that will advance their own well-being at the expense of aggregate well-being. Our intuitive exploitation detectors should be activated when they make such a claim. Our utilitarian argument about the dangers of exploitation should give us a very good reason not to allow these tortures.

What of the Roman arena case? Perhaps the utility information we could gather from a single sadist might not be plausible enough to outweigh the sufferings of the victim; but even if millions of people have only minor sadistic leanings, the televised torture of a single victim might reasonably lead to a case in which utilitarianism would seem to require that torture.

The Roman arena is definitely a harder case for utilitarianism, and one can extend the following rebuttal. For utilitarianism to recommend the construction of a Roman arena, two unlikely facts would have to jointly obtain: (1) the satisfaction of the sadism of the masses would necessarily require the real suffering of a real victim, and so a simulation of the kind now provided by many of our mass entertainments would not suffice; (2) the sadism of the masses would have to be of a particularly durable—perhaps genetic—kind, which resists efforts of extirpation by civilization and cultivation.

If it is cheaper in utility terms to civilize a population than to inflict horrible sufferings on a handful of individuals, utilitarianism clearly requires the former course. The evil that lurks in human hearts may be impossible to extirpate entirely; but as a general fact it does seem plausible to at least divert the worst in us away from doing actual harm into fantasized harm. One can be cynical and misanthropic enough to believe that the Roman masses may have experienced genuine personal good in the arena, while still being optimistic enough to believe it may have been possible through cultural change to get them to realize other personal goods. If they were to refuse to endure such changes when the changes were less costly than the sufferings in the arena, they would be behaving exploitatively, and utilitarianism would rule out their enjoyment.

A factual universe in which widespread sadism is of the particularly obdurate kind does not seem to be the one in which we live. It is small wonder that we find sadism to be intolerable.

Society-wide cases

The principle of self-ownership effectively rules out any institution of slavery. It simply does not seem plausible that there is any kind of activity that could be performed by slaves that could not be performed by paid workers. The existence of markets in employment, in which workers are free to move in and out of employment—markets that could not exist without self-ownership—is a powerful exploitation-preventing device. Other things being equal, workers are far less likely to be exploited, or at least exploited to a lesser degree, if they must be compensated to the extent that their work is more strenuous, dangerous, or unpleasant, that is, productive of a greater amount of disutility in itself. And workers free to move will receive such compensation since, if they are rational, they will simply move out of such jobs unless some compensation is introduced. Workers who are not free to move, serfs and slaves, can be subjected to exploitation to a much greater degree. When we see serfdom and slavery, then, we are almost certainly correct in inferring that these institutions exist to exploit serfs and slaves. Our historical experience with real venal oligarchies confirms this intuition. Our exploitation-detection mechanisms, and hence our sense of wrongness, should be triggered.

Of course, exploitation does not exist only in slave and feudal societies. Utilitarians define exploitation as that which takes place when *A* and *B* interact in such a way that A is better off than he or she would be if A and B had acted to bring about the utility-optimal outcome. The deal struck between a capitalist and a worker under actually existing conditions of bargaining power may be to the capitalist's personal advantage, whereas a potential deal that could be struck between them if bargaining power were more evenly distributed could be utility-superior to that which is actually struck. The possibility for this kind of capitalist exploitation seems especially likely if there is any mass of poor persons in a labor market for whom working cheaply is preferable to the even deeper poverty of unemployment. Given that in many societies the differences in bargaining power—because of differences in wealth and skill—are sufficiently great to raise worries about exploitation, there can be doubts about whether the institutional solution here proposed for utilitarianism is adequate to take care of our intuitive worries about the distributive fairness of the doctrine.

In chapter 5 worries of this kind were brushed aside by assuming an egalitarian baseline for the institutions of Imperfectia. Of course, it is unlikely that any known society starts from an egalitarian baseline, and this problem was addressed in chapter 6 with a theory about redistribution. The question now becomes one of how well this theory handles intuitive objections about possible arrangements under capitalism.

It should be clear that the existence of a social minimum and of educative redistribution will handle many cases of capitalist exploitation. Capitalists cannot drive wage bargains that will make any person worse off than he or she would be under the social minimum: workers would simply opt out of the labor market rather than settle for such wages. And persons who have been well educated will have open to them a much greater range of ways to make a living. They, too, can simply walk away from excessively exploitative offers.

To be sure, utilitarian institutions may have built into them some toleration of inegalitarian distribution and the resultant capitalist exploitation. But to the extent that they do tolerate such inequality, they do not actually wander far from common intuitions about what is fair. There is broad moral and political support in advanced industrial societies for providing all children with adequate educational and vocational preparation for decent, humane existences. That differences in advantage should be allowed to accumulate to the point where some people live in squalor seems deeply offensive; that we should continue to be so interested in the fate of schoolchildren in bad urban neighborhoods is a tribute vice pays to virtue in this regard.

At the same time, most people seem intuitively willing to tolerate a large measure of inequality among adults as long as a social floor protects against the most brutal kinds of economic deprivation. This position seems to be a very utilitarian-institutionalist one: when people are asked to justify inequality, they often cite as central concerns economic efficiency and the personal liberty to dispose of one's self and talents in accordance with one's personal good.[3] Most Americans (though perhaps not most residents of industrial democracies) are quite happy with a political economy that sends children into the world of the market well prepared and then lets the chips fall where they may. The gap between what utilitarianism seems to recommend for the political economy of an imperfect world and what commonsense justice also recommends thus seems not to be too wide. Of course, there may be quite a gap between existing conditions and what either a commonsense theory of justice or a utilitarian political economy would recommend, a problem I consider in my discussion of local injustice.

Utilitarianism as an Alienating Doctrine

The central problem of alienation in utilitarianism lies in morality's excessive demands. The total amount of good one could achieve for others by imposing vast sacrifices on oneself is very great, and thus utilitarianism would appear to demand just such a set of sacrifices. Commonsense morality, however, seems to excuse individuals from doing good when the costs of achieving it are too great for the do-gooders. Hence, there would appear to be another gap between utilitarian and commonsense requirements for justice.

The institutions of political economy in an imperfect world, however, may be close to commonsense morality in that they have the effect of combating moral alienation by combating moral exploitation. We may rightly balk at an apparent moral requirement for us to impoverish ourselves; if we actually acted in such a way, we would leave ourselves open to exploitation in a variety of ways, which the institutions of an imperfect world are designed to prevent.

The institutions that protect self-ownership and limited world ownership are in large part predicated on the assumption that it is easier to coordinate the care of individuals if they are charged with looking after themselves. It often makes a great deal more sense for me to look after my body and for other persons to look after their bodies, respectively, than does any other arrangement. Of course, such an arrangement, in which each looks after one's own, is not the only one imaginable: I could be partly responsible for the well-being of 100 other people, 100 other people could be partly responsible for me, and moral care could be shuttled around to whomever needs it most. To a limited extent, this sharing of responsibility is what occurs among friends and within families. But spreading care too thin seems too likely to open up opportunities for individuals who wish to exploit others to shirk their duties.

Frank Jackson, in his article on the nearest and dearest objection to consequentialism,[4] develops a helpful analogy for understanding why an intelligent consequentialist doctrine would be unlikely to sanction unlimited involvement by every agent in the well-being of every other agent, even if the goal of that doctrine is maximization of the well-being of agents. Suppose that a group of us are charged with maintaining order in a large and potentially unruly crowd—say, a group of English football fans. Disturbances might occur in any part of the crowd at any time, but they may be more likely to occur if a security person is absent. Nonetheless, it is easier for more rather than fewer guards to put down a disturbance.

What would be a better strategy for keeping order in the crowd? Would it be best if we were given a section of the stadium and the responsibility for keeping order there, being allowed to leave our posts in none but the direst emergencies? Or should we rove about as a unit, rushing to whatever point seems to be having a disturbance at the moment? Which would keep better order? Often the former, "static defense" strategy will be superior. We each should stay by our posts and do our parts there, even though from moment to moment we might be better able to maximize security by leaving it and rushing off.

What is often true for guards in keeping order is also often true for individual moral agents in attempting to maximize utility: each should stand by one's post— oneself, one's family, and one's projects, for the most part—and maximize utility there, rather than constantly rushing off to whatever point of need seems to have arisen at the moment. Reasonable distributive institutions should guarantee that other agents will not suffer too much from one agent's not being constantly attendant to their needs.

The fact that other agents may be exploiters makes it even more important that one agent is not willing to abandon his or her own projects and own nearest and dearest at sudden moments. Other agents may neglect their posts if they know that someone may come rushing to bail them out; they may waste their time and energy, fail to take care of their bodies, dissipate their physical capital, and so on.

The willingness of others to pitch in when benevolence is called for is also relevant. In chapter 3, I briefly discussed a three-person redistribution problem in which a utilitarian could be exploited indirectly by a greedy agent who refuses to help a third, needy person. The possible existence of such kinds of exploitation provides a second, and in most cases weaker, reason for not abandoning one's own closest persons and projects. It is reasonable to ask whether other agents are doing their fair share to help persons in need. If utilitarians or their close analogues are few and far between and misery is widespread, it is entirely possible that utilitarians could burn themselves out, using up their own resources while the selfish invest their resources prudently and selfishly and thereby prosper.

It should be made clear that the existence of reasonable conditions of distribution are a necessary background for attending to one's own projects. It is one thing to ignore the suffering of a person who wastes his or her own resources; it seems quite another to ignore that of a person who was born impoverished and never had any resources to waste. In actually existing worlds, quite a few people are born with few resources. There is inherited poverty and, consequently, *local injustice*. What obligations does a utilitarian have to struggle against such injustice? Is it not possible that the struggle even here might be so alienating as to bring back the alienation objection with force?

Local injustices may take a number of possible forms. In the grossest kinds, individuals may be denied the rights necessary for securing self-ownership; they may be subject to private violence or to inequities in procedures designed to protect rights. An historical example is the more blatant forms of oppression suffered by black Americans, that is, lynchings, segregation, biased legal proceedings, and so on. More subtle kinds of local injustice may occur when there are inequities in world ownership. The social minimum may be so negligible that some people are allowed to suffer severe poverty; or the distribution of educational resources may be so inequitable that certain children are locked into conditions of failure, penury, and diminution.

The interesting question that utilitarians must ask themselves about local injustice, however, is not what form it takes but the level of *tractability* particular local injustices have. At its most tractable, a local injustice may simply be the artifact of outdated institutions; as noted in chapter 4, the quality of the available equilibrium may be held hostage to history, as well as to local circumstances. A too low social minimum may reflect redistributive institutions that were established to deal with a different era's technical or moral circumstances. For instance, the absence of a decent system of social security may reflect either a different era's lesser wealth or greater worries about exploitation by the work-shy. Or perhaps older institutions that functioned as a kind of a social security—for example, extended families—have subsequently atrophied and not been adequately replaced. Likewise, educational institutions that fail to provide adequate opportunities for children may once have been quite adequate for a simpler world.

What makes local injustices tractable, however, is not just the logical possibility of institutional reform but the existence of a body politic in which a sufficiently large group of citizens is motivated to fight for and sustain institutional changes. The conditions for self-enforcing rules of civic cooperation, noted in chapter 5, must be met. Correcting local injustices can require sacrifices of individuals in two ways: first, there are costs of political participation for those who fight injustices. If we assume that any democratic institutions exist at all, citizens bear costs in becoming informed, in working in political campaigns to elect reformers to office (or to frighten existing officeholders into enacting reforms), and in monitoring officeholders to make sure that reforms stick and that there is no backsliding. Second, once reforms to correct local injustices are enacted, expenditures are often required to get new institutions up and running. Raising the social minimum or improving education usually means raising expenditures, which inevitably means raising taxes.

Bearing these costs raises collective action problems, of course. Even if we interpret "living in a more just society" as a benefit for everyone (which is probably a mistake since some people care not a bit for justice as long as their personal prosperity is guaranteed), the first class of costs to provide it fall specifically on those who struggle for reform, while the benefit itself is spread generally throughout society. The second class of costs is yet more problematic since it generally falls on persons who would be more fortunate if the old local injustice still existed. Given these collective action and redistribution problems, it is unlikely that any reforms are likely to come about in a society that does not already have efficient self-enforcing rules. It is possible that a society may have welfare-maximizing political participation rules but bad ownership and redistribution rules. In such a society, reform is a feasible project, but not all societies operate in this way.

So when utilitarians look around and see local injustice, they should ask themselves whether the right set of social rules is in place to reform a set of antiquated or misfunctioning social institutions, or whether citizens in their political lives are so functionally selfish and short-sighted that the social will to bear the cost of reform simply does not exist. In either case, they will find limits on the costs they can expect morality to impose on them.

In the former case, there are enough other individuals sufficiently like the utilitarians to bear a portion of the costs of political participation. If the local injustice is sufficiently salient and many people are motivated by a sense that something must be done about injustice, that local injustice will call forth many persons who will try to eliminate it. The overall cost of participation will thus be spread among many individuals, limiting the costs that a single individual will have to bear.

In the latter case, the argument for limits on the costs morality will probably impose is a bit more subtle. If the right rules not are in place, attempts to eliminate local injustice through institutional reform are very likely to fail. Political participation in a venal oligarchy or in a bad version of the imperfect world is going to be, more likely than not, simply wasted effort; the expected general utility of any individual's action is likely to be so small that even an act-utilitarian calculation would recommend not becoming engaged.

Thus a utilitarian would have limited public obligations in a world in which others are noncontributors and exploitation is a strong possibility. But what about one's private obligations? It is likely, after all, that one could be obliged to expend large amounts of one's private resources through private charity to the point of impoverishing oneself. Such an impoverishment would be just as alienating when undertaken through private action as it would be through public action.

In a bad world, an individual utilitarian might have some moral obligations of private charity, but these, too, would no doubt be limited by the need to avoid exploitation. The amount of time and energy that a utilitarian could be expected to give to perfect strangers would be relatively small. *Ex hypothesi*, an individual picked at random from a population in a bad world would be an individual likely to try to exploit another. Thus, utilitarians would owe perfect strangers some acts that count as easy rescues—such as throwing a drowning man a life preserver. In these instances, the costs of allowing exploitation are smaller than the benefits that could be realized by the easy rescue. But utilitarians would not owe perfect strangers highly costly rescues.

In a bad world utilitarians would owe to certain other persons close to them more costly assistance: friends and family can certainly make greater moral claims on them than strangers. In this regard, utilitarianism again would coincide with common sense, and for a good reason: the friends and family of a utilitarian are not strangers drawn at random from a potentially exploitative population. If we pick our friends wisely, they are not likely to exploit us either in exchanges or in gifts. And it is also true that our families are less likely to exploit us, in part because they are bound to us by sympathy and in part because a common socialization makes them more likely to share our moral decision rules.

Thus, what utilitarianism recommends for private charity in a mediocre-to-bad world is not far from common sense, either. There can be a rational foundation for the limits of moral obligation both through the welfare state and through one's activity as a private person.

A brief digression on international justice may be in order here. It is an ugly fact of contemporary life that the world is divided between rich and poor countries, and in some of the poorest countries, the material needs of life are so scarce that there is considerable suffering among the population. It is not unreasonable to believe that a large-scale transfer of resources from the rich to the poor would alleviate a great deal of suffering while leaving the inhabitants of richer countries in poorer but still reasonably comfortable circumstances. It would therefore appear that utilitarianism would require such transfers. In many cases, however, they would impose costs on the populations of wealthier countries that some would deem too excessive to be plausibly required by justice.

Of course, there is an interpersonal version of the alienation problem in international distributive justice as well. Individual actors have the capacity to give up their personal time and resources to the amelioration of suffering across borders. They can give money to Oxfam or travel overseas to plant forests and or do any number of other things. Indeed, the fact that states do so little themselves to alleviate global misery may create a strong incentive for benevolent and impartial individuals to do so through their own efforts.

For the most part this book has concentrated on justice within a single society. But precisely because it is a global theory, utilitarianism points to global problems like international distributive justice. I cannot deal fully with the issue here by trying to divine just what utilitarianism requires of us in that realm. But I at least try to construct a reason for having the intuition that massive international transfers are not required by morality.

The most important actors on a global scale are not individual persons but individual states. And international society resembles at best a very imperfect Imperfectia and at worst either a venal oligarchy or a Hobbesian chaos. Exactly which it is depends on the era of history. During a well-functioning international equilibrium, the international society has been an imperfect world. When a single international actor or group of actors holds hegemony over the globe (a typical era is no doubt the high-water mark of European imperialism in the late nineteenth century), international society has been a venal oligarchy. When no actor has been dominant and war predominated, it is more of a Hobbesian chaos.

By now the reader can imagine what would happen to a purely hypothetical state of Utilitariana (perhaps a peaceful democracy full of genuine and self-conscious utilitarians) that attempted to undertake a large-scale utility-maximizing transfer of resources in this environment. It would almost certainly be the victim of terrible treatment by its neighbors, in a Hobbesian era, or by the hegemonic state, in a venal-oligarchic era. Its resources are what it must rely on to compete economically and ultimately militarily with other states. Should it transfer them away, it would be weaker and less able to defend its interests. Utilitariana would face conquest and colonization at worst, pauperization at best, and the individual utilitarians within would probably, in their diminished state, cease to be effective as utilitarians at all.

Private persons who attempt to alleviate global miseries may also find themselves exploited, albeit in a variety of different ways. They will make themselves worse off vis-à-vis more selfish persons who do not make such efforts: the problem of fair contribution to redistribution applies to global justice just as much as it does to local justice. Moreover, their meliorative efforts in other polities may help elites in societies that are themselves venal oligarchies. Many of the poorest countries have elites who are fantastically rich and maintain their riches by monopolizing political power. By providing outside relief of suffering, utilitarians may blunt domestic political forces within those societies, which would otherwise be pushing for more just local arrangements.

Thus, at the very least, the intuition that there may be limits to obligations in global justice may not be entirely mistaken. Utilitarianism need not be alienating, even on a divided globe.

Another brief digression on law-abidingness in a moral tyranny may help the reader to see how utilitarianism faces problems of moral alienation. Readers will remember an objection advanced in the introductory chapter against utilitarianism because it might endorse the establishment of a totalitarian party or religion, metaphorically called a Church Universal, through the use of state power and inquisitions if that is what would make a sufficiently large part of a population well off. Such an establishment seems to be an intolerable affront to our moral intuitions, an attack on liberty and decency.

In chapter 5 the possibility of a particular kind of bad society, the moral tyranny is discussed. In this bad world, an elite holds a society together not for the sake of pursuing its own material gain—as in the case of a venal oligarchy—but for the sake of imposing on it a collective pursuit of some symbolic or psychic good. It should be simple enough to infer now why the establishment of a Church Universal, while theoretically permitted by utilitarianism, should be counterintuitive. The Church Universal's ends can in theory reflect the goods of most individuals in a society. But it seems more likely that it is really a form of moral tyranny: an imposition of ends that are not personal goods. Because the kinds of spiritual ends that a church seeks to promote are classical cases of low-κ goods, it is highly unlikely that we can verify about any society in which a Church Universal exists that it is not a moral tyranny. It is certainly in the interest of the leaders of such a church to claim that it is not (rebellion may ensue should people begin to think otherwise). But the utility realized by spiritual consolation is too idiosyncratic and too much locked in the heads of individuals to be made interpersonally comparable with any high degree of accuracy.

Where a Church Universal already exists, then, an Imperfectia or a venal oligarchy could well exist in its place. For reasons cited in chapter 5, it is highly plausible that such a society would be preferable to a moral tyranny. Where a Church Universal does not yet exist, but where there is a movement to establish one, intelligent moral agents should be suspicious for the kinds of reasons brought up in chapter 6.

Given that some persons at least see it as in their interest to oppress the goods of other persons, and given that it is hard to verify their claims of utilitarian justification for their policies, it seems more likely than not that attempts to establish a Church Universal are a kind of spiritual rent seeking, that is, attempts to establish the non-pecuniary or psychic well-being of certain persons at the expense of others through the manipulation of the political process. Our suspicions of forthcoming exploitation should be raised, and our intuitive sense that something very wrong is about to happen should be triggered. There is thus a good utilitarian reason for the commonsense libertarian position taken against state enforcements of ideological purity.

Utilitarianism and the Publicity Objection

We saw in chapter 1 that one possible objection to utilitarianism was that it might attempt to solve the various problems it raises through some form of undemocratic and systematic deception of the people. This is what Bernard Williams derisively calls "Government House utilitarianism" and what John Rawls worries about in his claim, explicated in chapter 2, that in proper theories of justice terms must be publicly knowable and defensible.

We now have available the analytical machinery to answer this particular objection. What utilitarianism appears to require are institutions in which the kind of Government House deception about which Williams is exercised must be forbidden. Communia and Libertaria would lack any kind of Government House because, strictly speaking, they would be societies without states. In those worlds, everyone simply knows the rules and follows them. In the various Imperfectias, various open political procedures are an institutional requirement of utilitarian political theory. The omnipresent possibility of exploitation through manipulation of the process makes any kind of Government House untenable. No sane citizenry would ever tolerate the existence of an elite, which makes choices about what morality the rest of us are to believe, for the excellent institutionalist reason that would-be exploiters would find their way into Government House like ants into a picnic basket. And that invasion would lead to an outcome that would be disastrous in utilitarian terms. In an Imperfectia, the rules must be publicly understood by the citizens for the utilitarian political logic of such a place to work at all.

In the bad moral universes, deception about morality may go on, but that can hardly be a problem with utilitarianism. In a venal oligarchy, of course, open political procedures may not exist, or such open political procedures as do exist may be largely impotent to oppose the will of the ruling elite. But the activities of this elite, however repugnant, are not the activities of a utilitarian Government House. Also, the kinds of suppression of open discussion of the truth that would occur in a moral tyranny seem to be ruled out as unacceptable in almost any plausible circumstances.

If the kind of world we live in is an Imperfectia, in which some complex set of rules of political procedure is justified by utilitarianism, Bernard Williams asks another question: given that utilitarianism has justified a world in which very little direct aggregation takes place, what is left of utilitarianism?

> If utilitarianism gets to this point [i.e., where it does almost all of its work indirectly], and determines nothing of how thought in the world is conducted, demanding merely that the way in which it is conducted be for the best, then I hold utilitarianism has disappeared, and that the residual position is not worth calling utilitarianism.[5]

It would seem that a highly protean doctrine has frozen into a shape in which it is no longer recognizable: Once everyone has rights that are recognized, once some kind of welfare state is put in place, it seems that the doctrine has little work to do at all. Furthermore, it is far from clear that it does us much service even as a public philosophy since it is quite possible to reason from any number of other plausible principles to the kind of institutions that utilitarianism has endorsed. Egalitarian principles or justice as fairness or ordinary common sensibilities about justice arguably converge on an endorsement of an institutional world very similar to that which utilitarianism appears to endorse. To put the objection another way: once we have gone to such great lengths to show how utilitarianism is at least congruent with common sense, why should we bother with it at all? Why not just keep common sense?

What Is Left of Utilitarianism?

Even in a world full of rules and institutions—like that of Imperfectia—there is still normative work for utilitarianism to do. The foundation for this work stems from an argument in chapter 1 that the work of utilitarianism is more likely a form of local rather than global maximizing, of making the best use of new information and opportunities on the margin rather than a complete revolution of social relations. In imperfect worlds, this work thus includes *local maximization, constitutional* change, and *exceptional case guidance.* In addition there is a kind of distinctive normative work specifically for utilitarians in venal oligarchies.

To provide anything like a full theory of any of these things here would require an entire new book. What I do provide is merely a series of thumbnail sketches of the problems. The aim is to show that there is still plenty of value in a consciously held global theory of utilitarianism, and therefore we should not fall back only on common sense and whatever reasonable institutions are lying about.

Bread-and-Butter Politics

Even within a system in which rights of self-ownership and world ownership are protected from direct utility maximizing, there are still plenty of local maximization problems that can be better or worse solved in utilitarian terms. Utilitarianism does not have to be just the theory in the background that justifies a set of institutions; it can provide serious help in showing how they can best be run.

First, there is the problem of *protecting rights.* It is all very well to talk of protecting rights in the abstract, but actual policymakers have to make decisions about how to protect them concretely. Rights do not protect themselves. Even if the vast majority of people in a society respect the rights of others in the absence of enforcement, there will still be opportunists who will ignore them when there are opportunities for private gain. Some form of enforcement is necessary, and enforcement is never to be had for free. Inside each problem of protecting commonly recognized rights there is an implicit maximization problem.

Consider a concrete example: one right that all persons in any plausibly decent society would have would be the right to be protected against violent assault. Unhappily there are people who will commit violent assault when they can get away with it. They will commit assaults for the sake of gratifying their own psychological urges toward sadism or dominance, for the sake of avenging perceived insults, or for more strategic reasons like extorting property or services from their victims. There are various ways to prevent such assaults. It may be possible to avert such acts in advance by educative efforts to shape the character of the offenders so that they will either lack or be able to suppress inclinations for domination or vengeance. It is also certainly a good idea to attempt to deter assaults by detecting and punishing them. And—this is more controversial—some would-be assailants may be so committed to violence that they are beyond the reach of education, rehabilitation, or deterrence. If such persons can be reliably identified, a strategy for preventing assaults would be to incapacitate them, possibly through permanent incarceration or lifetime supervision of their conduct.

The maximizing problem involved in protecting people from assault is not a simple one. Any one of these three strategies has costs: all three will require the expenditures of public resources; the second two will have additional costs. Punishing people to deter them causes a direct utility loss to the punished, and that loss cannot be ignored by a utilitarian. It is implausible that there could be a good utilitarian justification for torturing convicted assailants to death, even if such a policy would have a significant deterrent effect. Preventative detention or other forms of incapacitation of those judged to be irredeemably violent imposes a cost on detainees in the form of lost liberty.

Punitive and incapacitative measures also have a more subtle cost in the incentives they create for both official corruption and other forms of criminal behavior. If the punishment for criminal conviction is too savage, potential convicts will have a strong incentive to attempt to avoid conviction through bribery, and that incentive in turn creates another incentive for officials to pursue individuals with criminal charges that might otherwise be ignored. And, unhappily, if punitive sanctions are too harsh, those who might be subject to them will also have incentives to engage in other forms of illegalities: forcible and violent escapes from officers of the law, threats and coercion against persons involved in judicial proceedings, and so on.

It is a difficult duty for society's legislators to try to solve a maximizing problem under these conditions. Utilitarian considerations can play at least two explicit roles in the process. First, they can provide a guide to the relative importance of the right in question to be protected. Keeping people safe from violent assault is an important social end, but it cannot be allowed to override everything in sight. As I have just noted, we could not realistically expect to justify torturing people to death slowly and painfully for the crime of unarmed assault, even if such a policy would lead to a significant decline in the incidence of that crime. Neither could we plausibly lock people up on the mere suspicion, even if reasonable, that they might commit assault. By comparison, we might be justified in interning persons in wartime on the mere reasonable suspicion[6] of their being spies or saboteurs: here the goal is sufficiently important to provide a warrant for more extreme action. So first, utilitarian reasoning can provide a sort of *upper bound of severity* with which a legislator is entitled to deal with a problem. Utilitarianism can help elaborate constitutional standards like due process (no locking people up on mere suspicion, at least in peacetime) and limits on cruel and unusual punishments (no torturing people to death).

Second, utilitarianism can provide a standard for good legislation and appropriations within the bounds it establishes. Different levels of taxation can be established to raise revenue to suppress crime, and there are different ways of allocating those funds among teachers, officers, and prison warders. Some of these will be superior, in utilitarian terms, to others, and utilitarianism recommends seeking this latter class. This standard is one that may well be distinct from that provided by our unaided intuitions or from other theories of justice. But since we have reasons to believe that our unaided intuitions cannot solve cognitive problems of arbitrarily great complexity, and we have reasons for thinking utilitarianism the correct theory of justice, we have reasons for following its suggestions in this kind of local maximization problem. We especially have reasons for following its advice, given that over time both the information we have about the relative efficacy of different policies and the relative efficiency with which we can process this information change.

In addition to the special good of security, there is the problem of the provision of public goods more generally. Well-constituted polities do not normally exist only to protect the rights of their constituents. They also have considerable responsibilities for the provision of public goods, that is, those goods that, because of jointness of supply nonexcludability in their enjoyment, will not normally be provided in socially optimal quantities by private actors in a market. National defense and environmental protection are obvious examples. I cannot be excluded from enjoying the benefits of defense against a foreign invasion of the United States as long as I remain within its frontiers, nor can I realistically be prevented from enjoying all the clean air I can breathe. So, usually, the only way to see that these things are provided is to levy a tax on a populace or, in the case of clean air, either to subject air-polluting emissions to regulation or to create and enforce property rights in emissions.

In the provision of public goods, utilitarianism again engages two kinds of normative work. First, through the semirigidity principle for Imperfectias, which is argued in chapter 6, it provides a bound on the sorts of policies that might be enacted in the pursuit of public goods provision. To cite my toy example again: free public concerts of classical music may be a nonexcludable good, but their policy effect might be nothing more than a utility windfall for a (politically influential) faction of classical music lovers. This bound exists to prevent certain kinds of rent seeking, for example, by any constituency that will benefit a great deal by the provision of some non-excludable good at the expense of everyone else. Second, utilitarianism provides distinctive normative guidance concerning how much and what kinds of public goods are to be provided. Within the constraints provided by the semirigidity principle, the principle of utility can give us at least a rough answer about, for example, how much and what kind of national defense is a good amount.

Finally, there is the problem of *setting the social minimum*. The social minimum argued for in chapter 6 also provides an area for local maximizing in which utilitarianism matters. An important part of the trick for legislators here is to try to set the level of this minimum to that level where the welfare-enhancing effects of transferring resources to those who are in deep need of them is balanced by the best estimate of the bad effects of potential exploitation. Here, as elsewhere, the kind of normative guidance that a utilitarian theory provides is distinct from common sense and from other theories of justice. A more egalitarian or prioritarian theory would probably urge us to be more tolerant of exploitation by the worst off, while commonsense justice would probably drag in a farrago of competing notions about needs, just deserts, fairness, and so on.

So it is clear that in local maximizing—the problems of bread-and-butter politics—utilitarianism maintains a distinct role and does not simply collapse into common sense. I now turn to the question of what role utilitarianism might have beyond bread-and-butter politics.

Change-of-constitution questions

Hitherto in my discussion of Imperfectias I have written as if the kinds of utility information that are interpersonally available are relatively static, and I have assumed that the distribution of choice rules among individuals is fairly static as well. But in reality such a stasis need not obtain. Possible advances in moral and scientific understanding may change our assessment of the utility effects of different kinds of policy. For example, we may become convinced through economic research that certain goods cannot be delivered adequately through a free market; perhaps an optimal free market in health insurance may be unfeasible because asymmetric information makes it a "market for lemons." Or psychological research may convince us that the kind of harm done to members of a racial or cultural minority through hate speech and other forms of stigmatization is much graver and more pervasive than we had hitherto believed. Consequently, it may become reasonable to believe that some kind of institutional change is necessary. The establishment of some form of national health care may require a bend in the principle of semirigidity and put a crimp in previously existing economic liberty. And placing limits on some previously existing constitutional protection of free expression may require an exception to be made in a general prohibition against legislation for or against purely symbolic behaviors because of their alleged utility effects.

Utilitarianism recommends some procedure for institutional change in Imperfectia —a procedure for a constitutional amendment, for example—that meets the following standard. The procedure should be difficult enough to make it unlikely that it will be profitable for any group of rent seekers to take advantage of it. But it should be simple enough that—as long as there is a large (probably a super-majority-sized) and enduring body of moderately well-informed and conscientious citizens capable of realizing the long-term optimizing effects of a change—change can take place. The amendment provisions of the U.S. Constitution are at least plausible candidates for such utilitarian meta-rules. That an amendment must be approved both by two-thirds of the national legislature (or a constitutional convention) and by two-thirds of the states is a difficult requirement to meet, and it is unlikely that most groups of rent seekers will attempt to amend the Constitution to achieve their ends. But the requirements are not so difficult that amendment is impossible: the basic document has been amended over twenty times in two centuries—often achieving far-reaching consequences.[7]

Utilitarians should be willing to trust that such a process would not become an opportunity for even a supermajority to prosper at the deep expense of a small minority; their theory of how Imperfectia can be governed at all depends on citizens following rules that give them at least some regard for one another. Furthermore, utilitarians will be willing to tolerate a worse-off effect on a minority, but only if it is clear that the gains to the majority will outweigh the losses to the minority.

The utilitarian recommendation is distinct from that which would be made by other theories of justice. A prioritarian theory of justice would probably recommend giving a constitutional veto to some potentially worse-off minority to make sure that its interests are not harmed by an aggregating majority. A libertarian theory would probably insist on making it even more difficult or impossible to abridge constitutional guarantees through amendment. And an egalitarian theory might try to make it difficult or impossible to amend a constitution in ways that might diminish the egalitarianism of the institutional outcome of such an amendment.

Defenders of theories of justice other than utilitarianism should be quick to argue the superiority of their theories on the grounds that we may not even want a supermajority interfering in certain kinds of institutional arrangements. Would we really want to put a crimp in freedom of speech, the libertarian should argue, just because two-thirds of the population has an enduring conviction that such would be the optimal thing to do? Would we really want to allow some minority to be oppressed, the egalitarian should argue, just because two-thirds of a national electorate has an enduring belief that it would be best overall for that oppression to occur?

Of course, in any world in which citizens have no moral regard for at least some other citizens, there is a danger that the utilitarian's provisions for large-scale institutional change will be used by supermajorities to exploit superminorities. But, *ex hypothesi*, a world in which citizens have no moral regard for at least some other citizens is only doubtfully an Imperfectia since its norms would make it more likely to choose the rules that set up a venal oligarchy, albeit one in which the "oligarchy" is an enduring majority of the population. Such a world seems more like a venal *polyarchy*, which differs from a venal oligarchy only in the number of exploiters.

The charge that utilitarianism is out of line with our intuitions in its recommendations for constitutional change may implicitly be using our worries about what goes on in a "badish" world of a venal oligarchy. To show that utilitarianism is inadequate in its recommendations, it would be necessary to show that horrible results would take place in a world in which citizens have norms or follow rules that bring about the functional equivalent of mutual regard. Until such a demonstration is forthcoming, I see no reason to imagine that the distinctive advice utilitarianism gives us about constitutional change should be rejected. And furthermore, I think that the utilitarian advice has a strong point that other theories lack: its sensitivity to changing empirical realities and its democratic willingness, at least in the right kind of moral worlds, to allow people to collectively control their own lives in accordance with these changing conditions.[8]

Exceptional Cases

No matter how well adapted a society's institutions might be to the task of maximizing aggregate utility, there can still be opportunities for an individual act that optimizes better than the rules allow. An emergency may require the disposal of another person's property when his or her consent to do so is unavailable or unforthcoming. A person—either a private person or a state official—may come into possession of information that must be acted upon promptly but without proper authority in order to avert some disaster. A soldier or other official may be lawfully ordered to do something that he or she knows on the basis of private information will result in a bad outcome.

Here the principle of utility seems to give conflicting advice since the institutions that it justifies (property, behavioral constraints, and legitimate lines of authority) lead to an outcome it cannot sanction. What should an individual agent do? Simply to allow agents to maximize as they see fit would lead to disaster since then every kind of exploiter could get away with anything on the grounds that at the time it was done, it seemed to be a utilitarian course of action. Such an unchecked individualism raises the specter of the utilitarian-Hobbesian state of nature briefly discussed at the end of chapter 3.

A possible resolution, one in which the principle of utility does some explicit work, is as follows: an agent who sees no other course of action but to break the rules and avert disaster (or possibly realize some great good) should do so, promptly owning up to the deed and submitting to punishment if need be. Of course, a reasonably humane set of institutions, like those that would exist in a decent Imperfectia, would allow for mitigation and even in some cases exoneration of persons who break the rules. A jury in a criminal trial in Imperfectia could, for example, review the rule-breaking agent's actions to see if it really was based on a reasonable belief that there was no course other than to break the rules or risk a great loss in utility.

If the standards of review are sufficiently stringent, potential exploiters will be deterred by the likelihood of punishment for acts that are not really utility maximizing, while agents who find themselves in difficult moral situations will not be deterred from doing the right thing under the principle of utility. These standards of review could be more or less self-consciously utilitarian, requiring a jury to consider the seriousness of rule breaking as potential exploitation. And if we consider the conditions of Imperfectia—in which citizens are utilitarian enough to care about preserving a good society for one another—there is reason to believe that citizen juries would do a good job of applying these standards of review.

Outside of Imperfectia, utilitarianism would still provide a role for some kind of individual calculation. In a venal oligarchy, it can sanction disobedience to rules that exist primarily to benefit the oligarchs (such as respecting the property rights of a wealthy man who withholds aid from the starving) while still respecting those rules that have a clearer utilitarian justification (rules against assault, killing, etc.). In a moral tyranny, a utilitarian calculator might cultivate—to the extent that prudence allows—breaking those rules that attempt to impose a nonpersonal theory of the good. The utilitarian would keep the flame of individuality alive; protect the banned thoughts and the banned books; and perhaps hope for a better day, if only under a venal oligarchy.

If utilitarians do find themselves in a venal oligarchy that seems unlikely to change into something more desirable in the near future, they may have an additional useful service to offer: they can make the arguments found in chapter 5 about quasi compliance to the rulers of that society. They can advise, not unreasonably, the venal oligarchs that they will be more successful in the long run if they guarantee stability, peace, and a modicum of liberty to their subjects. Subjects allowed enjoyment of their own property will generate more wealth than those constantly subject to pillage and rapine. And subjects allowed at least the liberty of personal conscience and conviction are less likely to be provoked to that bitter resentment that is the bane of princes. If there must be a prince, a good utilitarian can at least serve the end of good by being the voice of prudence and moderation.

Utilitarianism thus provides agents with a certain freedom to act according to its precepts. Like so many other moral theories, it provides room for morally motivated, conscientious objections. Indeed, given that even a well worked-out set of social institutions may fail to anticipate certain moral problems, utilitarianism might be best served by agents who keep it and its derivative principles close to awareness in moral deliberation.

It is thus not the case that utilitarianism vanishes entirely into institutions and common sense: it can and should remain in agents' moral deliberations as an explicit theory. It retains a distinctive content in ordinary politics, in constitution-making politics, and in the individual deliberations of agents.

Conclusion

I have begun this book with a series of objections against utilitarianism drawn from common intuitions of its wrongness. In providing a theory in which moral intuitions play the part of inferences and in trying to show what it is that utilitarianism would actually recommend in the real world, I have tried to answer these objections. Utilitarianism, I have shown, only recommends our doing the counterintuitive thing in factual worlds in which exploitation does not exist and the evolutionary stability of utilitarianism is nonproblematic. Utilitarianism only recommends horrible acts in those worlds in which there is no problem with interpersonal comparisons and no great probability that others will act exploitatively. And utilitarianism only requires us to act in ways that would be morally alienating in worlds in which there is no realistic possibility that what would be alienating is also exploitative.

I have also tried to show that attempts to subvert utilitarianism through appeals to formal properties about theories of justice—such as finality and publicity—do not work either. The finality of utilitarianism is unlikely to be in jeopardy in a world in which people cannot suffer horrible acts as patients or alienating acts as agents. The rules protecting self-ownership, which are necessary to prevent exploitation, also forbid the horrible acts and allow individuals the liberty to do much of what they see as best with their lives. The question of utilitarianism's subversion in its finality by grossly unfair distributive arrangements is answered by a set of institutions in which no deep suffering is allowed and a generous provision is made for educational opportunities for all. The question of inadequate publicity is answered by showing that utilitarian arrangements would not permit a Government House and would also continue to permit some kind of consciously held utilitarianism to work as a public philosophy.

I believe that these arguments, while hardly comprehensive, airtight, and unanswerable, are adequate to make a case for the plausibility of utilitarianism. What institutions utilitarianism could plausibly require in a world like our own has been explained. If these are not, in fact, the institutions that it would require, it is up to my critics to point out why. I myself, having gone through this account, think it plausible to stay with utilitarianism. Barring a thorough criticism of these institutional arrangements or some other pillar of the theory, a hybrid prioritarian or egalitarian account of the sort I sketched in chapter 1 is neither desirable nor warranted.

This book has been, in effect, a sketch. Much work remains to be done in filling out the painting. I see two areas in which further work would be particularly fruitful. First, the concept of utility needs much refinement. Here I have had to work with a mostly intuitive and commonsensical concept of interpersonally comparable utility. This concept can do only the roughest kind of normative work. Careful theoretical refinement is needed, possibly through a formal axiomatization that would provide interpersonally comparable cardinal scales similar to the von Neumann–Morgenstern utility functions. An even more ambitious refinement would be to provide a more comprehensive theory of what utility is; such a theory might draw on new advances in neuropsychology and provide more than just a measure of utility. Even a von Neumann–Morgenstern type of measure would only be a kind of moral thermometer. A theory of utility would be a theory of moral heat.[9] Extending the analogy further, we might think of Bentham's hedonistic theory of utility as being like the old caloric theory of heat. Whatever new and scientific theory of utility might be forth-coming could be the moral equivalent of the mean molecular kinetic energy theory of heat. Whatever form it might take, a more sensitive concept of utility would help us to refine much further our answer to what kind of institutions utilitarianism would require. This advance would be a great boon both to moral reflection and to political practice.

Second, more research should be done in endogenizing institutions. Only the first and most tentative steps have been taken to show how a society of individuals, who are to some extent rational and self-interested, solves the problem of order and holds together. The subsidiary question of the origins of norms and rules, their relation to evolved human psychology, their propagation through populations via an "epidemiology of representations," and their institution-creating effects is a rich and rewarding area for research by social science. And whatever rewards are reaped by that research can be brought back into moral theory, as they will provide an even richer account of the institutional requirements of theories of justice. This richer account can, in turn, be used to deepen reflection on the acceptability of moral theories.

But both the further exploration of the concept of utility and of the work done by decision rules is a subject for another day. I have taxed the reader's patience enough with this account of utilitarianism. If have even slightly vindicated the doctrine while spurring further work, my task is done.

NOTES

CHAPTER 1

1. For a discussion of the distinction between rule and act versions of utilitarianism, see David Lyons, *Forms and Limits of Utilitarianism* (Oxford: Clarendon, 1965).

2. See Robert Adams, "Motive Utilitarianism," *Journal of Philosophy* 71 (1980): 476–82.

3. Or more reasonably, there are acts about which one should have the strongest possible reservations: intentionally killing an innocent human being is a paradigm of such an act. Perhaps one could commit such acts to prevent a moral catastrophe, such as the deaths of thousands of innocent people, but one must surely refrain from such acts under any normal circumstances.

4. I owe this example to Shelley Kagan. See his *Limits of Morality* (Oxford: Clarendon, 1989), 25–7.

5. I owe the term *personal good* to John Broome, who formulated it and gave it this name. See his *Weighing Goods: Uncertainty, Equality, and Time* (Cambridge and London: Basil Blackwell, 1991), 165.

6. See G. E. Moore, *Principia Ethica* (1903; reprint, Cambridge: Cambridge University Press, 1956), 83–5.

7. For a discussion of welfare economics and its approaches to social welfare, see Dennis C. Mueller, *Public Choice II* (New York: Cambridge University Press, 1989), 1–43, 374–407.

8. The emphasis is mine in the first instance, Bentham's in the second and third. See Jeremy Bentham, *The Works of Jeremy Bentham*, ed. John Bowring (Edinburgh: William Tait, 1843), vol. 1, 1.

9. See Mill in Mary Warnock, ed., *John Stuart Mill: Utilitarianism, On Liberty, Essay on Bentham, together with selected writings of Jeremy Bentham and John Austin* (New York: New American Library, 1974), 258–62. For an elegant contemporary reconstruction and defense of Mill's views on value, see Wendy Donner, *The Liberal Self: John Stuart Mill's Moral and Political Philosophy* (Ithaca, N.Y.: Cornell University Press, 1991).

10. Such articulations actually begin a little earlier than the twentieth century with F. Y. Edgeworth, *Mathematical Psychics* (London: Kegan & Paul, 1881), who introduced differential and integral calculus into utilitarian analysis. Edgeworth did not break, however, with the hedonist tradition of earlier utilitarianism.

11. For the original axiomatization, the influence of which over contemporary economics and decision theory cannot be easily overestimated, see John von Neumann and Oskar Morgenstern, *Theory of Games and Economic Behavior* (Princeton, N.J.: Princeton University Press, 1944), 8–29. For a simpler axiomatization (one of many) and a rebuttal of common misunderstandings of axiomatic utility theory, see R. Duncan Luce and Howard Raiffa, *Games and Decisions* (New York: Wiley, 1957), 12–38.

12. For expositions of the view that persons are not necessarily better off when their preferences are satisfied, see Cass Sunstein, "Preferences in Politics," *Philosophy and Public Affairs* 20 (1991): 3, and James Griffin, *Well-being: Its Meaning, Measurement, and Moral Importance* (Oxford: Clarendon, 1986), 10–20.

13. See Broome, *Weighing Goods*, 180–2.

14. I have in mind here especially Mary Ann Glendon, *Rights Talk: The Impoverishment of Political Discourse* (New York: Free Press, 1991), 1–17. See also L. W. Sumner, *The Moral Foundations of Rights* (Oxford: Clarendon, 1987), chap. 1. Sumner makes an apt analogy between contemporary rights discourse and an arms race, in which competing powers engage in a futile and ultimately self-defeating escalation.

15. In his successful Senate campaign, Mr. Wofford of Pennsylvania made frequent use of the slogan "If every criminal has a right to see an attorney, why shouldn't every law-abiding citizen have a right to see a physician?"

16. Indeed, in certain contexts pornography may actually have a positive causal effect on the egalitarianism of gender norms. It may do so by breaking down traditional, less egalitarian sexual roles or by being so disgusting that its viewers develop a greater commitment to gender egalitarianism. For a brief review of some of the legal and empirical issues at stake in the debate of pornography and gender egalitarianism, see Deborah L. Rhode, *Justice and Gender* (Cambridge, Mass.: Harvard University Press, 1989), 263–73.

17. I do not mean to suggest that utilitarianism boils down the question of conflicting rights in the pornography case to a simplistic question of whether or not it should be banned. Obviously it is a necessary but not a sufficient condition that the losses due to tolerating pornography must be greater than the gains to justify banning it. Alternative strategies, such as the use of education to change norms of intersexual interaction, may be superior to a prohibitive strategy.

18. Apparently at least one federal appeals circuit answers this rhetorical question in the affirmative. In the majority opinion of *American Bookseller's Assn. v. Hudnut*, 771 F. 2d 323 (7th Cir. 1985), Judge Frank Easterbrook accepts the contention that pornography may be the source of massive harm to women, but he insists that the free-speech provisions of the U.S. Constitution prevent a legislature from doing anything to redress those harms.

19. I am grateful to Derek Parfit for making the difference between these two views clear to me.

20. Derek Parfit's apt description. I've often heard him use it as an expository device in seminars, although I do not think it has yet appeared in his published writing.

21. The connection between intertemporal divisions within our own lives and divisions between persons is one that some utilitarian thinkers have exploited to throw doubt on the idea that theories of justice should be distribution-sensitive. Metaphysical arguments have been advanced by Derek Parfit to show that the differences in personal identity between lives and within lives may be the same kinds of differences; hence those principles that we use within our own lives and those that we use across lives should be the same. See Parfit, *Reasons and Persons* (New York and Oxford: Oxford University Press, 1984), 341–2; and John Broome, "Utilitarian Metaphysics?" in *Interpersonal Comparisons of Well-being*, ed. Jon Elster and John E. Roemer (New York: Cambridge University Press, 1991), 70–97, at 93.

22. Mark Johnson provides an example of such a view:

> There is nothing scientific about any of this [utilitarianism] whatsoever, for there is no scientific calculation possible, given our present lack of knowledge of causal connection and our inability to decide in any satisfactory way where to terminate our consideration of the indefinitely long chains of effects issuing from a given action. . . . And it would require of us a psychologically impossible awareness of all the actions available to us at a given moment that might possibly affect the well-being of others.

See *Moral Imagination: Implications of Cognitive Science for Ethics* (Chicago and London: University of Chicago Press, 1993), 122.

23. The story was told by Eddy Zemach of the Hebrew University of Jerusalem, who was visiting at Williams College in the spring of 1986.

24. Assuming, of course, that the Third Reich and its associated train of horrors are not a necessary causal condition for some future event of which we would strongly approve but cannot foresee. It is logically possible, for instance, that our having had the experience of Auschwitz may allow us to head off some even worse horror further in the future, by making us sensitive to the kinds of things that can happen if certain people are allowed to get political power. But, of course, this possibility strengthens rather than weakens the case against utilitarianism.

25. It could be that we are all profoundly deluded when we think we are acting prudently; perhaps the universe is sufficiently full of fatality and chaos that we really have no control over our destinies even when planning only for ourselves. Such a contention is fascinating and radical, but it raises metaphysical issues too deep for a mere political scientist to try to address. I can only ask dedicated Heracliteans to bracket their worries in this book.

26. See Henry Sidgwick, *The Methods of Ethics*, 7th ed. (1907; reprint, Indianapolis: Hackett, 1981), 411–3.

27. Robert Nozick has, as a thought experiment, advanced the idea of such an "experience machine" and argued that few if any people would allow themselves to be plugged into it. See *Anarchy, State, and Utopia* (New York: Basic Books, 1974), 42–5. His thought experiment and its conclusion have influenced a number of subsequent thinkers. One of the most important is natural law theorist John Finnis, who uses the thought experiment to make an antihedonist argument in his *Natural Law and Natural Rights* (New York: Oxford University Press, 1981), 85–8.

28. Examples like these are used to raise the possibility that personal good may be more than experiential; see Parfit, *Reasons and Persons*, 149–53; and also Thomas Scanlon, "The Moral Basis of Interpersonal Comparisons," in *Interpersonal Comparisons of Well-being*, 22–3.

29. For sophisticated accounts and defenses of hedonism, see Sidgwick, *Methods of Ethics*, 123–98; see also J. C. B. Gosling, *Pleasure and Desire: The Case for Hedonism Reviewed* (Oxford: Clarendon, 1969); and Rem B. Edwards, *Pleasures and Pains: A Theory of Qualitative Hedonism* (Ithaca, N.Y.: Cornell University Press, 1979).

30. There are many ways of describing the logical foundations of utility theory. This particular set of requirements is an adaption of John C. Harsanyi, "Normative Validity and Meaning of von Neumann–Morgenstern Utilities," in *Frontiers of Game Theory*, ed. Ken Binmore, Alan Kirman, and Piero Tani (Cambridge, Mass.: MIT Press, 1993), 307–30, at 309–10.

31. See Brian Barry, *Political Argument* (London: Routledge & Kegan Paul, 1965), 3–15.

32. A brief exposition of the money pump can be found in Ken Binmore, *Fun and Games: A Text on Game Theory* (Lexington, Mass.: D.C. Heath, 1992), 95. There is a hidden assumption built into this argument, however, which may not always hold. This assumption is that it is always rational to prefer to have more money than less, that the effect on well-being of a

greater amount of wealth is always positive. In most real-world cases, this assumption is fairly plausible, but it is not guaranteed to be true in all cases. If the effect of having a certain amount of wealth on well-being is negative, so that one is better off with A and less wealth than with A and more wealth, going through a money pump or a Dutch book like cycle is anything but irrational. But the argument from the money pump can be made stronger by generalizing its premise. A generalized version of the argument would be a reductio ad absurdam, which can be made by adding the additional following premises. Call the first the *premise of complementarity*. Suppose for any given set of alternatives {A,B,C} there is some complementary alternative S such that A and S are preferred to A, B and S are preferred to B, and C and S are preferred to C. This premise seems close to self-evident: it is hard to think of any set of alternatives such that there is not one thing which if added to them would make all of them better. Now for some probability p, it would follow that A and pS (probability of S) is preferred to just plain A, and likewise for the other alternatives. This, too, should be close to self-evident since something and a chance of some other good thing is surely preferable to plain old something. Now let us grant further the *premise of small margins*, in which there exists some probability $p^* < p$, such that if A is preferred to B, A and p^*S is preferred to B and pS; that is, a sufficiently small gain in the probability of achieving some additional good should not be sufficient to change one's preference over two alternatives over which one has a noticeable preference. This additional premise should not be too controversial since it is hard to imagine a clear preference over alternatives that would switch in such a way.

That A and pS is preferred to A and p^*S results as an application of the axiom of monotonicity. It also seems a sound proposition (given that S is good and $p^* < p$), so anything that contradicts it will amount to a reductio. Such a reductio, however, can be made if we grant nontransitive preferences over {A,B,C}. Suppose that one prefers A to B, B to C, and C to A. By the premise of complementarity, one should prefer B and pS to C and pS, so if one starts with C and pS one will exchange that for B and pS. By the premise of small margins, there is a p^* such that one will prefer A and p^*S to B and pS, so one would then exchange B and pS for A and p^*S. Then by complementarity, one prefers C and p^*S to A and p^*S, so one would exchange to get to C and p^*S. But then one has in effect exchanged C and pS for C and p^*S, which violates the axiom of monotonicity.

33. See Binmore, *Fun and Games*, 118.

34. Decision theorist Paul Anand, in his elegant little book *Foundations of Rational Choice under Risk* (Oxford: Clarendon, 1993), denies that a rational agent would necessarily have transitive preferences. That is, he denies that if one prefers A to B and B to C that one should prefer A to C. Some early decision theorists thought that transitivity resulted as a matter of simple logic from binary preference relations, or that transitivity was a pragmatic necessity whenever one would be faced with a set containing more than two alternatives. After all, if one prefers A to B, B to C, and C to A, how would one choose from a set containing A, B, and C? But as Anand shows, this implication does not follow. A rational individual may have separate binary and ternary rankings over alternatives and thus select A from the choice set {A,B}, B from {B,C}, C from {A,C} and (say) A from {A,B,C}. Anand correctly argues that a rational agent may extend these orderings to whatever order is necessary, from ternary to tetranary to pentanary to N-nary, as needed, and avoid logical and pragmatic contradiction. He therefore concludes that the transitivity of preference is unnecessary for rationality. For Anand, rational is as rational does. Since agents often violate transitivity in experimental settings, he concludes further that the most plausible conception of rationality is one without transitivity. Specifically, he thinks that rationality requires something much weaker: a principle of nondominance that requires that if one has a binary preference of A over B, one is rational if one does not choose B over A.

Anand rejects the money pump with the following argument. (In the following, read the expression *XpY* as "*X* preferred out of the set {*X,Y*}," *XpYpZ* as "*X* preferred out of the set {*X,Y,Z*}," and so forth.) If we assume that an agent has preferences defined up to all the relevant higher order relations and can see what sequence of choices are forthcoming, the agent can simply refuse to engage in the kinds of trades that will make him or her worse off over a whole sequence of trades. So even if an agent has a set of binary preferences *ApB*, *BpC*, *CpA*, and *CpC'* (where *C'* represents *C* less some quantity of some positive good), the agent's independent tetranery preference ordering (which could be *ApBpCpC'* or any other sequence in which *CpC'*) will keep him or her from going into the cycle.

I do not think that there is any way to attack Anand's argument on purely logical grounds, but it can be subject to serious question on pragmatic grounds. One might get at these pragmatic grounds by trying to think about how one might design an algorithm for making choices so that one does not end up with dominated outcomes. It would not be adequate to simply instruct a chooser to stop choosing whenever it comes across a dominated outcome. This assertion can be illustrated as follows. Suppose a chooser has preferences according to the binary relations *ApB*, *BpC*, *CpD*, and *DpB* and the tetranary relation *ApBpCpD* and is offered the following sequence of possible trades, starting with *D*:

1. *C* for *D*
2. *B* for *C*
3. *D* for *B*
4. A for D or for C

Trades 1–3 are a money pump, but trade 4 is designated as clearly preferred by the tetranary and binary relations. So a sophisticated algorithm should be able to see forward to trade 4 and execute the appropriate series of steps. But note an important consideration: even where all the appropriate preference relationships are defined, an algorithm that guarantees arrival at nondominated outcomes is only logically possible when the last decision node is known. In real life, unfortunately, we seldom know what the last decision node will be since our knowledge of the future is always imperfect. What choice sets tomorrow will bring cannot be known. If a hypothetical step 5 is added to the choice set that the algorithm in question cannot foresee, it will be possible to fool the chooser into arriving at a dominated outcome. An algorithm working with transitive preferences, however, cannot be fooled in such a manner, even if it does not have perfect information about the future.

35. This is a view held by John Finnis, who believes that it can never be rational to weigh different dimensions of the good against one another. See *Natural Law and Natural Rights*, 111–25.

36. For many neo-Thomist natural lawyers and some perfectionist liberals, incommensurability is *the* weapon against utilitarianism. See, for example, Robert P. George, *Making Men Moral: Civil Liberties and Public Morality* (Oxford: Clarendon, 1993), 88–90; Germain Grisez, "Against Consequentialism," *American Journal of Jurisprudence* 23 (1978): 21–72; John Finnis, *Fundamentals of Ethics* (Oxford: Oxford University Press, 1983), 86–93; and Joseph Raz, *The Morality of Freedom* (Oxford: Clarendon, 1986), 321–68. But this literature, while it may have a good case against old-fashioned hedonistic utilitarianism, does little damage to more contemporary versions of the doctrine. I have combed through it at some length, looking in vain for any serious engagement with the modern axiomatic utility theory used here. Much of the argument in these sources seems to invoke problems of decision, which are difficult in practice, and to declare them, with little or no subsequent analysis, to be unsolvable in principle. But nowhere in either the natural law or perfectionist liberal literature have I found an argument that a rational individual *should* fail to satisfy any of the logical requirements for the elaboration of a von Neumann–Morgenstern utility function or even a Paul Anand-like argument that they *could* fail to do so.

37. See Michael Fumento, *Science under Siege: Science, Technology, and the Environment* (New York: William Morrow, 1993), 267.

38. Some philosophers who have thought about the use of thought experiments take this position. See Roy Sorenson, *Thought Experiments* (New York: Oxford University Press, 1993).

39. James Griffin gives an example: "The French government knows that each year several drivers lose their lives because of the beautiful roadside avenues of trees, yet they do not cut them down. Even aesthetic pleasure is (rightly) allowed to outrank a certain number of human lives." Griffin, *Well-being*, 82.

40. I owe this example to Gilbert Harman. See his *Nature of Morality* (New York: Oxford, 1977), 3–4. It has been a central part of the case against utilitarianism for some important moral philosophers for quite some time. For a lengthy analysis of the problem, see Judith Jarvis Thomson, *The Realm of Rights* (Cambridge, Mass.: Harvard University Press, 1990), 134–52.

41. The problem of moral alienation is explicated most elegantly by Kagan, *Limits of Morality*, 1–2, and by Peter Railton, "Alienation, Consequentialism, and the Demands of Morality," *Philosophy and Public Affairs* 13 (1985): 134–71.

42. This is an argument one very prominent utilitarian makes. See Peter Singer, "Famine, Affluence, and Morality," *Philosophy and Public Affairs* 2 (1972): 229–43.

43. For a good brief exposition (and response to) this "nearest and dearest" objection, see Frank Jackson, "Decision-theoretic Consequentialism and the Nearest and Dearest Objection," *Ethics* 101 (1991): 461–82.

44. The use of an appeal to cost in the sense that the excess of costs on agents may excuse them from otherwise binding moral duties is found extensively in the work of Shelley Kagan. See *Limits of Morality*, 231–70.

45. See John Rawls, *A Theory of Justice* (Cambridge, Mass.: Harvard University Press, 1971), 500–1. Rawls suggests that the costs of utilitarianism are so high that in a society in which it became a general theory of justice, persons might succumb to exhaustion and "self-hatred."

46. A case in point: most persons of my acquaintance react to Gilbert Harman's hospital case with an immediate rejection of the notion that sacrificing the one healthy patient is morally warranted. C. M., a close friend of mine, had a rather different reaction. "It's easy," he said. "Kill that person, and save the five others." Then he paused for a few seconds before adding, "As long as it's not me."

47. A good consequentialist should object that distributive indifference is not the problem at the heart of my involuntary organ donor case since we are contemplating the appropriate distribution of equally large portions of bad (i.e., death) among different persons. This is correct in the purest case of the example, but if the "inferential theory" of moral intuitions I present in the next chapter and the "nonexploitation heuristic" I argue for in chapter 3 jointly obtain, there is a strong case to be made that our intuitions about this case are being driven by the suspicion that we are making one person's life go very badly for the sake of a lesser benefit spread over a large number of people.

48. See R. M. Hare, *Moral Thinking: Its Levels and Its Point* (New York: Oxford University Press, 1981), 44–64. For another interesting and recent example of a strategy of "indirect consequentialism," see Conrad Johnson, *Moral Legislation: A Legal-Political Model for Indirect Consequentialist Reasoning* (New York: Cambridge University Press, 1991).

49. Parfit, in *Reasons and Persons*, describes "collective consequentialism" and argues that it might be considerably less alienating than a purely individualist consequentialism. Jackson, in "Decision-theoretic Consequentialism," makes use of a similar argument in attempting to rebut the nearest and dearest objection.

50. See Amartya Sen and Bernard Williams, Introduction to *Utilitarianism and Beyond* (Cambridge: Cambridge University Press, 1982), 16.

51. William James, "The Moral Philosopher and the Moral Life," in *The Will to Believe and Other Essays in Popular Philosophy* (New York: Longmans, Green, 1905), 188. Russell Hardin brought my attention to this spectacular piece of moral rhetoric. See his *Morality within the Limits of Reason* (Chicago: University of Chicago Press, 1988), 23.

52. It might be possible to insist that the suffering of the one soul could be so extreme that it would outweigh even the greatest bliss of the rest of humanity. A latter-day William James could resist this dodge by qualifying the conditions of the story so that the fate of the one lonely soul is horrible but not horrible enough to outweigh everyone else's flourishing.

CHAPTER 2

1. See Brian Barry, *Democracy, Power, and Justice: Essays in Political Theory* (Oxford: Clarendon, 1989), 413–6.

2. Judith Jarvis Thomson also uses the death penalty to demonstrate the irreducibly moral content of certain moral questions. See her *Realm of Rights*, (Cambridge, Mass.: Harvard University Press, 1990), 22–5.

3. For a trenchant critique of some of the worse excesses of pop sociobiology, see Richard Lewontin, Steven Rose, and Leon Kamin, *Not in Our Genes: Biology, Ideology, and Human Nature* (New York: Pantheon, 1984).

4. The classic statement of Hume's Law is to be found in his *Treatise of Human Nature*, bk. III, chap. 1:

> In every system of morality, which I have hitherto met with, I have always remark'd, that the author proceeds for some time in the ordinary way of reasoning, and establishes the being of a God, or makes observations concerning human affairs; when of a sudden I am surpris'd to find, that instead of the usual copulation of propositions, *is* and *is not*, I meet with no proposition that is not connected with an *ought* or *ought not*. This change is imperceptible; but is, however, of the last consequence. For as this *ought* or *ought not*, expresses some new relation or affirmation, 'tis necessary that it shou'd be observ'd and explain'd; and at the same time that a reason should be given, for what seems altogether inconceivable, how this new relation can be a deduction from others, which are entirely different from it. But as authors do not commonly use this precaution, I shall presume to recommend it to the readers; and am persuaded, that this small attention wou'd subvert all vulgar systems of morality, and let us see, that vice and virtue is not founded merely on the relations of objects, nor is perceiv'd by reason.

See David Hume, *A Treatise of Human Nature*, ed. E. C. Mossner (New York: Penguin Books, 1984), 521.

5. The analogy between moral and mathematical reasoning was first suggested to me by some illuminating remarks of Thomas Scanlon. See "Contractualism and Utilitarianism" in *Utilitarianism and Beyond*, ed. Amartya Sen and Bernard Williams (Cambridge: Cambridge University Press, 1982), 105–6. The analogy is also to be found (not surprisingly) in the work of Richard Hare. See *Freedom and Reason* (New York: Oxford University Press, 1963), especially 88–9.

6. One knows one has really finished a proof with rigor when even a computer can approve its results. See Ken Binmore, *Playing Fair*, vol. 1 of *Game Theory and the Social Contract* (Cambridge, Mass.: The MIT Press, 1994), 235.

7. Of course, if there are such things as "mathematical facts," which we can "discover"

rather than simply derive, perhaps there could also be moral facts, which we could discover in the same way. At this level of philosophical abstraction, I fear, my mind simply wanders away, so I do not speculate about this possibility beyond this note.

8. Jeremy Bentham, *An Introduction to the Principles of Law and Legislation*, chap. 1, para. XI, cited from *The Works of Jeremy Bentham*, vol. 1., ed. John Bowring (Edinburgh: William Tait, 1843), 2.

9. The unjustly forgotten Alexander Smith (1794–1851) elaborated a sophisticated approach to utilitarianism on self-evident first principles, in which he considered multiple principles from which utilitarianism could be derived. He thus anticipated by over a century the idea of treating morality as a deductive mathematical or logical system. See Alexander Smith, *The Philosophy of Morals: An Investigation*, 2 vols. (London: Smith, Elder, 1841), I, 195–206. For one of the few critical discussions of Smith, see J. B. Schneewind, *Sidgwick's Ethics and Victorian Moral Philosophy* (Oxford: Clarendon, 1977), 82–8.

10. Shelley Kagan describes such a system as one of "extremism plus (side-)constraints" and ascribes it to William Godwin. See *The Limits of Morality* (Oxford: Clarendon, 1989), 10.

11. See Robert Nozick, *Anarchy, State, and Utopia* (New York: Basic Books, 1974).

12. Even I, as poor a mathematician as I am, have occasionally had such experiences. Some years ago, when I first began to study utility theory, I had a flash of intuition about a consequence of being able to make a pair of interpersonal comparisons between two agents on interpersonal comparisons between those two agents generally. I worked intermittently for two days on a proof before discovering that John Harsanyi had proved the result I had intuited some fifteen years before. For his proof, see *Rational Behavior and Bargaining Equilibrium in Games and Social Situations* (New York: Cambridge University Press, 1977), 50–5. The chagrin I felt at my lack of originality was tempered by the pleasure of knowing that at least I had been right.

13. Judith Jarvis Thomson, I think, comes close at times to advocating a fairly pure view of intuitions as straightforward moral facts. For example, she sees the common reaction to the organ transplant case discussed in chapter 1 as a kind of irreducible moral "datum" on which all theories must build. See *Realm of Rights*, 143. This is not to say that she thinks that moral data are straightforward natural facts. In her analysis, there are some propositions—for example, "one ought not torture babies to death for fun"—that would be true in all possible worlds. See *Realm of Rights*, 18. Thus in her view moral propositions are more like propositions from mathematics, which would be true in all possible worlds, rather than natural facts, which are true only in some possible worlds. Where my view differs from hers is that on the inferential theory of moral intuitions, there are no *irreducible* moral data.

14. There are few book-length studies on intuition, but all those that I have come across take this position. An important empirical source is Malcolm R. Westcott, *Toward a Contemporary Psychology of Intuition: A Historical, Theoretical, and Empirical Inquiry* (New York: Holt, Rinehart & Winston, 1968). A general psychological study, which proposes mechanisms for making intuitive judgements, is Keith Holyoak and Paul Thagard, *Mental Leaps: Analogy in Creative Thought* (Cambridge, Mass.: MIT Press, 1995). A short discussion of the use of thought experiments in ethics is to be found on pp. 178–82. A general philosophical study, which focuses on the use of thought experiments in plumbing out intuitions about both scientific and moral matters, is Roy Sorenson, *Thought Experiments* (New York: Oxford University Press, 1993). A more recent empirical study, which pays close attention to the role of tacit knowledge in decision making is Arthur S. Reber, *Implicit Learning and Tacit Knowledge: An Essay on the Cognitive Unconscious* (New York: Oxford University Press, 1993). For a discussion of epistemic intuition and its role in the natural sciences, see Efraim Fischbein, *Intuition in Science and Mathematics: An Educational Approach* (Dordrecht: Reidel, 1987). For one of the few relatively comprehensive reviews of the notion of intuition in different kinds of moral theory, see T. K. Seung, *Intuition and Construction* (New Haven, Conn.: Yale University Press, 1993).

15. Scanlon uses a slightly different formulation in his article "Contractualism and Utilitarianism": "Those rules for the regulation of behavior which no one could reasonably reject as a basis for informed, general agreement." He argues that both Rawls and Harsanyi go awry in using the "rational acceptance" formulation. He is not alone in this suggestion, which has been picked up and developed at considerable length by Brian Barry in *Justice as Impartiality* (Oxford: Clarendon, 1995).

The problem with Scanlon's formulation, which applies mutatis mutandis to Barry, is that it appears to make the adverb "reasonably" do all the necessary work. Thus, to call an action like accepting or rejecting a proposed set of rules "reasonable" is to make a kind of evaluative judgment of that action. When I say of a man that he "reasonably" responded to a demand I made, it seems that I am saying that he responded to it according to some norms of justice or morality. Contrast this with a claim that a man responded "rationally" to a demand of mine to see the evaluative force of "reasonably." It may be unreasonable of my noisy neighbors to keep me awake all night, but it is hardly irrational for them to do so, if they enjoy the activity that keeps me awake and no sanctions against that activity are forthcoming.

Whence, then, the force of "reasonably"? It seems that Scanlon's formula is simply a means of allowing one to use one's intuitions to evaluate potential systems of moral rules. This formulation is fine as far as it goes—it may turn out to be a rather useful heuristic device—but it does not seem to be capable of solving those problems that a contractualist methodology are supposed to solve since people seem to have just as many conflicts as confusions over what is reasonable as over what is moral.

16. These five conditions are laid out and discussed in John Rawls, *A Theory of Justice*, 130–6.

17. Political anarchy, though, might be viable. In chapter 5, I discuss the possible conditions under which a working political anarchy might subsist.

18. See John Harsanyi, "Cardinal Utility in Welfare Economics and in the Theory of Risk-taking," *Journal of Political Economy* 61 (1953): 434–5; and John Harsanyi, "Cardinal Welfare, Individualistic Ethics, and Interpersonal Comparisons of Utility," *Journal of Political Economy* 63 (1955): 309–21.

19. See Harsanyi, *Rational Behavior*, pt. I. See also his "Morality and the Theory of Rational Behavior" in *Utilitarianism and Beyond*.

20. Iris Marion Young is perhaps representative. See *Justice and the Politics of Difference* (Princeton, N.J.: Princeton University Press, 1990), 99–107.

21. But for a very elegant exposition of the notion of what it would be like to see something from no particular perspective, see Thomas Nagel, *The View from Nowhere* (New York: Oxford University Press, 1986).

22. Strictly speaking, the Baysian method of dealing with choice under uncertainty would require us only to assign some subjective numerical probability to our being any person. But the assignment of equal probabilities is the outcome of a conjunction of Baysian decision making and the impartiality requirement.

23. The most interesting recent discussion is probably to be found in Jon Elster and John E. Roemer, eds., *Interpersonal Comparisons of Well-being* (New York: Cambridge University Press, 1991).

24. Even John Rawls, though he expresses some skepticism about them, thinks that it would be hard to get rid of the notion of interpersonal comparisons in moral philosophy altogether:

> I do not assume, though, that a satisfactory solution to these problems [of interpersonal comparisons of well-being] is impossible . . . skepticism about interpersonal comparisons is often based on questionable views: for example, that the intensity of pleasure or of enjoyment which indicates well-being is the intensity of pure sensa-

tion; and while the intensity of such sensations can be experienced and known by the subject, it is impossible for others to know it or infer it with reasonable certainty. Both of the contentions seem wrong. Indeed, the second is simply part of a skepticism about the existence of other minds, unless it is shown why judgments of well-being present special problems which cannot be overcome.

From *Theory of Justice*, 91.

25. At least this is the case if the decision maker is not to be vulnerable to the charge of having some kind of ethical analogue to a Dutch book.

26. See Rawls, *Theory of Justice*, 172–4.

27. See Harsanyi, *Rational Behavior*, chap. 4.

28. An anomaly emerges if choices are to be made for populations of indeterminate size. There are two possible principles of utility, one that requires the *average* utility to be maximized, another that requires the *aggregate* utility to be maximized. For populations of the same size, these two principles coincide. But they offer differing recommendations for populations of differing sizes since it might be possible for a large population with a low average level to have a greater aggregate than a smaller population with a high average level. This difference will lead to tricky ethical questions of how large a population to have. Taken to extremes, either utilitarian principle seems to lead to absurd results. The application of the aggregate principle indicates that a sufficiently huge population of persons with lives barely worth living is morally preferable to a smaller population of persons with very good lives; Derek Parfit calls this result the "Repugnant Conclusion" (see *Reasons and Persons* (New York and Oxford: Oxford University Press, 1984), chap. 17). The application of the average principle indicates that it would be morally wrong to add persons to a population of persons who have very good lives if the added lives are only slightly less good than those of the rest. Parfit calls this latter problem the "Absurd Conclusion" (*Reasons and Persons*, chap. 18.) and uses it to derive a paradox for the average principle, which he calls the "Mere Addition Paradox."

These appalling conclusions seem to apply to versions of utilitarianism that I call in this chapter "fundamentalist," that is, those in which the principle of utility is morally basic. In contractualist versions of utilitarianism like Harsanyi's, the conditions of just contracting and not the principle of utility are morally basic. I do not think Harsanyi has any means for solving these vexing questions—but neither, I think, does Rawls or any other contractualist. It seems hard to figure into contractualist reasoning, or place behind a veil of ignorance in the contracting parties, whether or not they are to actually exist. To get problems of population ethics at all into contractualist reasoning, we would have to do some very fancy and probably very dubious metaphysical reasoning. Personally, I think that it would be best to simply give up on the idea of solving such problems through contractualism at all.

29. His theory began to develop in R. M. Hare, *The Language of Morals* (New York: Oxford University Press, 1952), and continued in *Freedom and Reason* (New York: Oxford University Press, 1963). Its high-water mark and fullest development are to be found in *Moral Thinking* (New York: Oxford University Press, 1981), which introduces a number of complications I lack the time to consider here but which, as become clear later, have strongly influenced the way in which I think about utilitarianism.

30. Given that Kant himself seems to have been strongly attached to deontological side constraints, it seems odd to imagine a Kantian utilitarianism, but that is what Hare provides. He argues that there is no necessary contradiction between Kantian reasoning and utilitarianism, and I concur. For a similar point of view, see David Cumminsky, "Kantian Consequentialism," *Ethics* 100 (1990): 586–630.

31. Before any reader tries to kill *me* for what seems to be an outrageous and amoral perspective, let me remark that in the morality of common sense there are cases of legitimate

killing, for example, self-defense. Thus it seems unlikely that many persons other than paci-fists would opt for an absolute rule against killing. Most would want to recognize some cases of legitimate killing—to preserve one's life against aggressors, to uphold the rule of law against certain dangerous criminals, and so forth. Thus it is legitimate to consider the preferences of those who have "a reason to kill."

32. Those who are inclined to grumble about the alleged fantastical nature of examples in moral philosophy should be advised that cases of deliberate sacrifice of some to save others were a not-uncommon feature of nineteenth-century naval disasters. A case of throwing pas-sengers, in some cases unwilling passengers, overboard from an open boat actually occurred in the aftermath of the wreck of the American emigrant ship *William Brown* in 1841. Instruc-tions given to the jury in the subsequent manslaughter case have an oddly utilitarian cast since the judge held that the jury could consider the possibility that the necessity of preserving the lives of the many justified the sacrifice of the few. *U.S. v. Holmes*, 1 Wallace Junior 1, 26 Fed. Cas. 360 (1842). For an account of the disaster and subsequent trial, see A. W. Brian Simpson, *Cannibalism and the Common Law* (Chicago: University of Chicago Press, 1984), 161–77. And of course, the notorious case of the *Mignonette* in 1884 involved the sacrifice of one to save four.

33. Rawls has an additional argument against the use of subjective probabilities in the original position, to the effect that for choosers to do so would require them to take a special attitude toward risk, that is, a willingness to gamble with one's entire fate. See *Theory of Jus-tice*, 166. But this argument appears to be founded on a misconception, at least with respect to Harsanyi's version of utilitarianism. As Kenneth Arrow has pointed out, because individu-als' utility functions are constructed out of their preferences over risky prospects, any special attitudes individuals happen to have about risk—whether they be risk seeking, risk neutral, or risk aversive—would be built into their choices to begin with, whatever decision rule they happen to use behind a veil of ignorance. See Kenneth J. Arrow, "Some Ordinalist-Utilitarian Notes on Rawls's Theory of Justice," *Journal of Philosophy*, 70 (1973): 245–63; reprinted in *Collected Papers of Kenneth J. Arrow*, vol. 1 (Oxford: Basil Blackwell, 1984), 96–114, at 107.

34. See Rawls, *Theory of Justice*, 187–90.

35. Readers will recognize this parable as an abstract version of the story of Wilt Cham-berlain told by Nozick in *Anarchy, State, and Utopia*.

36. See *Morality within the Limits of Reason*, 182–92.

CHAPTER 3

1. I include a note, however, for those who are not quite familiar with the game. The name "Prisoner's Dilemma" comes from a story attributed to A. W. Tucker. Two men are ar-rested and held in separate cells. A conniving prosecutor wishes to convict them of a serious crime but lacks sufficient evidence. He does, however, have sufficient evidence to convict each man on a number of more minor crimes. He therefore proposes to each prisoner the follow-ing deal: "If you rat on your fellow prisoner, I will not prosecute you on any of the minor charges and arrange for you to be treated leniently by the court for turning state's evidence. If not, I will convict you of all the minor charges that I can substantiate with evidence of my own." Both prisoners know that if they fail to rat on their fellow and he rats, they will be treated very severely. If both rat, both will be treated less severely but more severely than if neither had ratted. This game is quite destructive because each player has a strong incentive to rat. Each is better off ratting no matter what the other does (hence ratting *dominates* remaining silent.) The prosecutor therefore knows that he is quite likely to get each man to rat on the other. For an old but still timely discussion, see R. Duncan Luce and Howard Raiffa, *Games and Decisions* (New York: Wiley, 1957), 94–6.

2. I must note that I use the description of Prisoner's Dilemma to include a much wider array of game-theoretic interactions than orthodox game theorists do. Many of the interactions in this chapter on which I hang the label would seem strange to an orthodox theorist because, to the latter, it is a tautology that if players are engaging in strategies other than mutual defection, the underlying game must be something other than a Prisoner's Dilemma because, in accordance with the axiom of revealed preference, preference is determined by choice rather than the other way around. If a player is observed choosing alternative *A* over alternative *B*, then a fortiori *A* is preferred to *B*. Thus to an orthodox theorist, the idea that players should cooperate when cooperation is a dominated strategy is nonsense: if they are cooperating, by definition that strategy is not dominated. I must emphasize, then, that whenever I use the term *Prisoner's Dilemma* to describe a game, I mean a game in which purely self-interested players who do not expect to interact again in the future will defect. Players whose decisions are governed by norms will not, however, necessarily defect. The coherence of my usage turns on the fact that unlike orthodox game theorists, I do not rely on the axiom of revealed preference. I use the concept of personal good as that which would be measured by a von Neumann–Morgenstern utility scale that would be arrived at if people were perfectly well informed about how their lives would go, based on certain choices, and not just by that scale that can be inferred from behavior.

3. The concept of Pareto optimality, named after the early twentieth-century Italian political economist Vilfredo Pareto, is that condition or state of affairs in which it is not possible to improve the outcome for one person without making at least one other person worse off. If a change can be made from a state *A* to another state *B*, in which at least one person is made better off while no other person is made worse off, this change is called a *Pareto improvement*. *A* is Pareto-inferior to *B*, and *B* Pareto-dominates *A*.

4. Thus the Prisoner's Dilemma is a central analytic device in Gregory Kavka's contemporary reconstruction of Hobbes's political philosophy. See Kavka's *Hobbesian Moral and Political Theory* (Princeton, N.J.: Princeton University Press, 1986).

5. See Russell Hardin, *Morality within the Limits of Reason* (Chicago: University of Chicago Press, 1988), 40–2.

6. See Derek Parfit, *Reasons and Persons* (New York and Oxford: Oxford University Press, 1984), 5–7, 55–62.

7. A classic example of minimalist reasoning is provided by David Gauthier, *Morals by Agreement* (New York: Oxford University Press, 1986). A minimalist is a kind of *rule egoist*, someone who does not calculate the payoffs to oneself of every action but rather follows those rules that, if one sticks by them, will tend over the long run to make one best off overall. For an explication of the notion of rule egoism, see Kavka, *Hobbesian Moral and Political Theory*, chap. 9.

8. For readers unfamiliar with the concept of Nash equilibrium, it is simply this: a Nash equilibrium to a game exists when a given player's strategy is the best response to the strategies of all other players, which strategies are in turn the best response to it. For further and more formal exposition see Ken Binmore, *Fun and Games: A Text on Game Theory* (Lexington, Mass.: D. C. Heath, 1991), 47; and Eric Rasmussen, *Games and Information: An Introduction to Game Theory* (Cambridge, Mass.: Basil Blackwell, 1989), 30–6.

9. The great contemporary pioneer of the concept is Thomas Schelling. See his *Strategy of Conflict*, rev. ed. (Cambridge, Mass.: Harvard University Press, 1980), as well as Schelling, *Arms and Influence* (New Haven, Conn., and London: Yale University Press, 1966). Another highly readable discussion of commitment as strategy is Avinash K. Dixit and Barry J. Nalebuff, *Thinking Strategically: The Competitive Edge in Business, Politics, and Everyday Life* (New York: Norton, 1991). Actually the common term used by strategic theorists is not *commitment* but *precommitment*. Cliff Landesman, however, in a personal conversation, has convinced me that

the term *precommitment* is redundant and thus an abuse of the language, so I stick simply to *commitment*.

10. The source of the following nasty little story is Schelling, *Strategy of Conflict*, 43-6.

11. Robert Frank has advanced an intriguing proposal to the effect that our moral emotions (anger, guilt, gratitude, etc.) might serve as internal commitment devices that compel us to do the right thing, thus making us capable of doing that which serves our strategic interests even in cases in which there might be a strong short-term temptation not to. See Frank, "If *Homo economicus* Could Choose His Own Utility Function, Would He Want One with a Conscience?" *American Economic Review* 77 (1987): 593–605; and his subsequent book, *Passions within Reason: The Strategic Role of the Emotions* (New York: Norton, 1988). While I find Frank's speculations illuminating, the use of moral emotions as a commitment device suffers the same drawbacks as other possible commitment devices in overcoming the problem of exploitation. An egoist could just as well commit emotionally to certain courses of action as could a utilitarian, perhaps by cultivating powerful, self-centered, and infantile emotions. A great virtue of Frank's account is that it helps to develop an evolutionary account of norms, which I have put to use later in this chapter. An account similar to Frank's is Jack Hirshleifer, "On the Emotions as Guarantors of Threats and Promises," in *The Latest on the Best: Essays on Evolution and Optimality*, ed. John Dupré (Cambridge, Mass.: MIT Press, 1987).

12. Cliff Landesman.

13. The concept of evolutionary stability was first studied (not surprisingly) by biologists like Robert Trivers, William D. Hamilton, and John Maynard Smith. For an exposition, see John Maynard Smith, *Evolution and the Theory of Games* (New York: Cambridge University Press, 1974). The concept was imported into social science by Robert Axelrod, whose work will be discussed at greater length in the following chapter. See his *Evolution of Cooperation* (New York: Basic Books, 1984) and "An Evolutionary Approach to Norms," *American Political Science Review* 80 (1986): 1095–111.

14. E. O. Wilson is the most famous representative. See *Sociobiology: The New Synthesis* (Cambridge, Mass.: Harvard University Press, 1975).

15. See the previously mentioned work of Robert Frank.

16. Ken Binmore has appropriated the fine old word "librations" to describe processes like natural selection, which allow agents to reach equilibrium without consciously thinking about their behavior. For an elementary exposition, see *Fun and Games*, 393–434. He has also adapted evolutionary reasoning to his use of game theory in moral philosophy. See *Playing Fair* vol. 1 of *Game Theory and the Social Contract* (Cambridge, Mass.: MIT, 1994), 187–92. He promises more use of evolutionary arguments in the forthcoming second volume.

17. Allan Gibbard invokes an evolutionary model to explain the emergence of coordination between the moral emotions of different people. See Allan Gibbard, *Wise Choices, Apt Feelings* (Cambridge, Mass.: Harvard University Press, 1990). Danny Soccia in a recent paper has argued that utilitarianism faces a serious potential problem because communities of utilitarians face "invasion" from without by groups of egoists. While the conclusion he wishes to draw is not the same as mine (his argument is to establish a lemma in a more general argument for rejecting the "ought implies can" principle), his thoughts on the matter have influenced my own. See Soccia, "Utilitarianism, Sociobiology, and the Limits of Benevolence," *Journal of Philosophy* 87 (1989): 329–43. Even Bernard Williams has been willing to begrudge evolutionary considerations a role in moral theory. See "Evolutionary Theory, Epistemology, and Ethics," in *Evolution and Its Influence*, ed. Alan Grafen (Oxford: Clarendon, 1989).

18. See Axelrod, "Evolution of Norms" and *Evolution of Cooperation*. It is interesting to note that the latter contains a chapter cowritten with biologist William D. Hamilton on the evolution of cooperation in biological systems.

19. See Dan Sperber, "The Epidemiology of Belief," in *The Social Psychology of Widespread Belief*, ed. Colin Fraser and George Gaskell (Oxford: Clarendon, 1990).

20. Most recently, James Q. Wilson, *The Moral Sense* (New York: Free Press, 1993), 40–4, 70–2.

21. Leda Cosmides and John Tooby—beginning from the major premise that human beings are likely to have innate, domain-specific cognitive mechanisms for solving recurrent problems, and the minor premise that cooperation was such a recurrent problem in human evolution—have developed a hypothesis that human beings have a specific cognitive ability for detecting potential cooperators and cheaters. They have tested this hypothesis—achieving impressive results—with a series of experiments based on the Wason selection task. For a summary of their results, see "Cognitive Adaptions for Social Exchange," in *The Adapted Mind: Evolutionary Psychology and the Generation of Culture*, ed. Jerome H. Barkow, Leda Cosmides, and John Tooby (New York: Oxford University Press, 1992), 163–228.

22. See Daniel Dennett, "Memes and the Exploitation of Imagination," *Journal of Aesthetics and Art Criticism* 48 (1990): 127–35; and Dennett, *Consciousness Explained* (Boston: Little, Brown, 1990).

23. This particular three-part exposition is adopted from Dennett, "Memes and the Exploitation of Imagination."

24. Dennett, following a suggestion and employing a term invented by Richard Dawkins, wishes to use the word *meme* for such psychological traits. The term is found in chapter 11 of Richard Dawkins's *Selfish Gene* new ed., New York and Oxford: Oxford University Press, 1989.) Dennett builds and intriguing theory around the notion of memes, but since the theory is a bit underspecified, I shall avoid his term, and hope that my argument about the development of norms and knowledge can stand on its own.

25. Robert Boyd and Peter Richerson have done extensive formal modeling of various possible processes of cultural transmission, replication, and selection of traits. See *Culture and the Evolutionary Process* (Chicago: University of Chicago Press, 1985).

26. It is likely that seeking a certain level of utility satisfaction is hard-wired into us by the process of biological evolution. The original biological function of most of our modes of enjoyment (of food, sex, etc.) seems to be to direct our attention to achieving those things that would result in evolutionary selection.

27. Derek Parfit, for one, considers the possibility that it may be best for a believer in consequentialist morality to self-efface. See *Reasons and Persons*, 40–5. Rawlsians can and should object that for a set of principles of right to be self-effacing would be a violation of the publicity constraint on principles of right. I have not denied the publicity constraint, not because I think such a constraint is necessarily morally basic, but because, as I argue in the final chapter, there are reasons to believe that utilitarianism does its work best as a public doctrine.

28. The term is mine, although the analysis is not entirely original. Games with very similar normative properties are discussed briefly by Robert C. Ellickson in his study of the emergence and maintenance of social norms, which he calls "specialized labor games." See *Order without Law: How Neighbors Settle Disputes* (Cambridge, Mass.: Harvard University Press, 1991), 162–4.

29. I know that if I do not put double emphasis on the ceteris paribus, there will be some libertarian who has not been reading carefully who will complain—not unjustly—about the unfairness of making Egoist surrender even one dime of his or her income. Granted, it might be unfair in many circumstances, especially if Egoist's income comes from work and Needy's lack of income comes from nonwork. So perhaps one assumption that should go along as part of ceteris paribus would be that none of this income comes from work. This distribution should be thought of as a kind of manna from heaven. Perhaps Egoist and Utilitarian have inherited trust funds and Needy has not.

30. The idea of using oneself as a model or mirror of every other person for making judgments of interpersonal comparisons is elegantly defended in Alvin I. Goldman, "Simulation and Interpersonal Utility," *Ethics* 105 (1995): 709–26.

31. Mimicry in butterflies is a fascinating topic. See John R. G. Turner, "Mimicry: The Palatability Spectrum," in *The Biology of Butterflies*, ed. R. I. Vane-Wright and P. R. Ackerly (London: Academic Press, 1984), 141–62.

32. Cliff Landesman has brought to my attention another interesting possibility. Every undergraduate has at some time or another had fun playing with a thesis known as *psychological egoism*. According to this thesis, everything that anyone does is really part of a complicated strategy to ensure one's own private well-being. Apparently public-spirited or moral acts are undertaken only for self-interested reasons: those improving one's reputation or as part of an implicit contractual arrangement to get help from others in the future. One may well imagine a mirror-image thesis to psychological egoism, which we might call *psychological utilitarianism*. In this thesis, everyone is really a utilitarian. Apparently private-spirited or selfish acts are really undertaken for utilitarian reasons: defending oneself against exploitation, acquiring a reputation as nonexploitable, and so on. Each of these theses is completely nonfalsifiable, which I suppose goes to show the truth of the old generality that extremes meet.

CHAPTER 4

1. This definition is taken from Jack Knight, *Institutions and Social Conflict* (New York: Cambridge University Press, 1992).

2. This analysis is thus a simplification of what Elinor Ostrom calls a "grammar of institutions." It can be made considerably more complex, but for the expository purposes of this section the simple analysis should do. For a more complex case, see Sue E. S. Crawford and Elinor Ostrom, "A Grammar of Institutions," *American Political Science Review* 89 (1995): 582–600.

3. See John Searle, *The Construction of Social Reality* (New York: Free Press, 1995), especially 95–126.

4. This example is used in Daniel Dennett, *Consciousness Explained* (Boston: Little, Brown, 1991), 24, to show how certain kinds of facts can depend for their existence on concepts. It is explored at greater length in Searle, *Construction of Social Reality*, 41–4.

5. Such seems to be the view of sociologists like Talcott Parsons, who remarks about individual choices, "In a figurative sense, it might be said that the value-orientations . . . come to make the choice rather than the actor." See Talcott Parsons and Edward A. Shils, "Values, Motives and Systems of Action," in *Toward a General Theory of Action*, ed. Talcott Parsons et al. (Cambridge, Mass.: Harvard University Press, 1951), (Footnote) 70. It appears to be the position as well for anthropologists like Clifford Geertz, who makes an explicit analogy between a culture's values and a controlling computer program. See *The Interpretation of Cultures* (New York: Basic Books, 1973), 44–5. In general, such views tend to be held by those who hold that there is a large amount of plasticity in human nature, so that the preferences of individuals might be shaped by culture to be anything or almost anything. This is certainly the case with Geertz, with social scientists strongly under the influence of behaviorism, and with Parsonian sociologists. (Parsons and Shils refer explicitly to "plasticity" of the organism; see "Values, Motives, and Systems of Action," 71). This view of human beings as being exceedingly plastic with respect to their preferences and beliefs—the so-called "standard social science model"—is now being convincingly criticized by Darwinian social scientists. For an overview, see John Tooby and Leda Cosmides, "The Psychological Foundations of Culture," in *The Adapted Mind*, ed. Jerome Barkow, Leda Cosmides, and John Tooby (New York: Oxford University Press, 1992), 19–136.

6. Agents often find it easy to coordinate even though a rigorous formal analysis of coordination, which properly pins down the knowledge necessary for agents to coordinate, is often distressingly complex. To see just how complex, see David K. Lewis, *Convention: A Philosophical Study* (Cambridge, Mass.: Harvard University Press, 1969), and Christina Bicchieri, *Rationality and Coordination* (New York: Cambridge University Press, 1993).

7. Schelling gives a number of remarkable examples of salience in *The Strategy of Conflict*, rev. ed. (Cambridge, Mass.: Harvard University Press, 1980). One of the most famous is the decision rule that allows two people to find each other in New York City on a given day. There seems to be a strong tendency to coordinate on meeting at the information kiosk in Grand Central Terminal at noon. I myself have seen this result replicated for Cambridge, Massachusetts, in an undergraduate game theory class at Harvard College, where almost all students in a class of thirty-five managed to coordinate on meeting at the Harvard Square kiosk at noon.

8. See Robert Axelrod, *Evolution of Cooperation* (New York: Basic Books, 1984), 55–72.

9. For a formal discussion, see George W. Downs, David M. Rocke, and Randolph M. Siverson, "Arms Races and Cooperation," *World Politics* 38 (1986): 118–46.

10. For a simple proof, see Ken Binmore, *Fun and Games* in *A Text on Game Theory* (Lexington, Mass.: D. C. Heath, 1991), (373–6. The folk theorem seems to be a quite robust result, and it holds up under many conditions, including the introduction of many players into the game and constraints on information available to them (with some exceptions). See Drew Fudenberg and Eric Maskin, "The Folk Theorem in Repeated Games with Discounting or with Incomplete Information," *Econometrica* 54 (1986): 533–54.

11. Equilibrium selection in general is a complex problem for theorists that raises quite a lot of disagreement even in simple games, even though in real life it seems that people manage to select equilibria reasonably well. In a brief discussion, Binmore emphasizes the importance of focal points, a suggestion that seems to be at least congruent with my emphasis on rules. (See *Fun and Games*, 295–9.) Reinhard Selten and John Harsanyi provide an interesting discussion of equilibrium selection for finite games but largely avoid the kinds of folk-theoretical problems I raise here. See *A General Theory of Equilibrium Selection in Games* (Cambridge, Mass.: MIT Press, 1988).

12. See Barry Nalebuff and Avinash Dixit, *Thinking Strategically* (New York: W. Norton, 1991), 113–5.

13. See Michael Taylor, *The Possibility of Cooperation* (New York: Cambridge University Press, 1987), 82–108.

14. See Randall Covert, "Rational Actors, Equilibrium, and Social Institutions" in *Explaining Social Institutions*, ed. Jack Knight and Itai Sened (Ann Arbor: University of Michigan Press, 1955), 57–94. For a good introductory review of some relevant literature, see N. Schofeld, "Anarchy, Altruism, and Cooperation," *Social Choice and Welfare* 2 (1985): 207–19; and for an introduction to theoretical issues, see Binmore, *Fun and Games*, 377–81.

15. Such self-enforcing rules, in which others punish one for one's defections, are common in the explanations of social institutions. Simple models, in which children make a decision about whether to support their parents conditional on their parents' having supported their parents, are often used to show how self-interest can be the cement of society—even of families—in the complete absence of altruism or familial sentiment. For expositions of such simple and elegant models, see Partha Dasgupta, *An Inquiry into Well-being and Destitution* (Oxford: Clarendon, 1993), 212–7; and Binmore, *Fun and Games*, 380–2.

16. Randall Calvert, personal communication, February 1995.

17. In representing a social game in this way, I am closely following the practice of Ken Binmore. See *Playing Fair*, vol. 1 of *Game Theory and the Social Contract* (Cambridge, Mass.: MIT, 1994), 44–9.

18. Sadly, it is an equilibrium. If the other person is constantly making use of all the aids of war, one cannot do better for oneself by unilaterally seeking peace.

19. But not only the Nash bargaining solution. There have been other proposed solutions to the problem of bargaining between selfish players, such as the Kalai-Smordinsky solution or the so-called "minimax relative concession." See Gauthier *Morals by Agreement* (New York: Oxford University Press, 1986), 129–50. The technical difference between these solutions is of little import here. As Ken Binmore points out, for convex sets they will seldom be far apart (see *Playing Fair*, 88), but they will tend to diverge from utilitarian solutions. So the analysis that follows will tend to hold no matter which of these bargaining solutions is thought most appropriate.

20. For succinct expositions of the Nash bargaining solution, see Dasgupta, *Inquiry*, 337–40; and Binmore, *Fun and Games*, 180–91.

21. A still more complicated problem arises when we consider whether evolutionary stability would be jeopardized in those instances in which both X and Y are utilitarians but one is badly off when the equilibrium is a point in the potentially optimal set. If the tendency for a selection pressure against utilitarian norms is directly proportional to how well they fare in life and equal for both agents, we could expect that whatever losses to evolutionary stability are incurred by X's being in a bad equilibrium might be offset by gains to Y. But if there is a marginally increasing selection pressure against utilitarian norms as their carrier becomes worse and worse off, or if the selection pressure against X's utilitarian norms increases at a rate faster than it diminishes for Y's, the selection of at least certain points in the potentially optimal set could diminish the overall evolutionary stability of utilitarianism. In this latter case, utilitarians might again be pressed back toward something like an exchange-optimal equilibrium. But because the question of what conditions exactly hold cannot be investigated further here, I can only note the existence of the problem. Since the institutional recommendations in the next chapter tend toward the exchange-optimal anyway, it is not a deep issue for the main argument.

22. Such a small minority may flourish in conditions in which there is a lack of rules in a population as a whole that enables the population to resist it. Russell Hardin calls this a situation of "dual coordination power." See *One for All: The Logic of Group Conflict* (Princeton, N.J.: Princeton University Press, 1995), 29–31. See also Keith M. Dowling, *Rational Choice and Political Power* (Brookfield, Vt.: Edward Elgar, 1991), 84–114.

23. A graphical representation of where Abel and Cain find themselves would thus show lines with slopes −0.5 to −2 running through an exchange-optimal point on the Pareto frontier. The measure of the angle between these two lines is roughly 0.62 radians, so in this case κ would equal approximately 0.41.

CHAPTER 5

1. I refer, of course, to Marx's famous line in his "Critique of the Gotha Program," in *Karl Marx: Selected Writings*, ed. David McLellan (New York: Oxford University Press, 1977), 566–8. Marx clearly did seem to believe that the "higher phase" of communism would effectively abolish what we think of as ordinary mechanisms of distributive justice in place of social formations, the end of which would be "free association" and the promotion of human flourishing in general. Marx is openly disdainful of Benthamite utilitarianism; see Karl Marx, *Capital*, trans. Samuel Moore and Edward Aveling, ed. Frederick Engels (New York: International Publishers, 1967), 571n. But Marx's conception of free association seems not incongruent with that which a society of utilitarians could achieve without worries about exploitation, and his conception of human flourishing seems not inconsistent with the non-Benthamite conception of utility outlined in chapter 1.

2. This discussion owes a great deal to Russell Hardin's discussion of "Utilitarianism without Interpersonal Comparisons," in *Morality within the Limits of Reason* (Chicago: University of Chicago Press, 1988), 75–114.

3. It is important to note that it is not the case that a unilateral defection is always utility-superior to mutual defection. While in all gift-optimal and in many exchange-optimal Prisoner's Dilemmas unilateral defections are utility-superior to mutual defections, it is easy to construct cases in which mutual defection is superior to unilateral defection.

4. It is only "quasi" because, as far as I can tell, the original Pareto principle referred only to outcomes that were mutually preferred rather than defined in terms of more fundamental utilities. If I referred only to preferences in the principle, this libertarian version of utilitarianism would be vulnerable to the attacks on pure preference utilitarianism, which I briefly discussed in chapter 1. Thus this Pareto principle is only "quasi."

5. A theory of how such exchanges might be worked out is provided in the Samuelsonian theory of pure public goods provision. See Paul A. Samuelson, "The Pure Theory of Public Expenditure," in *The Collected Scientific Papers of Paul A. Samuelson*, ed. Joseph E. Stieglitz (Cambridge, Mass.: MIT Press, 1965), vol. 2, 1223–5.

6. See Michael Taylor, *The Possibility of Cooperation* (New York: Cambridge University Press, 1987).

7. Could it not be the case that advances in technology and psychological sophistication might allow us to make determinations of the contribution of lordship and sadism to a person's well-being with greater precision, thus raising the κ value of that information? I am sure this case could be realized not just in principle but also in practice. But no doubt if we were to actually make such advances, the vividness of our beliefs about true sadism would change in significant ways, and our underlying moral intuitions should shift also. An innate, incurable, and psychologically well-understood sadism might very well be considered not a mark of the devil but a severe psychological disability. But if such a discovery were to be made, it would be possible to treat sadists in a manner similar to that of the other severely disabled, a manner that I describe subsequently.

8. Moral hazard, as has been noted, is a ubiquitous problem for any institution of insurance, whether explicit or, as it is here, merely implicit. For an excellent overview, see Carol A. Heimer, *Reactive Risk and Rational Action: Managing Moral Hazard in Insurance Contracts* (Berkeley: University of California Press, 1985).

9. Derek Parfit, in a Harvard seminar on problems of ethics, which I attended, provided the following intuition pump on forcible organ donation: suppose that henceforth, because of a bizarre panspecific genetic mutation, all human beings are born as twins, one of whom has two good eyes and one of whom is blind. Suppose further that in a reliable surgical procedure an eye could be transplanted from the sighted to the sightless twin, leaving two one-eyed but sighted twins. Would it be morally acceptable to mandate such operations universally? Parfit polled the graduate students present and found that ten out of eleven (including myself) thought that it would be so acceptable. "Better tell Nozick," he said with a grin. This outcome is surely not surprising, though, if my theory of moral intuitions as unconscious inferences is correct. There is no issue of moral hazard here since on no plausible account can we be responsible for producing the equipment with which we are born. Furthermore, newborn infants do not engage in the right kind of strategic deception to raise moral hazard worries, and there is little or no case to be made *ex ante* that two-eyed sightedness for one agent outweighs total blindness for another.

10. See R. M. Hare, "What Is Wrong with Slavery," in *Essays on Political Morality* (Oxford: Clarendon, 1989), 148–66, at 155.

11. The solution, thus, to my problem of sadism in a psychologically sophisticated world might be something like this: if sadistic pleasures were really high-κ information, anyone who

can enjoy life only through sadism might be thought of as having a disability of a rather special kind. This person ought to be allowed to use his or her income to purchase the right to inflict pain. If I know human nature at all well, I should say that if the purchasing power is adequate, this person should be able to find buyers.

12. When I lectured on the subject of utilitarianism and horrible acts at the University of Rochester in February 1995, Andrew Dick, an empirical student of health-care policy, made the following objection: could it not be the case that there really is a residuum of persons in need of organs that are so clearly cases in which moral hazard is not involved (dying children, for example) that utilitarianism would force us to bite the bullet on forced transfers at least occasionally? Professor Dick's intuition was that in reality there were. He may well be right on the facts of the matter, but the force of his objection turns on a false alternative: either let innocent children die or start grabbing people off the streets for organ donation. But the world of policies is not exhausted by these alternatives. One might, for instance, deal with the problem of cases without moral hazard by changing organ donation policies, say, by having mandatory rather than voluntary (as is the case now) donation of organs from all persons already clinically dead. Were such a policy to be adopted (it may well be a reform utilitarianism would recommend), Professor Dick's problem could (I think) be solved. This policy would be a limit on the right of self-ownership, to be sure, but it hardly seems a deeply morally objectionable one (except perhaps for some people who have bona fide religious objections to such a procedure). After all, it's hard to see what is lost to a dead person by not being buried or cremated with all one's parts.

13. See Robert Nozick, *Anarchy, State, and Utopia* (New York: Basic Books, 1974), 151.

14. See David Gauthier, *Morals by Agreement* (New York: Oxford University Press, 1986), 209–32.

15. A version of the criterion is elaborated by John Locke in his *Second Treatise of Government*, para. 33: "Nor was this *appropriation* of any parcel of *Land*, by improving it, any prejudice to any other *Man*, since there was still enough, and as good left." In *Two Treatises of Government*, ed. Peter Laslett (Cambridge: Cambridge University Press, 1960), 291.

16. See Nozick, *Anarchy State and Utopia*, 178–82, and Gauthier, *Morals by Agreement*, 208–32, for their versions of Lockean provisos.

17. See Richard Epstein, *Simple Rules for a Complex World* (Cambridge, Mass.: Harvard University Press, 1995), 59–63.

18. Subject to a number of exceptions. Some very talented individuals might be able to produce more than the norm even with a zero allotment of material wealth. For a brief survey of the concept of a *value numeraire* and a demonstration of its calculability, see John Roemer, *A General Theory of Exploitation and Class* (Cambridge, Mass.: Harvard University Press, 1982), 147–73.

19. Rawls, for example, argues that while an imperfect society should engage in some economic accumulation—subject to the constraint of a just rate of savings—to achieve a decent social minimum, a truly just and sufficiently wealthy society would have no moral need for accumulation. He contrasts his position with utilitarianism, which might accumulate indefinitely, and would not recognize a just rate of savings constraint. See *Theory of Justice* (Cambridge, Mass.: Harvard University Press, 1971), 286–7.

20. See Marx, *Capital*, 667–724.

21. Rawls would probably not disagree with the need for progress over the nineteenth century, given his principle alluded to in the previous note. But exactly on what grounds he would rate the nineteenth century materially indecent (and the twentieth century decent?) are a bit unclear to me.

22. Thus Robert Nozick—that arch-libertarian—actually has a commitment to the view that community has an important role in human life. He merely denies to the state any legitimate role in using its coercive power to bring about the existence of any particular commu-

nity. See *Anarchy, State, and Utopia*, 297–334. A similar view is to be found in Epstein's *Simple Rules*, 42–9, 320–5.

23. I am willing to defend this last point against all comers for the society that exists at this historical time and place. I am not blind to historical contingency, however, and am willing to admit that it is possible that at different historical times and places there might be communitarian goods with much higher κ values than any such goods have now.

24. Strictly speaking, the severity of such punishments would not—for a utilitarian—be determined by their efficacy as deterrents alone, for if only deterrent power mattered, the most minor offenses would merit the severest punishments. The consequential seriousness of allowing violations to go undeterred would have to be weighed in a properly utilitarian calculus against the severity of punishment. Thus, one would be unlikely to prescribe hanging for the offense of spitting on a public sidewalk, for the disutility of even a single application of the penalty would likely outweigh the social disutility of even a very large amount of spitting.

25. For formal models and a review of real-world corruption in such problems, see Susan Rose-Ackerman, *Corruption: A Study in Political Economy* (New York: Academic Press, 1978).

26. For a discussion of the uses of feedback control in social organization, see Peter Richardson, *Feedback Thought in Social Science and Systems Theory* (Philadelphia: University of Pennsylvania Press, 1991).

27. See William Riker and Peter Ordeshook, "A Theory of the Calculus of Voting," *American Political Science Review* 62 (1968): 25. Derek Parfit, using this estimate, has an interesting discussion of why utilitarians would find it rational to vote in his review of mistakes in moral mathematics. I have drawn on it here. See *Reasons and Persons*, 73–5. The view that moral psychology is a necessary component of political participation is also defended in Robert E. Goodin, "Institutionalizing the Public Interest: The Defense of Deadlock and Beyond," *American Political Science Review* 90 (1996): 331–43, at 341.

28. Although it is not common to invoke any kind of sympathy of fellow feeling to explain political outcomes, it is surely a mistake to discount its existence entirely. David Hume put the matter very elegantly:

> Let us suppose a person ever so selfish; let private interest have ingrossed ever so much his attention; yet in instances, where that is not concerned, he must unavoidably feel *some* propensity to the good of mankind, and make it an object of choice, if everything be equal. Would any man, who is walking along, tread as willingly on another's gouty toes, whom he has no quarrel with, as on flint and pavement. . . . And if the principles of humanity are capable, in many instances, of influencing our actions, they must, at all times, have *some* authority over our sentiments, and give us a general approbation of what is useful to society, and blame of what is dangerous or pernicious. The degrees of these sentiments may be the subject of controversy; but the reality of their existence, one should think, must be admitted in every theory or system.

Enquiries Concerning Human Understanding and Concerning the Principles of Morals, ed. P. H. Nidditch (Oxford: Oxford University Press, 1975), 226. Given the modest costs of some political participation, the "degree of sentiment" necessary to motivate people to participate in the political life of Imperfectia should also be fairly modest.

29. Notoriously, and to his later sorrow, Robert Bork. See his "Neutral Principles and Some First Amendment Problems," *Indiana Law Journal* 47 (1971): 1.

30. For a full discussion, see Margaret Levi, *Of Rule and Revenue* (Berkeley: University of California Press, 1988).

31. Levi has an extensive discussion of devices for achieving what she calls quasi compliance. See *Of Rule and Revenue*, 48–70.

32. For Hellenophiles who object to this characterization ("Athens!"), I must point out that only a minority of residents of Athens were enfranchised, even in its most "democratic" period, and that the exploitation of women, metics, and slaves makes the interpretation of even Athens as a venal oligarchy highly plausible. For scholarly support of this view, see G. E. M. de Saint Croix, *Class Struggle in the Ancient Greek World: From the Archaic Age to the Arab Conquest* (Ithaca, N.Y.: Cornell University Press, 1981).

33. Richard Dawkins, and later Daniel Dennett, advance the hypothesis that there are bits of intellectual information analogous to computer viruses called "viral memes," which, while antiutilitarian in their content, are not so destructive or so virulent that they destroy themselves and, furthermore, are successful at reproducing themselves and driving out other memes. Dennett specifically refers to anti-Semitism as an example of such a pernicious meme. See *Consciousness Explained* (Boston: Little, Brown, 1991), 203; and Dawkins, *The Blind Watchmaker* (New York: Norton, 1987), 158. Dawkins, for his own audacious part, has suggested in a recent popular essay that all religious ideas may be the mental equivalent of computer viruses. See his article "Is God a Computer Virus?" *New Statesman and Society* 5 (18 December 1992): 223.

34. When orders of ruling priests come to care more about gratifying the lusts of the body than the aspirations of the soul, the resultant hypocrisy is thought to signify the moral turpitude of the rulers. Perhaps. But from the utilitarian perspective, it may be possible that such a development is something that would be morally welcome.

CHAPTER 6

1. The most prominent of these are probably Ronald Dworkin, Amartya Sen, Richard Arneson, and G. A. Cohen. John Roemer, "A Pragmatic Theory of Responsibility for the Egalitarian Planner," *Philosophy and Public Affairs* 22 (1993): 146–66, at 146, gives the following useful bibliography: Ronald Dworkin, "What Is Equality? Part I: Equality of Welfare," *Philosophy and Public Affairs* 10 (1981): 185–246; Ronald Dworkin, "What Is Equality? Part II: Equality of Resources," *Philosophy and Public Affairs* 10 (1981): 283–345; Richard J. Arneson, "Equality of Opportunity for Welfare," *Philosophical Studies* 56 (1989): 77–93; Richard J. Arneson, "Liberalism, Distributive Subjectivism, and Equal Opportunity for Welfare," *Philosophy and Public Affairs* 19 (1980): 158–94; Amartya K. Sen, "Well-being, Agency, and Freedom: The Dewey Lectures 1984," *Journal of Philosophy* 82 (1985): 169–211; G. A. Cohen, "On the Currency of Egalitarian Justice," *Ethics* 99 (1989): 906–44; G. A. Cohen, "Equality of What? On Welfare, Goods, and Capitalism," *Recherches Economiques de Louvain* 56 (1990): 357–82.

2. The most obvious defender of such principles is, of course, Nozick, but he is hardly the only one. F. A. Hayek can also be read as a defender of rule-based historical principles against patterned principles. See *The Mirage of Social Justice* (London: Routledge & Kegan Paul, 1975), 62–100.

3. As Nozick himself recognizes. See *Anarchy, State, and Utopia* (New York: Basic Books, 1974), 150–60.

4. It may be possible to counteract such a tendency by abolishing the family and having all children raised by the state. But unless human beings can be culturally reindoctrinated to a vast extent, and unless we can somehow imagine that the state's child-rearers are so good that they can produce children who are happier and better adjusted than their own parents could, it is quite hard to see how such an institutional shift could be justified on utilitarian grounds. Surely the utility losses (such as they are) to inequality are not so great that they can

easily outweigh the losses that most persons would experience in being deprived of the right to do something that they presently feel is a key part of their lives. It is also hard to see how one could easily square such an institutional shift with the institutions of property rights and personal liberty that would be presumed to exist in an Imperfectia. Consider this: surely not many women would bear the costs of pregnancy only to produce a child that would be taken from them at birth. Should such a "children to the state" policy take hold, it would seem quite likely that the birthrate would fall dramatically. How would a state respond to such an occurrence, which would probably be a disaster in utilitarian terms? By forcing women to become pregnant and carry children to term? How would that policy square with the institution of self-ownership?

5. Accidents that can be rationally anticipated, though, should create no grounds for redistribution when informational constraints permit the existence of working insurance markets. If economic agents can predict with some degree of accuracy the probability that they will be the victim of some misfortune, their most rational response would be to insure themselves against that contingency privately. Should they fail to do so and then expect subsidy through redistribution, we would create moral hazards by subsidizing excess risk taking. It may not be a good idea to subsidize the rebuilding of Floridian householders after hurricanes since those who live in Florida must know in advance that they are at risk from serious storms every few years.

6. The concept of a "market for lemons" in health insurance works something like this: since insurers do not have information as good as the insurees do about the health of their insurees, if insurance is offered at what would presumably be the market price (i.e., the actuarial cost of health care for a representative member of a population), the actual purchasers of insurance are likely to be sicker than the representative population. Insurance is thus not available to individuals at the actuarial price or, in some cases, not available at all. For an exposition, see George A. Akerlof, "The Market for 'Lemons': Quality, Uncertainty, and the Market Mechanism," *Quarterly Journal of Economics* 84 (1970): 488.

7. Of course, the issue is made more complicated by the fact that a regime that seeks to meet minimum basic needs—as I argue a utilitarian Imperfectia would—may also have universal health coverage as part of a package for meeting those needs. A national health service may kill two institutional birds with one stone by both overcoming market failures and helping to guarantee a social minimum.

8. See Mancur Olson, *The Logic of Collective Action* (Cambridge, Mass.: Harvard University Press, 1965). Olson also makes rent seeking through the rise of secondary associations a cornerstone of his argument in a noted later book. See *The Rise and Decline of Nations: Economic Growth, Stagflation, and Economic Rigidities* (New Haven, Conn.: Yale University Press, 1982).

9. For an overview of the literature about rent seeking in the political process see Mueller, *Public Choice II* (New York: Cambridge University Press, 1989), 229–46. The two seminal papers on rent seeking were written by Gordon Tullock and Anne Krueger. See Gordon Tullock, "The Welfare Costs of Tariffs, Monopolies, and Theft," *Western Economic Journal* 5 (1967): 224–32; and Anne Krueger, "The Political Economy of the Rent Seeking Society," *American Economic Review* 64 (1974): 291–302.

10. The metaphor of a leaky bucket to describe the redistributive process (implying there are losses in transferring a good from one group to another) is used by Arthur Okun, *Equality and Efficiency: The Great Tradeoff* (Washington, D.C.: Brookings Institution, 1975), 91–5.

11. See Anthony de Jasay, *The State* (New York: Basil Blackwell, 1985), 207–21.

12. See the U.S. Constitution, Amendment V.

13. For an elegant elaboration of the takings clause and an argument for increased rigidity in state prerogatives with respect to property, see Richard Epstein, *Takings: Private Property and the Power of Eminent Domain* (Cambridge, Mass.: Harvard University Press, 1985).

14. For an overview of U.S. constitutional jurisprudence concerned with the distribution of property, the development of the economic-libertarian line of cases in particular, see Walter F. Murphy, James E. Fleming, and William F. Harris II, *American Constitutional Interpretation* (Mineola, N.Y.: Foundation Press, 1986), 938–1003; and David M. O'Brien, *Constitutional Law and Politics*, 2nd ed. (New York: Norton, 1995), vol. 2, 252–96.

15. U. S. Constitution, Amendment XVI.

16. For a brief discussion of the possibility of constitutional constraints on rent seeking, see Richard E. Wegner, "Agency, Economic Calculation, and Constitutional Construction," in *The Political Economy of Rent-seeking*, ed. Charles K. Rowley, Robert D. Tollison, and Gordon Tullock (Boston and Dordrecht: Kluwer, 1988), 423–46; and Charles K. Rowley, "Rent-Seeking in Constitutional Perspective," in *Political Economy of Rent-seeking*, 447–64.

17. See Dworkin, "What is Equality?" (Parts I and II).

18. See Sen, "Well-being, Agency, and Freedom."

19. See Arneson, "Equality of Opportunity for Welfare."

20. See Cohen, "Currency of Egalitarian Justice."

21. See Roemer, "Pragmatic Theory of Responsibility."

22. This peculiar example (as far as I know) appears in Dworkin's "Equality of What?" but seems especially salient for Roemer. Apparently viniculture is an important preoccupation at Roemer's home institution. See Roemer, "Pragmatic Theory of Responsibility," 150–1.

23. For a mathematical elaboration of this idea, see Gary S. Becker and Kevin M. Murphy, "A Theory of Rational Addiction," *Journal of Political Economy* 96 (1988): 675.

24. This view is taken by several influential commentators on the metaphysical problem of free will, among them the ever excellent Daniel Dennett. See *Elbow Room: Varieties of Free Will Worth Wanting* (Cambridge, Mass.: MIT Press, 1989), 156–65. See also Ted Honderich, *The Consequences of Determinism* (Oxford: Clarendon, 1988).

25. See Roemer, "Pragmatic Theory of Responsibility," 150.

26. All this provision is, of course, dependent on the given society's being sufficiently wealthy and sufficiently competent at public administration. I doubt that wealth or competence are great barriers to present-day industrial societies.

27. For a view similar to mine, based on the assumption of marginal declines in utility to income, see Mancur Olson, "Why Some Welfare State Redistribution to the Poor is a Great Idea," in *Democracy and Public Choice: Essays in Honor of Gordon Tullock*, ed. Charles K. Rowley (New York: Basil Blackwell, 1987), 191–222.

28. See *Real Freedom for All: What if Anything Can Justify Capitalism?* (Oxford: Clarendon, 1995).

29. See van Parijs, *Real Freedom for All*, 25.

30. Economists generally maintain that one cannot make people worse off by giving them in cash the same value of goods one might give them in kind. But if either the poor are less rational than a typical consumer or if there are worries about certain kinds of administrative fraud, one may prefer to give goods in kind. See Hardin, *Morality within the Limits of Reason* (Chicago: University of Chicago Press, 1988), 162–3.

31. It may seem very strange that employers would pay such wages, but many economists think that in fact they do. Put very simply, the reason is something like this: if wages were market clearing, there would be no unemployment and labor discipline would be difficult. Each employer thus has an incentive to pay an above-market wage to ensure that the threat of dismissal is effective against unproductive workers. Consequently, in equilibrium, labor markets do not clear and there is always some unemployment in the system. For an account, see van Parijs, *Real Freedom for All*, 108–9, 112–6.

32. Of course, if there is no such good faith, an efficient social minimum is unlikely to be adopted as social policy, as has been shown by Allan H. Meltzer and Scott F. Richard, "A

Positive Theory of In-kind Transfers and the Negative Income Tax," in *Political Economy*, ed. Allan H. Meltzer, Alex Cukierman, and Scott F. Richard (New York: Oxford University Press, 1991), 53–75.

33. See Norman Frohlich and Joe A. Oppenheimer, *Choosing Justice: An Experimental Approach to Ethical Theory* (Berkeley: University of California Press, 1992).

34. Amy Gutmann has written an important critique of utilitarian approaches to education as a means of endowment boosting. See "What's the Use of Going to School?" in *Utilitarianism and Beyond*, ed. Amartya Sen and Bernard Williams (Cambridge: Cambridge University Press, 1982), 261–78; also Amy Gutmann, *Democratic Education* (Princeton, N.J.: Princeton University Press, 1987), 181–5. She has claimed that by directing education toward achieving the greatest happiness, utilitarianism is in conflict with a plausible liberal principle of allowing individuals to find their own best personal good. Utilitarianism, it seems, would require children to be so indoctrinated and trained to fit into society as comfortably as possible. Her critique seems to be on the mark for Benthamite utilitarianism, at least. I am not certain, however, how much purchase her critique has over my own use of utilitarianism since I take it that it is not the function of educational institutions to *directly* maximize utility; furthermore, my conception of utility is not necessarily one of happiness. Education in this scheme is meant to open possibilities for individuals in a property and contract world but not to fit them into it. And since individual utility functions may contain goods other than happiness in my account (given in chapter 1), which an individual may have to discover, the potential conflict between utilitarian education and liberal principles seems rather less than intractable.

35. There are exceptions to this generalization. In moments of hysteria, the uncorroborated testimony of children in courts of law can be used to condemn innocent adults; consider the Salem witch trials or some contemporary divorce or child-molestation proceedings. But even here it is doubtful that the bad behavior of children would have serious consequences were it not for the connivance—conscious or not—of some adults: witch-hunters, lawyers, judges, therapists, and so forth.

36. I should note in passing that the traditional goods associated with education—schools, books, classroom instruction, and so on—may not be the only ones a state may wish to provide as part of an "education." It would probably also want to provide a set of goods without which education would be impossible. Since children who are hungry, sick, or fearful are unlikely to benefit as much as they should from instruction, the state will probably wish to provide certain para-educational goods like nourishing meals, health care, and protection to children in need of it. The level of provision of these goods may be well above the social minimum when the general minimum is set low because of fear of exploitation.

37. At least, such is the opinion held by many economists who work in human capital theory. The pioneering work in this theory is Gary Becker, *Human Capital: A Theoretical and Empirical Analysis with Special Reference to Education* (New York: Columbia University Press, 1975). For a theoretical analysis of the effects of education on earnings, see especially pp. 14–44. An estimate of utility returns would be much more difficult, as Becker himself admits (see p. 67), because of the difficulties of comparing the different utility functions that would result from different processes of education. We would be required to make interpersonal comparisons of well-being between not just different persons but also different *hypothetical* persons. Difficult as this may seem, it need not be completely intractable if something known as the *Harsanyi doctrine* obtains. This doctrine maintains that if we have enough knowledge about someone's genetic endowments and environmental influences, we can know what is good for this person (for a brief exposition see Binmore, *Playing Fair*, vol. 1 of *Game Theory and the Social Contract* (Cambridge, Mass.: MIT, 1994), 61–67. This doctrine may seem quite peculiar in the abstract, but do not all parents who are concerned about the well-being of their

children apply it implicitly when they try to shape their children's tastes? I regret I cannot go into any details about how it might be applied here.

38. The possibility that one might make allocative decisions in such a way has been suggested in an education-financing proposal by Milton Friedman. He has suggested that an appropriate form of financial aid for impoverished students who wish to receive an expensive education would be for them to promise a proportion of their income over their lives to their institutions, their incomes presumably being much greater as the consequence of their education. See Milton Friedman, *Capitalism and Freedom* (Chicago: University of Chicago Press, 1982), 103–6.

39. In theory then, when citizens pay taxes to support education, they would as a matter of justice be paying for their own education, although as a matter of bookkeeping they may be paying for the education of a present generation of children. Society serves as the great creditor to us all—hence the justice of paying for schools even if one has no children oneself.

40. See Jonathan Kozol, *Savage Inequalities* (New York: Crown Books, 1991).

41. It is a commonplace in neoclassical welfare economics that we can make people no worse off by giving them an amount of money equal to the price of goods we would otherwise give them; if that basket of goods is utility maximizing, they will use the money to buy that bundle. If, however, another bundle is available for the same price that has greater utility for them, they will buy that bundle. Nothing is wrong in principle with this argument, but we should realize that in practice it would only apply to fully rational and well-informed individuals.

42. Amy Gutmann believes that the primary purpose of public education is to make citizens capable of engaging in democratic deliberation—hence the title of her book, *Democratic Education*. So our theories about what education is for are congruent on this point.

CHAPTER 7

1. This is also described by Gilbert Harman, *The Nature of Morality* (New York: Oxford University Press, 1977), 2, and discussed at considerable length by Judith Jarvis Thomson, *The Realm of Rights* (Cambridge, Mass.: Harvard University Press, 1990), 177–202. Thomson's analysis is curiously similar to my own, in that she thinks that different responses to the trolley problem should be based on what looks very much like the different degrees of moral hazard involved.

2. I am pleased to report that the existence of such an exploitation detector is not mere speculation on my part. As I noted in chapter 3, John Tooby and Leda Cosmides, using an evolutionary argument similar to mine, not only have postulated the existence of "social contract algorithms" built into human cognitive architecture but also have come up with a considerable body of experimental evidence to show that human beings have special cognitive competencies in detecting cheating on agreements. See "Cognitive Adaptions for Social Exchange" in *The Adapted Mind*, ed. Jerome H. Barkow, Leda Cosmides, and John Tooby (New York: Oxford University Press, 1992), 163–228.

3. Several informants in Jennifer Hochschild's important empirical study of beliefs about justice cite reasons very much like these. Even her poorer informants usually wanted not equality but *fair differentiation*. See *What's Fair: American Beliefs about Distributive Justice* (Cambridge, Mass.: Harvard University Press, 1981), especially 111–47. Hochschild's findings seem at least consistent with Frohlich and Oppenheimer's *Choosing Justice: An Experimentl Approach to Ethical Theory* (Berkeley: University of California Press, 1992), in which most respondents preferred a broad range of possible incomes, provided that there is a social floor.

4. See Frank Jackson, "Decision-Theoretic Consequentialism," *Ethics* 101 (1991): 461–82.

5. See J. J. C. Smart and Bernard Williams, *Utilitarianism: For and Against* (Cambridge: Cambridge University Press, 1973), 135.

6. Of course, the meaning of "reasonable" even in this context is something that utilitarians would want to police closely. National origin only seems like reasonable grounds for interning large numbers of people against the background of wartime hysteria compounded with racism, and I do not wish to side with the infelicitous majority decision in the notorious Japanese internment case, *Korematsu v. United States*, 323 U.S. 214 (1944). But other kinds of suspicion could be reasonable: one who was an outspoken Nazi sympathizer before the war against the Nazis probably should be locked up in wartime. For a discussion of related issues, in this case largely with respect to the detention of Nazi sympathizers in wartime Britain, see Richard Posner, *Overcoming Law* (Cambridge, Mass.: Harvard University Press, 1995), 159–68.

7. I do not mean to argue that U.S. constitutional provisions really are the optimal provisions that a utilitarian would approve of, and even less do I wish to argue that the framers of the Constitution were utilitarians in any *conscious* way. I merely wish to suggest that these provisions may be *consistent* with utilitarian recommendations.

8. Robert A. Dahl, one of the most careful students of democratic political systems now living, makes a utilitarian argument to democracy in *Democracy and Its Critics* (New Haven, Conn.: Yale University Press, 1989), 142–4. More interesting is his presentation of part of the Marquis de Condorcet's calculations that the probability of a group's coming to a "correct" decision rises (assuming a roughly equal distribution among individuals of each one coming to a correct decision) as the number of individuals in agreement rises. If something like utilitarianism is a general public philosophy, ceteris paribus it would thus seem prudent to use some kind of majoritarian procedure for arriving at policies that seem most likely to be utility maximizing.

9. The metaphor of temperature measures is von Neumann and Morgenstern's own. See *Theory of Games and Economic Behavior* (Princeton, N.J.: Princeton University Press, 1944), 17.

BIBLIOGRAPHY

Adams, Robert. "Motive Utilitarianism." *Journal of Philosophy* 71 (1980): 476–82.

Akerlof, George. "The Market for 'Lemons': Quality, Uncertainty, and Time." *Quarterly Journal of Economics* 84 (1970): 488.

Anand, Paul. *Foundations of Rational Choice under Risk*. Oxford: Clarendon, 1993.

Arneson, Richard J. "Liberalism, Subjectivism, and Equal Opportunity for Welfare." *Philosophy and Public Affairs* 19 (1980): 158–94.

———. "Equality of Opportunity for Welfare." *Philosophical Studies* 56 (1989): 77–93.

Arrow, Kenneth J. "Some Ordinalist-Utilitarian Notes on Rawls's Theory of Justice." In *Collected Papers of Kenneth J. Arrow*. Vol. 1. Oxford: Basil Blackwell, 1984. Originally published in *Journal of Philosophy* 70 (1973).

Axelrod, Robert. *The Evolution of Cooperation*. New York: Basic Books, 1984.

———. "An Evolutionary Approach to Norms." *American Political Science Review* 80 (1986): 1095–111.

Barry, Brian. *Political Argument*. London: Routledge & Kegan Paul, 1965.

———. *Democracy, Power, and Justice: Essays in Political Theory*. Oxford: Clarendon, 1989.

———. *Justice as Impartiality*. Oxford: Clarendon, 1995.

Becker, Gary. *Human Capital: A Theoretical and Empirical Analysis with Special Reference to Education*. New York: Columbia University Press, 1975.

Becker, Gary S., and Kevin M. Murphy. "A Theory of Rational Addiction." *Journal of Political Economy* 96 (1988): 675.

Bentham, Jeremy. *The Works of Jeremy Bentham*. Vol. 1, edited by John Bowring. Edinburgh: William Tait, 1843.

Bicchieri, Christina. *Rationality and Coordination*. New York: Cambridge University Press, 1993.

Binmore, Ken. *Fun and Games: A Text on Game Theory*. Lexington, Mass: D.C. Heath, 1991.

———. *Playing Fair*. Vol. 1 of *Game Theory and the Social Contract*. Cambridge, Mass.: MIT Press, 1994.

Bork, Robert. "Neutral Principles and Some First Amendment Problems." *Indiana Law Journal* 47 (1971): 1.

Boyd, Robert, and Peter Richerson. *Culture and the Evolutionary Process*. Chicago: University of Chicago Press, 1985.

Broome, John. "Utilitarian Metaphysics?" In *Interpersonal Comparisons of Well-being*, edited by Jon Elster and John E. Roemer. New York: Cambridge University Press, 1991.

———. *Weighing Goods: Uncertainty, Equality, and Time*. Cambridge and London: Basil Blackwell, 1991.

Calvert, Randall. "Rational Actors, Equilibrium, and Social Institutions." In *Explaining Social Institutions*, edited by Jack Knight and Itai Sened. Ann Arbor: University of Michigan Press, 1995.

Cohen, G. A. "On the Currency of Egalitarian Justice." *Ethics* 99 (1989): 906–44.

———. "Equality of What? On Welfare, Goods, and Capitalism." *Recherches Economiques de Louvain* 56 (1990): 357–82.

Cosmides, Leda, and John Tooby. "Cognitive Adaptions for Social Exchange." In *The Adapted Mind: Evolutionary Psychology and the Generation of Culture*, edited by Jerome H. Barkow, Leda Cosmides, and John Tooby. New York: Oxford University Press, 1992.

Crawford, Sue E. S., and Elinor Ostrom. "A Grammar of Institutions." *American Political Science Review* 89 (1995): 582–600.

Cumminsky, David. "Kantian Consequentialism." *Ethics* 100 (1990): 586–630.

Dahl, Robert. *Democracy and Its Critics*. New Haven, Conn.: Yale University Press, 1989.

Dasgupta, Partha. *An Inquiry into Well-being and Destitution*. Oxford: Clarendon, 1993.

Dawkins, Richard. *The Blind Watchmaker*. New York: Norton, 1987.

———. "Is God a Computer Virus?" *New Statesman and Society* 5 (18 December 1992): 223.

———. *The Selfish Gene*. New ed. New York and Oxford: Oxford University Press, 1989.

Dennett, Daniel. *Elbow Room: Varieties of Free Will Worth Wanting*. Cambridge, Mass.: MIT Press, 1989.

———. *Consciousness Explained*. Boston: Little, Brown, 1990.

———. "Memes and the Exploitation of Imagination." *Journal of Aesthetics and Art Criticism* 48 (1990): 127–35.

Dixit, Avinash, and Barry Nalebuff. *Thinking Strategically: The Competitive Edge in Business, Politics, and Everyday Life*. New York: Norton, 1991.

Donner, Wendy. *The Liberal Self: John Start Mill's Moral and Political Philosophy*. Ithaca, N.Y.: Cornell University Press, 1991.

Dowling, Keith. *Rational Choice and Political Power*. Brookfield, Vt: Edward Elgar, 1991.

Downs, George W., David M. Rocke, and Randolph M. Siverson. "Arms Races and Cooperation." *World Politics* 38 (1986): 118–46.

Dworkin, Ronald. "What Is Equality? Part I: Equality of Welfare." *Philosophy and Public Affairs* 10 (1981): 185–246.

———. "What Is Equality? Part II: Equality of Resources." *Philosophy and Public Affairs* 10 (1981): 283–345.

Edgeworth, F. Y. *Mathematical Psychics*. London: Kegan & Paul, 1881.

Edwards, Rem B. *Pleasures and Pains: A Theory of Qualitative Hedonism*. Ithaca, N.Y.:Cornell University Press, 1979.

Ellickson, Robert C. *Order without Law: How Neighbors Settle Disputes*. Cambridge, Mass.: Harvard University Press, 1991.

Elster, Jon, and John E. Roemer, eds. *Interpersonal Comparisons of Well-Being*. New York: Cambridge University Press, 1991.

Epstein, Richard. *Takings: Private Property and the Power of Eminent Domain*. Cambridge, Mass.: Harvard University Press, 1985.

———. *Simple Rules for a Complex World*. Cambridge, Mass.: Harvard University Press, 1995.

Finnis, John. *Natural Law and Natural Rights*. New York: Oxford University Press, 1981.

———. *Fundamentals of Ethics*. Oxford: Oxford University Press, 1983.

Fischbein, Efraim. *Intuition in Science and Mathematics: An Educational Approach*. Dordrecht: Reidel, 1987.

Frank, Robert. "If *Homo economicus* Could Choose His Own Utility Function, Would He Want One with a Conscience?" *American Economic Review* 77 (1987): 593–605.

———. *Passions within Reason: The Strategic Role of the Emotions*. New York: Norton, 1988.

Friedman, Milton. *Capitalism and Freedom*. Chicago: University of Chicago Press, 1982,

Frohlich, Norman, and Joe A. Oppenheimer. *Choosing Justice: An Experimental Approach to Ethical Theory*. Berkeley: University of California Press, 1992.

Fudenberg, Drew, and Eric Maskin. "The Folk Theorem in Repeated Games with Discounting or with Incomplete Information." *Econometrica* 54 (1986): 533–54.

Fumento, Michael. *Science under Siege: Science, Technology, and the Environment*. New York: William Morrow, 1993.

Gauthier, David. *Morals by Agreement*. New York: Oxford University Press, 1986.

Geertz, Clifford. *The Interpretation of Cultures*. New York: Basic Books, 1973.

George, Robert P. *Making Men Moral: Civil Liberties and Public Morality*. Oxford: Clarendon, 1993.

Gibbard, Allan. *Wise Choices, Apt Feelings*. Cambridge, Mass.: Harvard University Press, 1990.

Glendon, Mary Ann. *Rights Talk: The Impoverishment of Political Discourse*. New York: Free Press, 1991.

Goldman, Alvin I. "Simulation and Interpersonal Utility." *Ethics* 105 (1995): 709–26.

Goodin, Robert E. "Institutionalizing the Public Interest: The Defense of Deadlock and Beyond." *American Political Science Review* 90 (1996): 331–43.

Gosling, J. C. B. *Pleasure and Desire: The Case for Hedonism Revisited*. Oxford: Clarendon, 1969.

Griffin, James. *Well-being: Its Measurement, Meaning, and Moral Importance*. Oxford: Clarendon, 1986.

Grisez, Germain. "Against Consequentialism." *American Journal of Jurisprudence* 23 (1978): 21–72.

Gutmann, Amy. "What's the Use of Going to School?" In *Utilitarianism and Beyond*, edited by Amartya Sen and Bernard Williams. Cambridge: Cambridge University Press, 1982.

———. *Democratic Education*. Princeton, N.J.: Princeton University Press, 1987.

Hardin, Russell. *Morality within the Limits of Reason*. Chicago: University of Chicago Press, 1988.

———. *One for All: The Logic of Group Conflict*. Princeton, N.J.: Princeton University Press, 1995.

Hare, Richard M. *The Language of Morals*. New York: Oxford University Press, 1952.

———. *Freedom and Reason*. New York: Oxford University Press, 1963.

———. *Moral Thinking: Its Levels and Its Point*. New York: Oxford University Press, 1981.

———. "What Is Wrong with Slavery?" In *Essays on Political Morality*. Oxford: Clarendon, 1989.

Harman, Gilbert. *The Nature of Morality*. New York: Oxford University Press, 1977.

Harsanyi, John C. "Cardinal Utility in Welfare Economics and in the Theory of Risk-taking." *Journal of Political Economy* 61 (1953): 434–5.

———. "Cardinal Welfare, Individualistic Ethics and Interpersonal Comparisons of Utility." *Journal of Political Economy* 63 (1955): 309–21.

———. *Rational Behavior and Bargaining Equilibrium in Games and Social Situations*. New York: Cambridge University Press, 1977.

———. "Morality and the Theory of Rational Behavior." In *Utilitarianism and Beyond*, edited by Amartya Sen and Bernard Williams. Cambridge: Cambridge University Press, 1982.

————. "Normative Validity and Meaning of von Neumann–Morgenstern Utilities." In *Frontiers of Game Theory*, edited by Ken Binmore, Alan Kirman, and Piero Tani. Cambridge, Mass.: MIT Press, 1993.

Harsanyi, John, and Reinhard Selten. *A General Theory of Equilibrium Selection in Games*. Cambridge, Mass.: MIT Press, 1988.

Hayek, F. A. *The Mirage of Social Justice*. London: Routledge & Kegan Paul, 1975.

Heimer, Carol A. *Reactive Risk and Rational Action: Managing Moral Hazard in Insurance Contracts*. Berkeley: University of California Press, 1985.

Hirschliefer, Jack. "On the Emotions and Guarantors of Threats and Promises." In *The Latest on the Best: Essays on Evolution and Optimality*, edited by John Dupré. Cambridge, Mass.: MIT Press, 1987.

Hochschild, Jennifer. *What's Fair: American Beliefs about Distributive Justice*. Cambridge, Mass.: Harvard University Press, 1981.

Holyoak, Keith, and Paul Thagard. *Mental Leaps: Analogy in Creative Thought*. Cambridge, Mass.: MIT Press, 1995.

Honderich, Ted. *The Consequences of Determinism*. Oxford: Clarendon, 1988.

Hume, David. *Enquiries Concerning Human Understanding and Concerning the Principles of Morals*, edited by P. H. Nidditch. Oxford: Clarendon, 1975.

————. *A Treatise of Human Nature*, edited by E. C. Mossner. New York: Penguin Books, 1984.

Jackson, Frank. "Decision-theoretic Consequentialism and the Nearest and Dearest Objection." *Ethics* 101 (1991): 462–83.

James, William. "The Moral Philosopher and the Moral Life." In *The Will to Believe and Other Essays in Popular Philosophy*. New York: Longmans, Green, 1905.

de Jasay, Anthony. *The State*. New York: Basil Blackwell, 1985.

Johnson, Conrad. *Moral Legislation: A Legal-Political Model for Indirect Consequentialist Reasoning*. New York: Cambridge University Press, 1991.

Johnson, Mark. *Moral Imagination: Implications of Cognitive Science for Ethics*. Chicago: University of Chicago Press, 1993.

Kagan, Shelley. *The Limits of Morality*. Oxford: Clarendon, 1989.

Kavka, Gregory. *Hobbesian Moral and Political Theory*. Princeton, N.J.: Princeton University Press, 1986.

Knight, Jack. *Institutions and Social Conflict*. New York: Cambridge University Press, 1992.

Kozol, Jonathan. *Savage Inequalities*. New York: Crown Books, 1991.

Krueger, Anne. "The Political Economy of the Rent Seeking Society." *American Economic Review* 64 (1974): 291–302.

Levi, Margaret. *Of Rule and Revenue*. Berkeley: University of California Press, 1988.

Lewis, David K. *Convention: A Philosophical Study*. Cambridge, Mass.: Harvard University Press, 1969.

Lewontin, Richard, Steven Rose, and Leon Kamin. *Not in Our Genes: Biology, Ideology, and Human Nature*. New York: Pantheon, 1984.

Locke, John. *Second Treatise of Government*. In *Two Treatises of Government*, edited by Peter Laslett. Cambridge: Cambridge University Press, 1960.

Luce, R. Duncan, and Howard Raiffa. *Games and Decisions*. New York: Wiley, 1957.

Lyons, David. *Forms and Limits of Utilitarianism*. Oxford: Clarendon, 1965.

Marx, Karl. *Capital*, translated by Samuel Moore and Edward Aveling, edited by Frederick Engels. New York: International Publishers, 1967.

————. "Critique of the Gotha Program." In *Karl Marx: Selected Writings*, edited by David McClellan. New York: Oxford University Press, 1977.

Meltzer, Allan H., and Scott F. Richard. "A Positive Theory of In-kind Transfers and the Negative Income Tax." In *Political Economy*, edited by Allan H. Meltzer, Alex Cukierman, and Scott F. Richard. New York: Oxford University Press, 1991.

Moore, G. E. *Principia Ethica.* 1903. Reprint, Cambridge: Cambridge University Press, 1956.

Mueller, Dennis C. *Public Choice II.* New York: Cambridge University Press, 1989.

Murphy, Walter F., James E. Fleming, and William F. Harris II. *American Constitutional Interpretation.* Mineola, N.Y.: Foundation Press, 1986.

Nagel, Thomas. *The View from Nowhere.* New York: Oxford University Press, 1986.

Nozick, Robert. *Anarchy, State, and Utopia.* New York: Basic Books, 1974.

O'Brien, David M. *Constitutional Law and Politics.* Vol. 2, 2nd ed. New York: Norton, 1995.

Okun, Arthur. *Equality and Efficiency: The Great Tradeoff.* Washington, D.C.: Brookings Institution, 1975.

Olson, Mancur. *The Logic of Collective Action.* Cambridge, Mass.: Harvard University Press, 1965.

———. *The Rise and Decline of Nations: Economic Growth, Stagflation, and Economic Rigidities.* New Haven, Conn.: Yale University Press, 1982.

———. "Why Some Welfare State Redistribution to the Poor Is a Great Idea." In *Democracy and Public Choice: Essays in Honor of Gordon Tullock*, edited by Charles K. Rowley. New York: Basil Blackwell, 1987.

Parfit, Derek. *Reasons and Persons.* New York and Oxford: Oxford University Press, 1984.

Parsons, Talcott, and Edward A. Shils. "Values, Motives and Systems of Action." In *Toward a General Theory of Action*, edited by Talcott Parsons and Edward A. Shils. Cambridge, Mass.: Harvard University Press, 1951.

Posner, Richard. *Overcoming Law.* Cambridge, Mass.: Harvard University Press, 1995.

Railton, Peter. "Alienation, Consequentialism, and the Demands of Morality." *Philosophy and Public Affairs* 13 (1985): 134–71.

Rasmussen, Eric. *Games and Information: An Introduction to Game Theory.* Cambridge, Mass.: Basil Blackwell, 1989.

Rawls, John. *A Theory of Justice.* Cambridge, Mass.: Harvard University Press, 1971.

Raz, Joseph. *The Morality of Freedom.* Oxford: Clarendon, 1986.

Reber, Arthur S. *Implicit Learning and Tacit Knowledge: An Essay on the Cognitive Unconscious.* New York: Oxford University Press, 1993.

Rhode, Deborah L. *Justice and Gender.* Cambridge, Mass.: Harvard University Press, 1989.

Richardson, Peter. *Feedback Thought in Social Science and Systems Theory.* Philadelphia: University of Pennsylvania Press, 1991.

Riker, William, and Peter Ordeshook. "A Theory of the Calculus of Voting." *American Political Science Review* 62 (1968): 25.

Roemer, John. *A General Theory of Exploitation and Class.* Cambridge, Mass.: Harvard University Press, 1982.

———. "A Pragmatic Theory of Responsibility for the Egalitarian Planner." *Philosophy and Public Affairs* 22 (1993): 146–66.

Rose-Ackerman, Susan. *Corruption: A Study in Political Economy.* New York: Academic Press, 1978,

Rowley, Charles K. "Rent-seeking in Constitutional Perspective." In *The Political Economy of Rent-Seeking*, edited by Charles K. Rowley, Robert D. Tollison, and Gordon Tullock. Boston: Kluwer, 1988.

de Saint Croix, G. E. M. *Class Struggle in the Ancient Greek World: From the Archaic Age to the Arab Conquest.* Ithaca, N.Y.:Cornell University Press, 1981.

Samuelson, Paul A. "The Pure Theory of Public Expenditure." In *The Collected Scientific Papers of Paul A. Samuelson.* Vol. 2, edited by Joseph R. Stieglitz. Cambridge, Mass.: MIT Press, 1965.

194   *Bibliography*

Scanlon, Thomas. "Contractualism and Utilitarianism." In *Utilitarianism and Beyond*, edited by Amartya Sen and Bernard Williams. Cambridge: Cambridge University Press, 1982.

———. "The Moral Basis of Interpersonal Comparisons." In *Interpersonal Comparisons of Well-being*, edited by Jon Elster and John E. Roemer. New York: Cambridge University Press, 1991.

Schelling, Thomas. *Arms and Influence*. New Haven, Conn.: Yale University Press, 1966.

———. *The Strategy of Conflict*. Rev. ed. Cambridge, Mass.: Harvard University Press, 1980.

Schneewind, J. B. *Sidgwick's Ethics and Victorian Moral Philosophy*. Oxford: Clarendon, 1977.

Schofeld, N. "Anarchy, Altruism, and Cooperation." *Social Choice and Welfare* 2 (1985): 207–19.

Searle, John. *The Construction of Social Reality*. New York: Free Press, 1995.

Sen, Amartya, and Bernard Williams. Introduction to *Utilitarianism and Beyond*. Cambridge: Cambridge University Press 1982.

———. "Well-being, Freedom, and Agency: The Dewey Lectures 1984." *Journal of Philosophy* 82 (1985): 169–211.

Seung, T. K. *Intuition and Construction*. New Haven, Conn.: Yale University Press, 1993.

Sidgwick, Henry. *The Methods of Ethics*. 7th ed. 1907. Reprint, Indianapolis: Hackett, 1981.

Simpson, A. W. Brian. *Cannibalism and the Common Law*. Chicago: University of Chicago Press, 1984.

Singer, Peter. "Famine, Affluence, and Morality." *Philosophy and Public Affairs* 2 (1972): 229–43.

Smart, J. J. C., and Bernard Williams. *Utilitarianism: For and Against*. Cambridge: Cambridge University Press, 1973.

Smith, Alexander. *The Philosophy of Morals: An Investigation*. 2 vols. London: Smith, Elder, 1841.

Smith, John Maynard. *Evolution and the Theory of Games*. New York: Cambridge University Press, 1974.

Soccia, Danny. "Utilitarianism, Sociobiology, and the Limits of Benevolence." *Journal of Philosophy* 87 (1989): 329–43.

Sorenson, Roy. *Thought Experiments*. New York: Oxford University Press, 1993.

Sperber, Dan. "The Epidemiology of Belief." In *The Social Psychology of Widespread Belief*, edited by Colin Fraser and George Gaskell. Oxford: Clarendon, 1990.

Sumner, L. W. *The Moral Foundations of Rights*. Oxford: Clarendon, 1987.

Sunstein, Cass. "Preferences in Politics." *Philosophy and Public Affairs* 20 (1991): 3.

Taylor, Michael. *The Possibility of Cooperation*. New York: Cambridge University Press, 1987.

Thomson, Judith Jarvis. *The Realm of Rights*. Cambridge, Mass.: Harvard University Press, 1990.

Tooby, John, and Leda Cosmides. "The Psychological Foundations of Culture." In *The Adapted Mind: Evolutionary Psychology and the Generation of Culture*, edited by Jerome H. Barkow, Leda Cosmides, and John Tooby. New York: Oxford University Press, 1992.

Tullock, Gordon. "The Welfare Costs of Tariffs, Monopolies, and Theft." *Western Economic Journal* 5 (1967): 224–32.

Turner, John R. G. "Mimicry: The Palatability Spectrum." In *The Biology of Butterflies*, edited by R. I. Vane-Wright and P. R. Ackerly. London: Academic Press, 1984.

van Parijs, Phillipe. *Real Freedom for All: What if Anything Can Justify Capitalism?* Oxford: Clarendon, 1995.

von Neumann, John, and Oskar Morgenstern. *Theory of Games and Economic Behavior*. Princeton, N.J.: Princeton University Press, 1944.

Warnock, Mary, ed. *John Stuart Mill: Utilitarianism, On Liberty, Essay on Bentham, together with selected writings of Jeremy Bentham and John Austin*. New York: New American Library, 1974.

Wegner, David E. "Agency, Economic Calculation, and Constitutional Construction." In *The Political Economy of Rent-seeking*, edited by Charles K. Rowley, Robert D. Tollison, and Gordon Tullock. Boston: Kluwer, 1988.

Westcott, Malcolm R. *Toward a Contemporary Psychology of Intuition: A Historical, Theoretical, and Empirical Inquiry*. New York: Holt, Rinehart & Winston, 1968.

Williams, Bernard. "Evolutionary Theory, Epistemology, and Ethics." In *Evolution and Its Influence*, edited by Alan Grafen. Oxford: Clarendon, 1989.

Wilson, E. O. *Sociobiology: The New Synthesis*. Cambridge, Mass.: Harvard University Press, 1975.

Wilson, James Q. *The Moral Sense*. New York: Free Press, 1993.

Young, Iris Marion. *Justice and the Politics of Difference*. Princeton, N.J.: Princeton University Press, 1990.

INDEX